PETER KAY

T.V.

BIG ADVENTURES
ON THE SMALL SCREEN

HarperCollins*Publishers*

HarperCollins*Publishers*
1 London Bridge Street
London SE1 9GF

www.harpercollins.co.uk

HarperCollins*Publishers*
Macken House, 39/40 Mayor Street Upper
Dublin 1, D01 C9W8, Ireland

First published by HarperCollins*Publishers* 2023

1 3 5 7 9 10 8 6 4 2

© Peter Kay 2023

Peter Kay asserts the moral right to be
identified as the author of this work

A catalogue record of this book is
available from the British Library

HB ISBN 978-0-00-862331-9
PB ISBN 978-0-00-862332-6

Printed and bound in the UK using 100%
renewable electricity at CPI Group (UK) Ltd

This book is produced from independently certified FSC™ paper
to ensure responsible forest management.

For more information visit: www.harpercollins.co.uk/green

For Riley and Edie

Contents

In the Beginning ...

Miss Wild was our neighbour on the right when I was growing up. She always seemed very old to me and looked like Mother Teresa on stilts. Sometimes I'd watch her from my bedroom window, ambling around her backyard, struggling to rotate wet washing through a big Victorian mangle.

A spinster, and ex-baker, she'd occasionally make us a family apple pie, which my mum would graciously accept then scrape straight into the kitchen bin. 'That's a bit tight,' I'd whinge, gutted to see my favourite pudding disappearing into the bin bag. 'I was just warming up my custard.'

'I know,' she said, shaking her head sympathetically. 'I feel bad but we just don't know if her apples are ripe.'

There was a power cut once so my mum went round to see if she was alright. 'Are you okay?' she asked. 'There's been a power cut.' Then Miss Wild said, 'Well, I thought there had been, but then the bus went past with its lights on.'

You couldn't write it. Well, saying that, I just did.

But the main thing that sticks in my mind about Miss Wild was she was hard of hearing and would watch TV with the volume turned up full blast. It was so loud that it was easier

1

for us to watch our TV with her sound through the wall. If she changed channel, so did we. And it was pointless banging on the wall, as she couldn't hear us.

When she died we got her big old wooden-cased TV, so we went to being a two TV family. Very posh.

Mind you, her TV was out of the ark. It used to take about ten minutes to warm up. From a little tiny dot in the middle of the screen and then eventually, if we were lucky, we'd slowly get a full picture. Usually, my dad had to slap the side of the TV with the palm of his hand. It'd then turn either magenta or light green. But hey, it was a free TV.

The one thing I did love about it was that it had these huge buttons that'd leave an imprint on your finger when you pushed them to change channel. There were only four: they had written on them BBC1, BBC2, ITV and then the fourth one was just a star. Channel 4 was the stuff dreams were made of in 1977. And if we'd known they'd be producing shite like *Naked Attraction* one day, it probably still would be.

The really great thing about these big buttons was that if you twizzled them left or right you could tune the TV into other channels. I could get a visual haze of HTV or Yorkshire. I used to think that was amazing.

I'd shout to my dad, 'Look, it's Yorkshire TV!'

'Where? What am I looking at? I can't see anything.'

The picture was ghostly. In fact it was crap, but it felt like contraband, which made it all the more thrilling to me.

It was a bit like having a CB radio, which was all the rage at the time. Everybody had one. Well, everyone except us. My dad wouldn't let us have a CB as they interfered with the picture on the TV. I remember Craig Newton had a forty-foot aerial sneakily hidden up the side of a lamp post, and when he was giving it the old 'breaker, breaker, ten-four, good buddy' (which never sounded great in a Bolton accent) we could hear every word over *Rising Damp* or *Winner Takes All* and our TV picture would vibrate in sync with Craig's voice. My dad would go apeshit and go off wandering the streets to tear down his aerial.

Years later a taxi driver told me that he used to drive lorries and work with Peter Sutcliffe, and Sutcliffe's CB handle was Timberwolf. The driver said, 'Aye, wi wur gutted when wi found art that Timberwolf wur Th'ripper,' in his thick accent. Fucking Timberwolf! It still makes the hairs go up on the back of my neck. He also said that Sutcliffe posed for his works calendar. Jesus, he had some balls, that lad. I wonder what month he was? December? I can just see him leaning out of his lorry window, wearing a Santa hat with his thumb up.

One year my dad won a black and white portable TV in the raffle at our school Christmas fair. That was a really big deal. So now we were a three TV family. I forgot to mention the TV we were renting from Radio Rentals for a small fortune, but we kept that in the front room, or the 'good room' as my mum liked to call it, and weirdly nobody ever went in there (except for Christmas Day). We lived in a two-bedroomed terraced house with sod all room and we'd keep a whole room for best. Very working class, that.

On occasion when I had my Sunday bath, my mum would plug the black and white portable into the extension lead on the landing and sit it on a chair at the edge of the bathroom door. Just so I could watch *Open All Hours* in the bath. What a treat.

I commandeered the black and white portable out of my mum and dad's bedroom as often as I could, and I'd place it on the chair at the side of my bed (never had a bedside cabinet). Then I'd turn the TV on its side, so when I lay on my side in bed, I didn't have to strain my neck on an angle. Genius.

Once I'd waggled the aerial into the right position the picture was fantastic. I loved that telly and watched so many programmes and films on it over the years.

Right up until R Julie threw it at my dad's head one night when they had an argument, he ducked, and it shattered into a hundred pieces when it hit the bathroom door. I was gutted and so was the telly.

Another thing I liked to do was record programmes off the TV onto my cassette player. I'd record full episodes of *Coronation Street*, *Juliet Bravo* and *Benny Hill* and then listen to them later in bed, visualising the footage that I'd watched earlier. Bizarre, but this was before we got a video recorder.

I also recorded TV themes and built up a fantastic collection, which I've still got to this day. Occasionally you can hear my mum shouting, 'Peter, your tea's ready,' in the background. It would drive me mental at the time, hearing her in the middle of *Magpie* or *Rentaghost*, but now her shouting has become as endearing as the theme tunes themselves.

Every week I got a magazine called *Look-in* from the paper shop up the road.

I don't know if you remember *Look-in*. It came out every Tuesday and featured pin-ups of popular stars at the time: The Fonz, Adam Ant, Barry Sheene and Richard O'Sullivan. He became a bit of a heartthrob when he played Dick Turpin on ITV.

In fact, *Dick Turpin* got its own picture strip in *Look-in*. Other series and characters who had their own picture strips included Cannon and Ball, The Famous Five, *On the Buses*, *CHiPs* and Metal Mickey, to name but a few. Do you remember Metal Mickey? He was a robot who lived with a family and had his own sitcom on Saturday nights. It was on straight after *Mini-Pops*. And does anybody remember *Mini-Pops*? What a carry on that was. I can still vividly remember a schoolgirl in a nightie hoovering and miming to 'Morning Train' by Sheena Easton. 'Night time is the right time, we make love'. No wonder Channel 4 axed it after its first series. Perv central.

The weekly TV section in *Look-in* was always my highlight. Not only did you get to see what was on in all the other ITV regions, but you also got to see the logos of all the ITV regions at the top of each column: Tyne Tees, Grampian, Anglia, Thames, Yorkshire … and my own TV region, Granada. Which was an odd shape. A bit like a deformed letter 'G'.

I still believe to this day that Prince nicked it when he changed his name to a symbol. It was eerily similar to the shape used by Granada. Either that or he stopped at Granada motorway services on his Lovesexy tour and took a shine to it.

I'd spend ages comparing and contrasting the *Look-in* TV guide's schedules, grumbling, 'Why are Anglia showing *Grizzly Adams* on Saturday when we've got to make do with bloody *Gambit* with Fred Dinenage,' and, 'How have Yorkshire managed to wangle a new series of *The Incredible Hulk* two weeks before any bugger else?' I don't know why but I used to find it incredibly exciting. What a shame, I hear you cry, but I'd yet to discover my penis.

And if I was excited about the TV listings in *Look-in* then try to imagine how ecstatic I was when it came to the Christmas *TV* and *Radio Times*. I was like a pig in shit, every year, the second week of December. I would literally stalk the owner of our local paper shop for days. 'Has it come?', 'When's it coming? Any idea?'

You've also got to remember that you used to have to buy two TV guides in those days. The *Radio Times* just covered the BBC and the *TV Times* ITV. They were both on a right old screw until they joined forces in 1991. That's when *What's on TV* came out for 30p, and the gloves were off forever.

We'd only ever get a proper TV guide at Christmas and usually had to make do with Tony Pratt in the *Daily Mirror* when my dad finally brought his daily paper home from work. Then I'd only have half an hour to study the TV guide and read *The Perishers* before my dad would say, 'I'm just bobbing round to my mam's wi' the paper,' and it'd be gone. Why couldn't my nana and grandad buy their own bloody paper?

When I did manage to get my precious bumper Christmas *TV Times* and *Radio Times* I'd run home as fast as I could, grab a big felt tip and get ticking. My stomach just flipped, thinking about the excitement it used to give me. Slowly turning each page. Slowly building to the holy trinity of the TV guide: Christmas Eve, Christmas Day and Boxing Day.

You knew when you were there because the publishers would always splash out on a bit of colour shrouded by many a yuletide image dotted around the listings. And then just to ruin things they'd always shove the obligatory holiday guide right in the centre of Boxing Day. Arseholes.

I'd then spend the next few days carefully working out how many blank videotapes I'd need to ask Father Christmas for so I could tape all of my festive delights. Funny I still say 'tape' now after all these years. 'Can you tape the news for me later?'

Can you believe that I've *still* got all of my TV guides? They're all in a box in the attic and I have every single one since 1979. Actually, you can completely believe that, what am I talking about?

They're a bit tatty and torn now and I've actually seen one or two microscopic white insects wandering across the pages. Probably dining out on Noel Edmonds's face. I read through them a few weeks ago and that same excitement came flooding back. It's sadly not the same anymore. I still get a Christmas TV guide every year, but the glow has faded.

Most of the films that they show now we've seen already, and the big Bond film that used to always be on after the Queen's speech on Christmas Day has now been replaced with *The Chase, The Chase: The Bloopers* and *The Chase Celebrity Special* (in fact I think *The Chase* should be on seven nights a week … oh, wait, it already is). And then everything is bloody repeated the day after. Right, I'll get off my TV guide soapbox.

Each week formed its own televisual pattern which is still indelible in my memory to this day.

My daily dose of TV started when I got home from school, waiting impatiently for *The Young Doctors, Sons and Daughters* or occasionally *The Sullivans* to end on ITV. *The Sullivans* was an Australian period serial that followed the story of a family during the Second World War. I'll always remember the sweeping opening theme as the family posed for a photograph and one of the daughters mischievously pulled down the front of her brother's cap, prompting him to chase her down the street. Though *The Sullivans* would often be on at lunchtime/dinnertime, after *Rainbow* and *Chorlton & The Wheelies*, I'd get to see it when I was occasionally off school, usually after conning my mum into believing I was sick. Once I even resorted to putting talcum powder on my face and enquiring if she thought I looked pale. It worked, and before you could say the word 'skive' I'd made a bed on the front room couch and was slurping chicken soup. Meanwhile, my mum was down the chemist picking up a bottle of Lucozade (wrapped in orange cellophane, for some mysterious reason) while I watched daytime TV.

This consisted of schools telly, programmes like *Look and Read, Words and Pictures, How We Used to Live* and *Picture Box* (with its creepy Wurlitzer theme – look it up on YouTube, it's proper unsettling). We'd watch these programmes at school, when a teacher would wheel a telly on massive legs into the classroom and we'd idly pretend to shoot off the seconds from the countdown clock before it started.

In the afternoon it'd be a daily episode of *Crown Court* (where I'd become so engrossed in the plot I'd try to wangle another day off school just so I could find out if the accused was guilty), *A Country Practice*, *The Cedar Tree* and *Paint Along with Nancy* (an eccentric American lady who painted with a fecking knife). At least ITV made some kind of an effort; the BBC just used to show pages from Ceefax for hours on end with crap muzak playing underneath. Can you believe that was considered acceptable viewing? As if things weren't tough enough for the unemployed.

Sorry, I digress. I'd get home from school, head straight to the TV and, as the theme from some Australian serial was ending, I'd be knocking up a quick Dairylea or jam butty with a glass of milk just in time for classics such as *The Hair Bear Bunch!*, *The All New Popeye Show*, *Secret Squirrel* and *Battle of the Planets* (where I used to flip the armchair on its back, swivel it to face the telly and pretend I was sitting in a spaceship – much to my mum's frustration). We also had other treats available, such as *Stig of the Dump*, *Rentaghost*, some maths/science with Johnny Ball, *Jigsaw*, *Take Hart* (which could never return your pictures – tight BBC, just chucked them in a skip around the back of Broadcasting House), *Runaround* and *Razzmatazz*, but all of that paled into insignificance when *Grange Hill* started. Definitely the highlight of every child's viewing, though some parents banned their children from watching it, as it was considered corruptible.

My family lapped it up: the Tucker Jenkins era, Mr Bronson's wig, Clare Scott's crush on Mr Hopwood, Danny Kendall's death, Mr Bronson's wig, Gripper Stebson's bullying, Mr Bronson's wig and Zammo McGuire being a smackhead (which inspired the god-awful single 'Just Say No'). Some of the storylines in *Grange Hill* were controversial and ground-breaking for the time, especially Mr Bronson's wig.

As *Grange Hill* ended at 5.35 my dad would occasionally cook tea when my mum worked late at the supermarket. My dad would literally make a meal of his culinary prowess (or the lack of it), narrating his efforts like a TV chef and boasting of his achievements as he heated a tin of Heinz beans and mini sausages in a saucepan or attempted to cook a couple of burgers under the grill before almost always cremating them to the theme of the aforementioned *Grange Hill*, *Blockbusters*, *The Beverly Hillbillies* or *Neighbours*. Whenever I hear any of them now, I'm immediately transported back to my dad's crap teas.

Monday night was dull. It would kick off at 7 p.m. with *Wish You Were Here…?* (Judith Chalmers and Chris Kelly) or *The Krypton Factor*, followed by *Coronation Street* and *World in Action*, but things would go up a gear at 9 when it'd be a toss-up between *Quincy* on ITV or *Moonlighting* on BBC2.

Tuesday evening at 5.15 was either *Diff'rent Strokes* or *Mork & Mindy* (a personal favourite). I had a pin-up of them from *Look-in* on my bedroom wall until I was about fifteen, with Mork in his rainbow braces. Who needed Linda Lusardi?

After tea, I'd leg it round to my nana and grandad's house to watch *Laurel & Hardy* on BBC2. My grandad used to laugh so much that he would just choke and cough himself onto the floor. I know that sounds worrying but it is one of my most fond memories of him.

I still watch *Laurel & Hardy* today with my children, and now I'm the one who's choking and coughing on the floor. But that's probably Covid.

In March 1983 we finally got a video recorder (a Panasonic NV2010 and it's the one and only time I've ever performed a physical backflip). It weighed a ton and I used to carry it round to my nana and grandad's so I could watch videos with them. Thankfully they eventually bought their own video recorder, a Ferguson Videostar. I remember going round once and they were both sat in the kitchen in silence.

I said, 'I thought you were taping *Gone with the Wind*?'

My grandad said, 'We are.'

I said, 'Well, why are you sat in here, why aren't you watching it?'

My nan said, 'Well, we didn't want to talk cause it'll come out on the video.'

I said, 'WHAT? It won't record your voices!'

I can just see it now, Clark Gable saying, 'Frankly my dear, I don't give a … Stan, do you want a brew?'

Or Vivien Leigh: 'I'll think of some way to get him back. After all, tomorrow is another … Stan, it's time for your angina tablets.'

Meanwhile, on Wednesdays, *Minder* was on after *Des O'Connor Tonight* (where Freddie Starr always seemed to be dressed as a Nazi), but I'd have to go to bed before it started, so I'd always hear the theme tune to *Minder* muffled through my bedroom floor. 'I Could Be So Good for You' sung by Dennis Waterman.

Then I'd hear the front door close, and I knew my dad had gone to Chows chippy for fish, chips and peas. I'd lie in bed waiting for the sound of him coming back then I'd give it five minutes or so then stagger downstairs all disorientated, pretending I'd had a bad dream. 'I've had a bad dream, Mum … Oh, have you been to the chippy?'

My dad: 'Yes, I've been to the chippy, funny how you always have a bad dream every time I go to the bloody chippy … Go on, get yourself some bread so you can have "a" butty.' Heaven.

Thursday it was payday in our house, so, flush with his wages, my dad would send me back to the shop for some treats. Always the same order, 'a quarter of midget gems and a bottle of Midnight Rider', my mum would want a 'Fry's Five Centre or a Topic'. R Julie would get a packet of Smiths Salt 'n' Shake (with the blue sachet of salt somewhere inside). I'd get a packet of Minstrels (they melt in your mouth, not in your hand). I'd leg it out of the front door faster than Usain Bolt in my British Home Store slippers. Bit of sneaky penny tray mix with some of the change and back home in time for *Top of the Pops*. The highlight of the week.

That'd immediately be followed by *Porridge* with Ronnie Barker – who'd go on to be a huge influence on me as you'll find out later in this book. In fact, one of my earliest memories was watching Ronnie Barker win a BAFTA for his performance as Fletch in *Porridge*. The rest of Thursday night was *Tomorrow's World* and *Tenko* at half-nine.

Friday was the best night of the week, as we'd do the weekly big shop. Then walk home up the enormous hill of Mercia Street, pulling the tartan shopping trolley and a carrier bag each. Then we'd always go to the chippy for tea. Which I could never figure out, having just spent money on food shopping.

Plus, the pop man would come round on Fridays. We'd get a few bottles of orange cordial and lemonade. I'd make fizzy orange and then it'd be straight off into action-ville with either *The A-Team* or *The Fall Guy* followed by *That's My Boy*, *Me & My Girl* or *The Gaffer* (or *Dynasty* and *Points of View* if you were watching BBC1). Then it was *Flambards*, *We'll Meet Again*, *Shine on Harvey Moon* or *The Gentle Touch* followed by *Cheers* or *The Golden Girls* at 10 p.m. on Channel 4.

Saturday was always a full English breakfast for tea while watching *Final Score* on BBC1 and my dad checked his coupon. Then it would be *The Pink Panther Show*, which still reminds me of fried bread. Followed by *Doctor Who*, *The Dukes of Hazzard* or shitty *Tripods*. My mum and dad would get a taxi to the local working men's club and my grandad would come round and babysit. We'd watch all the big game-shows, *The Generation Game* and *3-2-1* with Ted Rogers (I still can't do the thing with my fingers), then a Clint Eastwood film and fall asleep.

Sundays I had that sad feeling that grew slowly throughout the day as the weekend was coming to an end and Monday was back to school. We'd watch *The Love Boat* and *Bullseye* after tea. Then listen to the Top 40 in the bath. Get my hair dried watching *Hart to Hart* or *Magnum, P.I.* Then as soon as *Mastermind* started, I'd have to go to bed. I still get butterflies when I hear that theme. As I got older, I was allowed to stay up and watch *That's Life!* with Esther Rantzen (I was quite chuffed my mum and dad let her come round).

What was *That's Life!* all about? Well, if it wasn't poor Ben Hardwick breaking our hearts needing a new liver then it was Doc Cox breaking our hearts having a singalong on the London Underground dressed as a giant turnip. They even had a dog saying 'sausages', where the owner was clearly moving its mouth. Then I was off to bed to the theme of *The South Bank Show* (the best part of the programme, if you ask me). And that, my friends, was my TV week.

Just for the record, I want you to know that I did play out as a child. I did sometimes leave the house and breathe fresh air. In fact, I was out almost every night. Down the park on my bike. Playing hide and seek and off-ground tig. In summer we'd play literally until the sunset, and you could do that without the fear of being thrown into the back of a van by a paedophile. Nobody knew what a paedophile was until the noughties when they started putting their names and addresses in the paper. But as much as I used to like playing out, I loved getting home and back in front of the telly.

And reading all of this opening back, it's apparent how much TV played a pivotal part in our lives. I just don't know whether that was us or whether other families were the same. Weren't we just a generation still fascinated with the magic lantern in the corner of the front room, which offered us escape? Does that ring any bells? Were you the same? Answers on a postcard to BBC TV Centre, London, W12 8QT. (Now that's a boy obsessed with TV.)

Help Yourself
to Biscuits

Living in Bolton meant we occasionally travelled into Manchester. We'd arrive at the north end of the city and I could see Granada Television. Looming on the horizon. The Hollywood of the North. Granada was the epicentre of everything televisual to me. I used to wake up in the mornings and listen to the station's opening theme by Keith Mansfield. Which incidentally always reminds me of 'Venus de Milo' on Prince's *Parade* album. Have a listen. I'm already convinced he nicked the Granada sign, so it all ties up.

I'd stay awake for closedown. Do you remember when we used to have those? A TV station closing down each night? Sounds alien now. The announcer would sign off with a bit of regional weather and then they'd bid us all goodnight. Play the Granada theme. The screen would go black. Then there'd be the obligatory pause before they'd pop back up to remind us to turn off the television and make sure we took the plug out of the wall. Brilliant.

As the years passed by I started to yearn to get into television myself. Every job I had when I left school always seemed to follow the same pattern. Two or three months working part-time in a supermarket, bingo hall or bar. I'd end up making the staff laugh. Somebody would inevitably say, 'You should be on television,' and then I'd get 'let go' (sacked), as I was crap at the job.

Deep down it hurt. Not because I'd lost the job, but I knew I had a natural gift for comedy and wanted to work in TV. Problem was, I didn't have any connections. I didn't have an uncle who was a cameraman or anything like that. I was from Bolton, things like that didn't happen to people like me.

I'd spend many a weekend down my local library with the IBA TV guide, copying the addresses of companies (I knew them all from the logos in *Look-in*). They all received a CV and a letter from me at some point. I just wanted a chance, a foot in the door, but I never once got a reply. But I still carried on, week after week after week.

I tell a lie, I did eventually get a reply. I was offered an interview for a job making tea at Granada Television. Oh, joy of joys. I went for an interview with a big executive with Perrier water on his desk (in a bottle, not just spilt everywhere). He said, 'I'll not lie to you, it's a shit job for crap money. You'll be brewing up for the editing staff but it's got potential. The lad you might be replacing is now working in Spain brewing up on *El C.I.D.* with Alfred Molina.'

When I got home I got a call telling me I'd got the job. I was beside myself, but it was to be short-lived. Especially when they told me what the pay was: one pound an hour for a fifty-eight hour week. That just wasn't enough. With travel and lunches, not to mention my mum's keep, I just couldn't afford to take the job and reluctantly I had to turn it down. I was devastated for a long time. I felt that I had missed my one chance.

Now, I'm aware that some of what I've just written is a slight duplication of content from my first book, *The Sound of*

Laughter (available from most charity shops for about a pound or less), but sometimes you've got to go backwards to go forwards, if you know what I mean. I just can't presume everybody will have read that first book. Anyway, it was only a tiny recap and I tried to make it as funny as possible.

I enrolled on a course at Salford College, an HND in Media Performance, where incidentally I would meet Sian Gibson (or Sian Foulkes as she was then). It was a two-year course where you did all aspects of showbiz-type things like acting, writing, editing, filming, dancing and movement (the last two were my least favourite).

I'd always been led to believe that academically I was a bit useless, but now that I'd found something I enjoyed I was getting merits and distinctions. I'd get the bus from Bolton every morning and be there for nine o'clock. Then I'd be one of the last to leave at night. I was thriving. Booking video cameras and editing suites. Spending hours writing and working on all kinds of projects. I'd never felt like this before.

In the second year, I ended up being chosen to take part in a TV directors' training course. Not as a director, though. As a performer. I wrote a monologue, a character called Leonard, based on a guy I once knew in Bolton. It was set at a bus stop and I even wrote a part for Sian. We got to go to Granada TV to film it. That was a huge thrill.

The monologue was filmed in a studio. They built an actual set. Bus shelter, railings, bushes, it all looked so real and professional. I was completely overwhelmed by the experience. The final performance would never be on actual TV, it was just a process Granada offered to help train new directors in television.

It certainly whet my appetite. Sian and I had a great time, and when it was over we snuck out back through a fire door and spent a few hours on the Granada Studios tour for free.

I also took an option in stand-up comedy in the second year of my HND course. Can you believe that was an actual option? It was the first time they'd ever offered it on the course. I took to it like a fish to water. Every Tuesday afternoon we'd meet up in a classroom and perform a routine we'd written that week for the rest of the group. There were nine of us and we did this for ten weeks, then we went to a pub up the road and held a 'comedy night', where we performed our material in front of a real audience and were marked by our tutors.

I did really well. In fact, I got a distinction star (not a clue?). It was the first time I'd ever performed stand-up. It was nerve-racking, I was terrified, but once I got on stage I felt completely at peace. Something I rarely felt in 'real' life. It was like coming home.

After college ended I was lucky enough to get on the books of a local acting agency in Manchester. They'd put me up for a few parts. All serious theatre. I remember once, they called saying, 'We've got you an audition for Chekhov's *Cherry Orchard* in Macclesfield,' to which I replied, '… and I've got a sore throat.'

I just didn't want to do serious acting. All I wanted to do was comedy but I was being unrealistic. It was tough enough getting work as an actor, let alone limiting yourself to just funny roles. But I couldn't help how I felt.

I'd seen other local comedians like Steve Coogan and John Thomson doing stand-up on local shows and, as a result, they'd been offered comedy acting roles on TV. So that's what I decided to try, use stand-up comedy as a possible stepping stone into being a comedy actor. I dusted off my college routine and put my name down as a competitor in the prestigious North West Comedian of the Year competition, whose previous winners included Caroline Aherne and Dave Spikey.

I arrived at the Buzz Club in Chorlton one hot August night (not to be confused with the Neil Diamond album of the same name, not that many of you did). I talked about my life, my part-time jobs and my family. Miraculously, I went on to win the heat. Then a few weeks later the Grand Final at the Levenshulme Palace (and trust me, it isn't). Dave Spikey hosted. In fact, that was the first time we met. Johnny Vegas was also a competitor and I thought he'd storm to victory.

I was last on the bill, and by the time I got on stage the audience were completely worn out. The room was roasting hot. I charged the stage with as much enthusiasm as I could muster in the sixty-degree heat and let them 'ave it.

The gods must have been smiling on me that night, because out of the fifteen finalists I won. That night my life literally changed forever. The next day I started getting calls from managers of comedy clubs wanting to offer me bookings. I was ecstatic, also the money was fantastic. I was still working part-time as a cinema usher, getting £45 a week for a twenty-hour shift. They were offering me £50 for a twenty-minute performance. Woo-hoo! Things were finally going to plan.

Now all I needed to do was get on TV.

I'd only been doing stand-up in the clubs for a few weeks when June West, a casting director, got in touch, offering me a part in a one-off comedy for Granada TV called *New Voices*. Oh, my giddy aunt, I was over the fecking moon, and to quote Hannibal from *The A-Team*: 'I love it when a plan comes together.' I just couldn't believe my plan was coming together so quickly.

The series celebrated new writers in television and the episode I was to be in was called 'Two Minutes', written by a really witty Liverpudlian girl called Johanne McAndrew. It was the story of three mates who decide to rob a pub. 'We pull up, we go in, we rob it, we come out, we drive off … two minutes,' hence the title. I was to be cast as the driver of the getaway car, George. The only problem was I hadn't passed my test, but I wasn't going to let something as trivial as that get in the way. Besides, they had all sorts of camera trickery, I doubted I'd even need to be driving a car. So when they asked me if I could drive, I said yes.

What was really fortunate was that the director was a man I'd met on the Granada directors' training course, Jonny Campbell. I must have stuck in his mind because he put in a request for June West to track me down. The rest of the cast was quite famous, Alexei Sayle, Paul Shane from *Hi-de-Hi!* and Lynda Baron who played Nurse Gladys Emmanuel in *Open All Hours*. With Ronnie Barker. There he is again. He'll no doubt keep cropping up in this book from time to time.

The three robbers were me, Matthew Dunster and Pearce Quigley (I know, I hadn't heard of them either). Matthew has since gone on to be successful in theatre as a writer/director, and Pearce is a renowned actor in his own right (he'll laugh when he reads that). I've been lucky to work with Pearce many times since and he's appeared in almost every production I've made in the last twenty-five years. We've also remained very good friends. In fact, I even turned up at his mum's eightieth for some buffet and a bit of a dance.

The plan was to rehearse for a couple of days at Granada TV and then film for three days on location in and around the Beswick/Ancoats area of Manchester.

I arrived for a rehearsal on a Monday morning and we all sat around a big table and read the script. I was still over the moon about being in Granada and finally working, in a proper acting job, with a proper wage. I think I got £300 but I would have done it for free.

There was Alexei Sayle sat at a table having a brew. I wanted to go over and tell him I'd bought ''Ullo John! Gotta New

Motor?' on 7-inch single, but I felt like an idiot. I decided to play it cool. Besides, he looked like he'd just punch me. Lynda Baron came over and said hello. She was exactly as you'd imagine her to be, all lovely and mumsy. I wanted to tell her about my mum putting the black and white telly on in the bathroom so I could watch *Open All Hours*, but again, I just couldn't. I just stayed quiet and overly polite.

I went over to the tea table and made myself a brew. 'Help yourself to biscuits,' said one of the crew, so I shoved a few packets in my pockets. Then I turned and bumped into Paul Shane. He had a massive head. 'Careful, son,' he said. 'I imagine you'd have been a big fan of *Hi-de-Hi!* when you were a kiddie? Fifty-eight episodes we made from 1980 to '88. I've still got the Ted Bovis suit at home and the shoes. The BBC were going to chuck them, use them as dusters, and I said, "I'll take them, thank you very much." Pass me the Bourbons, son,' and off he went. I never even got a chance to say hello.

Jonny the director was there and I thanked him for putting my name forward. June West was there too, and Johanne McAndrew. There was a cameraman there called Andy Hibbert and, unbeknownst to me, I would also go on to work with him on *Phoenix Nights*, *Max & Paddy*, right up to *Car Share*.

We read out the script; I had been reading it already at home, so I was familiar with most of my lines. I remember everybody performing it when they read, you know, acting a bit. Well, everybody except Alexei Sayle. He just mumbled through his part as if he didn't want to be there. Bizarre, I thought. Paul Shane was the complete opposite. He was delivering his lines as if he was performing *Hamlet*, with huge pauses between each line. We finished and had another brew. Paul Shane sidled over to me and said, 'Alexei's very quiet, isn't he? He'd better start opening his mouth or he's going to get fuckin' buried.'

Then off he went again. Confused, I just shoved a few more packets of biscuits in my pockets. Did he ever let anybody answer him?

The next day they sent a driver to pick me up from home. I felt like a competition winner. That felt weird. I've had many drivers over the years but I'm never able to relax. I had a driver on a job I did a couple of years back, nice fella but I'd always fall asleep on the way home and fart. Now I don't want you thinking I'm some kind of animal, I wasn't even aware I'd done it, not until a sudden rush of fresh air woke me and I'd catch the driver with tears in his eyes, discreetly lowering his window so he could breathe. I'd be mortified, sprawled in the back. That's why I prefer to drive myself.

We arrived at what they call unit base. This is usually a bit of spare land near the filming location that now looks like the circus has arrived. A convoy of big white wagons and units parked up. You'd often see a look of horror on the faces of the locals until they read signs on the vehicles such as 'Filming Services' or 'Television Caterers'. Phew! They probably thought the waltzers were about to be erected and the lead nicked from their roofs.

This convoy consisted of mobile units for make-up, costume, props, offices, and trailers where the actors would get changed. As well as a catering wagon and sometimes a double-decker bus for the cast and crew to eat on. I loved this magical circus. Especially catering.

That was the first thing I saw when I arrived for filming. I couldn't believe how much free food we could have. It was like being on an all-inclusive holiday but without the wristband. I kicked off with a couple of bowls of cereal, a full English breakfast, a selection of pastries … oh, and a few more packets of biscuits. Then I was off to the wardrobe truck to find my costume didn't fit me.

As I said, the story of 'Two Minutes' was about three guys trying to rob a pub, only to find that the regulars are so sick of being robbed they refuse to hand over any money. Frustrated and confused, the robbers threaten them at gunpoint, but the regulars retaliate by throwing bottles. The robbers eventually flee empty-handed. My character was waiting outside with a getaway car, which I'd bought because it was a bargain.

'You bought a getaway car?' says Pearce's character, grabbing me round the neck furiously. 'You were supposed to steal it, not buy it, you clown.'

We then see the car swerving, zig-zagging as it drives down the road.

That was a stuntman doing the zig-zag driving, thank the Lord. When they asked me about the other driving scenes I just nodded and stuck my thumb up. The truth is I'd had a lot of driving lessons so felt I could drive. Just not in the eyes of the law.

The car I had to drive was very old. I'd like to tell you what make it was, but I haven't got a bloody clue. I know it was light blue and the radio and heating didn't work, so we had to sit in it freezing during filming.

One thing we did have was proper guns, shotguns in order to rob the pub. For that we had to have an armourer on set all the time. Steve Tomko he was called, right character. He had a really strong Manc accent and was extremely proud of his firearms. 'This is a sawn-off shotgun and you should always hold it like this,' etc. None of the guns were loaded but Steve had to be on set while they were being handled.

He just wasn't able to drive with us in the car, as there wasn't enough room for him to be out of camera shot. So when we drove off around the block to get into position, we thought it'd be funny to go on a little bit of a detour via Netto with our shotguns.

'We're ready for a take,' the director said over the walkie-talkies.

'Coming,' I said, swerving into Netto car park, screeching the car past startled shoppers as we pretended to 'case the joint', Matthew and Pearce both looking mean as they held up their shotguns to nervous customers.

'Where are you?' said the director.

'We're on our way, over,' I said, just pulling out of the car park. 'We got a bit lost.'

That backfired. We got reported to the police and they turned up on set asking if we knew anything about three blokes down Netto with shotguns in a vintage car. We sheepishly confessed that we might have got a bit lost. The producer wasn't amused and we got a right bollocking over lunch. Which incidentally consisted of steak and ale pie, chips with mixed veg, and a pineapple upside-down cake for dessert.

After lunch, it was my big driving shot. Now, so far I'd sufficiently got away with driving. Fortunately, as it was an old car, the gears were a bit temperamental, so I was able to blame them a lot of the time. If I stalled the engine I'd just shake my head and shrug.

The director wanted me to drive up to a zebra crossing just as an actor was crossing and slam on the brakes, causing the pedestrian to leap out of the way. I nearly didn't stop twice and almost ran the poor fella over. On the third attempt they put cones out as markers, so I knew exactly when to stop, but then ran over the cones. The crew literally had to drag the traffic cones out from under the car. Pearce and Matthew were pissing themselves laughing, as I had confided in them that I hadn't passed my test. By now I'd noticed a few mumbles from the crew: 'Can this lad really drive?' On the fourth attempt, I hit my marks spot on and the director got his shot. Hallelujah!

On the last night of filming, I had a gig at the Frog & Bucket comedy club in Manchester. I invited some of the cast and crew down. Jonny the director came, and while I was on stage I told the audience what I'd been up to that week, that I'd been filming a comedy about driving a getaway car for a robbery and I also confessed that I hadn't actually passed my driving test. Surprisingly nobody from the crew was shocked in the slightest.

I was completely swept away with filming that week. The circus of it all. I was captivated by the dynamic. All of these strangers brought together through an abnormal set of circumstances generated an intoxicating camaraderie. Something I hadn't felt since my school trip to the Isle of Rum. Once it was over the magic stopped.

We were in a bubble. I completely lost touch with the outside world for those few days. The shoot was all-consuming and once it ended I was sad. Really bereft, perhaps in the knowledge that it might never happen again. I didn't want it all to end.

Why was I so down? I'd only known these people for a few days. I missed them, I missed filming, and I missed helping myself to biscuits. In fact, by the end of the week, I'd put on two stone, and I'd lifted enough biscuits to sink a ship.

But my stand-up to comedy-acting plan was working and I didn't have to wait too long to pick up another TV offer. The small role of groundskeeper in an ITV drama called *Butterfly Collectors*. It was written by Paul Abbott, who wrote *Clocking Off* and *Shameless*. I was only filming for a couple of days, but it was good fun and I got to meet Pete Postlethwaite, who was the star of the show. Great face, great actor. He'd been knocking about for years but his career had gone stratospheric thanks to performances in *The Usual Suspects*, *In the Name of the Father* and *Jurassic Park 2*.

What I did find strange was that hardly anybody talked to him when we were filming. Everybody wanted to give the big star some space. I felt a bit sorry for him, and after a while we struck up a conversation. It turned out that all he wanted to do was talk. He was fascinated with stand-up and he said that being a comic was one of the bravest jobs of them all. I've never forgotten what he said: 'I couldn't do it. Standing up there, living off your wits without any safety net and hoping that people will find you funny, bugger that.' I'd never thought of it like that really, but in return I found him being the star of a big ITV drama and carrying that responsibility far braver. The expectations were massive.

Another couple of bit parts followed. One was an appearance in a BBC police drama called *City Central* where I played a kind of an Alan Bennett-type character who lived with his mum. Though whether his mum was actually alive or not was never resolved. In the episode, the police used my character's house for surveillance on a gang of drug dealers and I was continually interrupting them with offers of tea and biscuits (if I'd known I could have brought some of my own biscuits).

Next, I got the part of a removal man in a comedy-drama, again for the BBC, called *Born to Run*, starring Keith Allen. He'd always struck me as high maintenance, but he turned out to be good company over the couple of days we spent together.

All of these parts were great experience. It felt as if I was getting a double apprenticeship, working in the clubs learning stand-up and getting the experience of filming in TV. I quickly learnt how the roles within a crew worked, who did what, and why they did it. I'd read end credits on programmes for years but now those roles started to mean something. Boom operator, grip, dolly, assistant director. Although I've still no idea what a 'best boy' is.

I found it all fascinating. Especially catering. Now, you can laugh, and I know I keep going on about it, but one thing I've learnt over the years is that good caterers are important. They're the backbone of any filming and the first thing I always book, sometimes months in advance, because if the cast and crew are happy with the food, filming will be happy. You'd be surprised how much that matters, but it does when you're stuck together for months in all kinds of weather.

The next TV offer I got was right up my alley. I was invited to write something of my own for a new Channel 4 comedy series called *Barking*. It would feature up-and-coming comedians, allowing them to create their own characters. *The Fast Show* had proved hugely popular in recent years and brought the sketch show and character comedy back to the fore. *Barking*'s cast featured unknowns like Catherine Tate, Mackenzie Crook, David Walliams and myself.

Writing my own material was a big deal for me. Creating my own characters was all I really wanted to do. I just couldn't believe the opportunity had arrived so fast.

I chose a character called Roy. A divorced painter and decorator who had joint custody of his child and whose only comfortable form of communication was discussing life through DIY. I wrote three short sketches and sent them off to the producers.

The ideas poured out of me. I'd experienced lots of custody dads while working as an usher at the cinema. They always tried that little bit too hard to please their children, and occasionally you'd overhear a comment of bitterness towards his ex-wife or her new boyfriend. 'He's taking you to Alton Towers? Well, I'm going to be taking you to Disneyland,' that sort of thing. 'Yes, sure, we could go bowling after the cinema … but your mum wants you back for five o'clock … the heartless cow.'

I also based my character on a second cousin of mine called Mick, who did painting and decorating for cash while he was still signing on. I'd spent a lot of time with him when he decorated our kitchen, front room, bedrooms and landing (well, the money was rolling in, plus it was a nice treat for my mum after all these years).

The only problem with Mick was that he'd talk more than he'd decorate while he chain-smoked. So even if your décor was top notch, it immediately stunk of Benson & Hedges. We tried to get him to smoke outside but that proved impossible. He'd say, 'Oh, yeah, no problem,' go to the kitchen door, then no sooner would you turn round than he'd be standing right behind you putting the world to rights with a fag in his mouth.

'They haven't got a bastard clue, this government. I mean look at Idi Amin,' he pronounced it Eye-dee Am-in, 'he slaughtered millions and they let him off scot-free. They should have had him stripping wallpaper as a punishment because this fucking woodchip's not for coming off, young Peter. I think whatever dickhead put this up must have used superglue.'

'It was my dad.'

'Oh,' he said, but he didn't give a shit. He was already off on another tangent: '... he's another clown who needs the birch, the Ayatollah Khomeini.' He pronounced it Eye-ya-toller Oh-mainy.

But I'll give Mick his due, he was cheap. I once went with him when he signed on.

'Any work since you last signed on?' the lady said.

'No, fuck all, love,' he said, wearing overalls covered in paint.

He was definitely a character and that's why I chose to write about him.

Word came back that the producers really liked my script and I was chosen to be included in the series. I was absolutely delighted.

Filming was to take place in London at a residential house somewhere in Pinner. The first scene was my character, now called Roy, arriving at my ex-wife's house to pick up my daughter.

*Doorbell ringing. Roy's young daughter, Charlotte,
opens the front door.*

Roy
Alright, flower, look at you, you're getting taller every time I see you. Are you ready for the offski? Look, I've got a big bag of pop and crisps for us. Is Alan in?

Charlotte shakes her head. Roy pushes her out of the way and strides straight into the house. Roy goes into the front room.

Jesus Christ. What has he done to my lounge? Look at that. He's wallpapered over woodchip, the maniac. What an abortion. Feel that wall. Stroke it. It's dog rough. What?! Where's my fireplace gone? Your mam never liked that fireplace – I say you never liked the fireplace, did you? Eh? She can't hear me. HEY, YOU COULD DO WITH PUTTING SOME SHELVES UP IN HERE, THEY'D LOOK NICE IN THIS ALCOVE

Ex-wife
(voice off)
Don't start, Roy

Roy
Well, you could. What do you reckon? I've got some offcuts of wood back at the flat. They'd be a perfect fit here. It wouldn't take me more than half an hour to bang them up. No time at all

You could put your nick-nacks on them. Maybe some books. You'd get about sixteen on there, easy. You could give me a lift if you fancied?

It'd be like old times. (*Reminisces*) Me and you together. Remember when we re-wired that back bedroom? When we did that grouting together at your mam's? You weren't born then, Charlotte. Re-lagging those tanks. Happy days. Where did it all go wrong? Is there no way we could …

We hear the front door bang. Roy quickly dives out of the front room and positions himself back in the hall.

Alan
I'm home, darling. Oh, hello, Roy. Saturday already, is it?

Alan greets Charlotte.

Alan
Hello, treacle, you had a good day?

Roy
I've told you, put your coat on, go on, do as your DAD says

Alan
(*gesturing to the doors into the lounge*)
Do you like the doors, Roy?

Roy
I like 'Riders on the Storm', it's a classic.
They played that at our wedding

Alan

No, these doors

Roy

Oh, yeah, was it your first time?

Alan

No. I got a new unit too. Distressed pine

Roy

Looks like it an' all. Come on, Charlotte, love, are we making
tracks? The film starts at two

Ex-wife

(voice off)

I want her back for five

Roy

Yeah, I thought you might

We were supposed to film everything in a couple of locations
but then something awful happened. The cameraman was
electrocuted. I'm not shitting you. Apparently the house we
were filming in hadn't been earthed properly (whatever that
means). The cameraman raised his hand just to alter a filming
light above his head and accidentally completed the circuit
within the house. Bang! The power in the house went off and
the poor cameraman fell to the floor right in front of me. It
was a shock, literally. I thought he was having a heart attack
but then I quickly realised the lights had all gone off. The crew
carried him outside to the garden and called an ambulance. It
was horrible and very frightening for everybody. The cameraman wanted to carry on filming, but the producer and director

wouldn't let him, understandably. Then, as we were waiting for the ambulance to arrive, the cameraman suddenly burst into tears. Delayed shock, the poor sod. Filming was cancelled for the rest of the day and I had to stay another night. The following day all of the scenes took place in a park where Roy has taken his daughter for the day. He told her the story of Hansel and Gretel.

Roy

The walls were made from spun sugar and the roof from gingerbread ... I mean that's bollocks straight away, because structurally it would be unsafe. There'd be absolutely no support. The whole lot would fall down on those two kiddies before the wicked witch would have time to eat either of them. That'd be Grimm. Get it?

The pinnacle of my bit parts came with a day working as a shopfitter on, wait for it ... *Coronation Street*. Now that was the Rolls-Royce of bit parts. To actually be on the world-famous cobbles. Well, I never actually saw any cobbles, as all my scenes were in the studio. Still, it was *Coronation Street* with Ashley Peacock, Fred Elliott and Maud in her wheelchair. Not Ken and Deirdre, I grant you, but still great to be there.

I had one line, 'Come outside, Mr Elliott, there's something I want to show you.' Not hard to learn. Though I must have said it to myself about three hundred times in preparation. In the scene, I accidentally dropped a piece of fish behind the shop counter, which would go on to fester into another episode and no doubt cause a huge palaver.

I arrived at the *Coronation Street* stage door, which was in a completely separate area of Granada Television. There were a few photographers lingering outside, ready to pounce on any unsuspecting cast, but they hadn't got a clue who I was.

Ten minutes later I was making myself a brew stood next to Rita Fairclough. Giggling to myself like a lunatic. I tried to act all nonchalant, casually asking Emily Bishop to pass me the semi-skimmed. I then heard a very familiar voice from behind. Deirdre Rachid-Langton-Barlow, asking for a teaspoon. It was all too much for me. It was like being among real-life waxworks that moved. I'd grown up with these people. Sadly, I just couldn't distinguish between their characters and real life.

I was sat in the green room (still don't know why it's called a green room, because I've been in a few over the years and none of them have ever been green) and a familiar man came over and introduced himself. As we chatted it suddenly clicked who he was. It was Jon Lindsay. Remember him? He was the shithouse who two-timed Deirdre. He took her for every penny and she even ended up in prison. 'Free the Weatherfield One'? It even got mentioned in parliament.

I couldn't concentrate on anything he was saying because every fibre in my body wanted to turn to Deirdre on the other side of the room and scream, 'THIS FELLA IS A LYING BASTARD, DEIRDRE. HE'S NOT A PILOT, HE WORKS IN TIE-RACK!' Of course I didn't. I just tried to get a grip of myself. It's not real, Peter.

Other bombshells that day included discovering that Fred Elliott talked posh in real life. I had a slash next to Mike Baldwin and found out that wheelchair-bound Maud could actually walk. We got to the end of the scene and she stood up and walked off. But she still let me wheel her all afternoon, the cheeky sod. I was glad I'd dropped that fish behind her counter, even if it wasn't real.

Up the Bird

Dave Spikey and I stayed in touch after the North West Comedian of the Year. We had a lot in common. Not just coming from Bolton, but we both had a similar sense of humour. At the time Dave was presenting a gameshow on ITV, *Chain Letters*. He asked if I'd like to write some jokes for the series. I was still working at the cinema at the time, ushering between stand-up gigs, so I said yes. What else did I have to do?

Dave was still working as a haematologist at Royal Bolton Hospital, which was about fifteen minutes away from my house. I was still living with my mum at the time and Dave would often come round in his dinner hour to write. He was asked by some producers at Tyne Tees television (where the series was filmed) if he had any other comedy ideas. He kindly invited me to submit some ideas with him.

Writing with Dave was something I looked forward to. He was easy-going and writing together just seemed to naturally flow. Of course, you never know if what you're writing is ultimately funny, you can only go with your instinct. If it makes you both laugh then hopefully you're on to something.

Ironically, describing the process of writing is quite hard to put into words. But usually one of us would come up with an initial idea, then the other would offer another suggestion, taking the idea a bit further or sometimes in a completely different direction. I'd never written with anybody before; I'd only ever jotted notes down for myself. But this new process was enjoyable, creating, sharing with somebody else.

Over the years I'd compiled books, ledgers, bags of scraps of paper brimming with thoughts, ideas, jokes, bits of conversations I'd overheard in the street, on the bus or at work. I'd no apparent reason for logging all these notes but I felt as though there was some higher purpose.

We came up with an idea based on a headline Dave once read on the front of a local newspaper: 'Dead Man Weds'. It inspired us to write about a small local newspaper and the challenges it faces. The first episode started with the funeral of Jack, the editor of the *Fogborough Gazette*. As his coffin was carried into the crematorium we could hear 'Jack in the Box' by Clodagh Rodgers.

The paper has now got a vacancy for a new editor. So, a local lad who's been working in London as a journalist for the past twenty years returns to take the job. He arrives at the train station and is greeted by a taxi driver who takes him to his accommodation. Unable to lower the volume because the button had snapped off, the car plays deafening music for the journey and they can only talk in the gaps between the music. It was all very silly but we liked it.

The new editor soon becomes suspicious that something sinister happened to his predecessor, and slowly he uncovers a conspiracy connected to a mysterious pharmaceutical company on the edge of town. Before you can say Erin Brockovich, the local water has turned bright green and there are sightings on the moors of twenty-foot-high turkeys.

We drafted out the series but it was dismissed when Dave and me were offered our own one-off special for Granada TV.

Mad for It was another series for new comedy writers. I've always been a big fan of road trips, and so I came up with the idea of driving from one end of the Granada region to the other in a motorhome.

We thought it could be in a documentary style, with Dave and me presenting to camera. There'd be a script of sorts, but it would also be improvised. We started in Buxton and stopped off at certain places of interest along the way, like an ice-cream parlour, Bolton Wanderers' football stadium and the Manchester Apollo, where we met up with the manager, played by Neil Fitzmaurice, or Neil Anthony as he was known then.

Neil was a brilliant stand-up from Liverpool who I'd met doing the clubs. He had a great mind for comedy and was sharp. Practically everything that came out of his mouth was funny, whether he was on stage or not. We really hit it off and crossed paths occasionally at stand-up gigs. Backstage, chatting in dressing rooms, or sharing a car to a gig. So when the offer of the Granada comedy came up I couldn't wait to get him involved in some way.

In his first scene, he limped across the stage at the Apollo theatre telling us how a light had fallen on his leg during a Status Quo gig. 'They were rocking all over the world while I was rolling around in agony,' he said in a very camp Scouse accent. To be fair, it was probably the highlight of the episode. There were a couple of other funny bits, like Dave standing by the side of the road pretending to do a speed check on passing motorists, using a hairdryer. The episode ended abruptly as we drove out of the Granada TV region. We realise when the picture breaks up, so we have to reverse and say our goodbyes.

The episode could have been better, but it wasn't bad for two comedians finding their feet. I considered it all a big learning experience, so it was worth doing it for that alone. Plus, the idea of two people sharing a motorhome would crop up again further down the line. My only frustration was not getting into the editing room, and so the director made different choices. I knew there was gold to be mined. Maybe I'd be able to get into the edit one day and help craft a show.

Meanwhile, my stand-up gigs were going from strength to strength. So much so that a presenter/producer from Granada TV called Iain Coyle got in touch asking if I'd like to do an interview about my career to date. What career?

The interview would be part of a series called *Funny Business* (I bet they were up all night thinking of that title) and could be recorded wherever I fancied. So being the eternal home bird, I suggested our house.

For years I'd dreamed about getting on TV, and now TV was coming to our house. The funny thing was I felt completely at ease with the crew being there. It didn't phase me at all.

The interview is great to look back on. To see our terraced house in Croston Street. The first half of the interview takes place with Iain Coyle and me sat on my mum's wooden 'emergency' chairs in the backstreet. Fortunately, no cars wanted to drive past.

In the distance down the hill, I can see Lever's Rope Works, where my mum and dad used to work in the 1960s. In fact, this is where they met. My mum had come over from Ireland and got a job there with her sister Bernie. Then she met my dad. Years later my dad would get a job working there again and I'd often meet him from work and we'd walk home together the full six hundred yards.

Iain Coyle

So, I just want to talk about you and what you do and why you want to be a comic?

Me

Well, I was working as a cinema usher in Bolton

Iain Coyle

Don't you still do that?

Me

Oh, yeah, that's where the real money is, £2.59 an hour

Iain Coyle

That's minimum wage now

Me

Is it? I don't think they've gone decimal down at the cinema
yet. But it's all showbiz, one minute you're on stage making
hundreds of people laugh and the next you're picking up
Toffos. That's real life

As we're talking you can hear chatter off camera, followed by
clattering and banging. The camera tilts to reveal some children scrambling across the backyard walls and wooden back
gates, noseying at what's going on.

Iain Coyle

So this is where you live, is it? It's not a prop or anything?

Me

No, this is where I live. I think what I'd like to do is make
enough money from showbiz so I can finally buy myself a meal
from motorway services and get out of this shithole

Then more children start to gather around us. Word must be spreading that there is a film crew in the backstreet and by now the whole neighbourhood is arriving, coming thick and fast from the nearby streets. Some women gather for a sneaky peek further down the backstreet but they quickly retreat when the camera points towards them.

Me

I think we should have got Ken Loach to direct this

Iain Coyle

Do your neighbours know that you do stand-up?

Me

They do. They've started acknowledging me. Women in leggings who never gave me the time of day before
I was on telly

Because of all the unwanted attention, we decide to relocate indoors. There's a quick shot of our front room décor (recently refurbished by Mick, my chain-smoking second cousin in Chapter 1). Then we head upstairs to my bedroom, where we get a glimpse of my beloved video collection. All positioned meticulously on shelves I'd put up the previous summer when I switched rooms with my mum.

Even though it's just a quick look, everything comes flooding back to me. I can see my *Beatles Anthology* that I bought with my prize money from the North West Comedian of the Year. Four tapes of *Porridge* next to twelve tapes of *Mork & Mindy*, all taped off TV. I used to spend hours crafting and designing the labels with coloured felt tips and individual letters cut from magazines. I imagine I might have been a virtuoso at the old ransom note.

Along the far wall at the back of my bedroom is an enormous mural of the Manhattan skyline that took Mick two days to put up with two packets of Solvite and sixty B&H. There's a small comedy book collection on an adjacent shelf, and I can see my wooden chair/bedside cabinet with my trusty cassette player sat on it. There's even a quick shot of my posters on the ceiling. *James and the Giant Peach* and *Digby: The Biggest Dog in the World* (the latter of which is worth a tidy sum. Handy to know if work dries up).

Iain Coyle

I'd like to talk about your name, as there seems to be a lot of Kays in comedy

There's Phil Kay, Paul Kaye, Danny Kaye and Gordon Kaye …

Me

He's just done a play at the Bolton Octagon Theatre

Iain Coyle

… and didn't you used to work there?

Me

I did, until I got sacked for telling Des Barnes from *Corrie* that he couldn't come in in white jeans. I'd already had a written warning for falling asleep on the front row of Alan Bennett's *Talking Heads* while wearing my work jumper

The mention of Danny Kaye reminds me I've one of his LPs, so I climb up a stepladder to my record collection. Before I eventually find it, I pull out *The Best of Tony Christie* on LP, which has '(Is This the Way to) Amarillo' on it. At the time I used to play it at the end of my stand-up so everybody could

41

sing along. I always thought it was a bit of a weird choice, as it only ever got to number 18 in 1972 and yet everybody still seemed to know it. I didn't yet know it would one day become such a huge part of my life.

I also dig out an official *Jim'll Fix It* Soap Medallion with Jimmy Savile on the box. This is basically a soap on a rope in the shape of a *Jim'll Fix It* badge that I'd bought at a car boot sale.

Funny how one thing leads to another. Somebody at the BBC saw my interview on *Funny Business* and made an enquiry: Would I like to do a screen test for *The Sunday Show*?

IMDb says that '*The Sunday Show* was an anarchic entertainment programme broadcast live on Sunday lunchtimes between March 1995 and December 1997' and that it 'launched the careers of Paul Kaye (who played the character Dennis Pennis) and Peter Kay'.

Obviously by cut and pasting that synopsis I've given away the fact that I got the job. I'd watched *The Sunday Show* occasionally, but I wasn't a fan. The comedy was always a bit too mean-spirited for me. Mean humour was all the rage in the late-nineties. Especially on a lot of panel gameshows. They often took the easy route of ripping the piss out of celebrities who couldn't defend themselves.

I've only ever done three panel gameshows or quiz shows. The first one was called *All Over the Shop* presented by Paul Ross. This was a gentle daytime show and the complete opposite of cruel. So much so that I even brought my mum with me when I appeared on it. It was recorded in the afternoon at Pebble Mill Studios in Birmingham. The only reason I did it was because I got to be on a team with Dame Thora Hird and Angela Rippon. Who could say no to that? Plus, I got £700 for the privilege.

All Angela Rippon did was moan about how the BBC had gone to rack and ruin: 'It was actually cheaper for me to buy the soundtrack of *Schindler's List* from an Our Price record shop in Shepherd's Bush with my own money than it was to get it from the BBC library. The lunatics, Peter, have taken over the asylum.'

I hadn't a clue what she was on about. I'd just sat down next to her in make-up and she was already on her soapbox.

Meanwhile, poor old Dame Thora was on her last legs, literally, as she was pushed into the studio in her wheelchair. I genuinely don't think she knew whether she was on a daytime gameshow or *Last of the Summer Wine*.

The second panel gameshow I did (which wasn't really a gameshow as such) was called *Night Fever*. Do you remember that? It was a karaoke show presented by Suggs that used to be on Saturday nights at 7 on Channel 5. That was great fun.

I did that five times because it was £900 a pop and you could help yourself to a buffet-style breakfast at the hotel the following morning. Each show had a musical guest, and one week I ended up eating a full English breakfast with Ottawan. You know, they sang 'D-I-S-C-O' and 'Hands Up'. In fact, I saw their 'hands up' waving at me to come and join them. Only problem was they're French and hardly spoke a word of the Queen's. The only French I know is *je m'appelle* Peter, *j'habite à* Bolton and *le pantalon* (which means trousers), so the conversation was pretty stilted.

The show was easy to film, all you had to do was sing karaoke, and the panel of guests was a virtual who's who (literally, because nobody knew who we were). Amanda Holden, Davina McCall, some wanker off *The Bill*, Handy Andy Kane, Jonathon Morris from *Bread*, Lionel Blair, Shaun Williamson (he loved it – a bit too much for my liking) and Keith Chegwin, to name but a few. We all took turns, boys versus girls, and Suggs dished out the points. What's not to love? Easy TV while drying your hair, before going clubbing on a Saturday night.

I was sat in the canteen once chatting to the lovely Keith Chegwin. He was being very candid about his drink problems and he was quite the sharer. He said things got so bad at one point he actually resorted to drinking the windscreen wash from his car's wipers: 'Maggie [Philbin, his wife at the time] got suspicious when I insisted on cleaning the car five times a day. She came outside and caught me spraying the wiper fluid while trying to catch it in my mouth.' Then suddenly we were interrupted by a very familiar voice: ''Ello.' We both turned to find it was Rod Hull, but without Emu.

That was freaky. He had two real arms; I was so used to seeing Emu and that shite plastic false arm.

I'd once tried in vain to get Rod Hull's autograph when he was visiting Bolton Town Hall for the Christmas lights switch-on, but his assistant said he couldn't sign any autographs because his writing hand was 'up the bird'. I was gutted. I suppose, on reflection, shoving a biro in Emu's mouth would've killed the magic.

Meanwhile, back in the *Night Fever* canteen (what a joy that line was to write), Rod Hull was sporting a rather fetching denim cadet cap, clasped at the front with a gold press stud. It was the kind you might have seen Huggy Bear wearing in *Starsky & Hutch*. The image of Rod in that hat has stayed with me for years, so much so that I had a similar one made for Brian Potter in *Phoenix Nights*. (Episode three, series one. Brian's wearing it while he's hanging out of his Cadillac shouting orders at Young Kenny, who's hanging a makeshift sign advertising a psychic (spelt pys-kick).)

Rod and Keith were clearly old friends and quickly dived into a conversation about the state of showbusiness, so I went to get some roly-poly. The dessert, that is. A month later Rod Hull died. He fell off the roof of his house trying to fix the TV aerial (I might love TV, but I wouldn't go to those lengths). I heard his funeral was a bit of a let-down but apparently the reception was fantastic.

I'm sorry. That was a bit of a tasteless joke at the expense of Rod and I apologise to any of Rod's family who might be reading this. By the way, if any of Rod's family are reading this, you wouldn't happen to know what happened to his denim cap? I'd pay good money for it. I bet Emu got it in his will.

The third and final panel gameshow I did was *Bring Me the Head of Light Entertainment*. Heard of it? No, neither has anybody else. It was on Channel 5 and it was presented by Graham Norton. I had to fly to Norwich, as it was filmed at Anglia Television, home of *Sale of the Century* and *Trisha*.

Now, I'll tell you something that shocked me, and call me naive, but the week before filming I was sent all of the questions for the show. Shock, horror. Apparently, that was standard practice with all panel gameshows. Who knew? I certainly didn't. I thought they made it all up on the spot. They don't, they get most of the info beforehand and most of them are still shit. Apart from *Would I Lie to You?* That one always makes me laugh.

When I turned up for the filming, we all met up in the green room (which still wasn't green) to chat through our answers before the show. A producer read out each question and each of us would read out our suggested answers. For example, 'What were John Lennon's last words when he was shot?' I'd written 'Oh no!' (Ono) and so had most of the other panellists.

There was an awkward silence and then one of the team captains said, 'I've got that answer too, but can we go with me as I'm on each week and I really need to keep my material strong.' So that was that. It felt like a closed shop. As for Graham Norton, I never saw him until we started filming.

The rest is a blur. I just felt like a fraud, the show was crap, and to add insult to injury the breakfast at the hotel was luke-warm with no beans.

Anyway, I've drifted ... where was I? Just let me go back and see ... ah, yes, I'd just got a job on *The Sunday Show*. On the first day, I arrived at reception at the BBC, Oxford Road in Manchester. I was taken up to the entertainment department on the fourth floor and introduced to a very buoyant man called Gary Monaghan. He was the series producer. We chatted about what he thought my role might be within the show each week. He asked me about things I liked, my hobbies. I told him that I'd always been passionate about TV. About all the videos I had at home, as well as my TV themes collection.

One thing I did mention was that I'd collected a lot of opening and closing credits to TV programmes and compiled them on VHS tapes. I know it sounds tragic (and probably went a long way to explaining why I was still single), but my VHS tape of TV credits always went down well at parties. Especially when everybody was drunk at two in the morning. I'd stick it on (whether they liked it or not), and before you could say *Hong Kong Phooey* everybody was singing along, from *The Fall Guy* to *Fraggle Rock*.

In the second year of my HND in Media Performance, we had a cabaret night at a local pub in Salford. Traditionally, the second years put on a bit of a show for the first years. Bravely, I'd put my name forward as compere for the night. I spoke to a friend from the technical department and they rigged a TV up to a video recorder so I could play my TV credits compil-ation in between the acts. It went down a storm (in my mind). No, really, it did. People love nostalgia. I should know, I've based my career on it.

I told this story to Gary Monaghan and he liked the idea of me doing something like that on the show. Within about fifteen minutes we'd come up with Peter Kay's World of Entertainment.

Cut to me live on a Sunday lunchtime stood beside a large TV monitor.

Me
(to the audience)
Give me an N

Audience
N!

Me
Give me a 'tertainment

Audience
'tertainment!

Me
Put them together and what have you got?

Audience
N-tertainment!

Me
I'm Peter Kay and welcome to my World of Entertainment

Then we had a singalong to the theme from *Monkey (Magic)*, and the audience went with it (mind you, most of them were still leathered from the night before). I was completely in my element.

I'd be lying if I said I wasn't nervous, especially knowing it was all completely live, but when they counted down in my earpiece and I started I was off. I was completely fine and even if I fluffed my words, I just laughed at myself and ad-libbed around it. Again, just like stand-up, I instantly felt completely comfortable and at home.

It'd been just over twelve months since I'd driven a getaway car illegally on ITV, and now I'd somehow wangled my own slot live on the BBC singing along to old TV theme tunes. How the hell had that happened?

Working on *The Sunday Show* was a proper full-time TV job. I even had my own desk, computer and, most importantly, a staff pass with a code that allowed me to plunder the BBC archives down in London. That was like being given the keys to Fort Knox for me. I was ordering everything and anything I could get my hands on. Old episodes of *Parkinson*, *The Flumps*, Mick Fleetwood and Sam Fox presenting *The BRITs*, the whole of *Live Aid*. There were boxes upon boxes of tapes arriving every day and I just put it all down to 'research'. Truth was, almost all of it was for my ever-growing personal collection. I even had to put more shelves up.

I'd also finally bought a car, after all those years of learning to drive. A red Ford Fiesta from a garage in Oldham. I'd won the money to buy it over the summer in the final of Channel 4's So You Think You're Funny? stand-up comedy competition in Edinburgh. Now, I don't want you thinking I'm being blasé about winning, but I talk about it all in my previous book, *Saturday Night Peter: Memoirs of a Stand-up Comedian* (which is also available from all good charity shops for under £1, or I can do you a signed copy for £3.50? I've still got two boxes in the attic).

One of the prizes was the opportunity to have your own TV special on Channel 4 (next chapter, coming up) and £1,500.

That's where the money for the Ford Fiesta came in. So now I could drive to work, clutching the wheel with both hands. Ten and two o'clock. The one thing I didn't get working on *The Sunday Show* was a parking space, so I always used to park in a space reserved for the head of religious programming. I thought, If *they* can't forgive me, something's wrong with the world.

The show would go out on Sundays, obviously, though people would still often ask me, 'What day is it on?'

'It's called *The Sunday Show*, when do you reckon?'

Then we'd get Monday off. Well, everybody except me. That's the day I'd come in and copy all the BBC archive to VHS.

It was weird because for the first time ever in my life I didn't really have a boss. I'd always had a manager or a supervisor, but with this job you were very much left to your own devices, which I found a bit disconcerting. On Tuesdays we'd all get together, Gary Monaghan, a few associate producers (still don't really know what they do), and we'd chat through ideas for that week's segment. Luckily, as it was autumn there was plenty going on with Halloween, Bonfire Night and Christmas coming up.

Wednesday, Thursday and Friday would be spent writing the script, searching through the archive and doing any filming that might be needed for my sequence on Sunday. I filmed a spoof of *Cracker*, where I played Robbie Coltrane interviewing Father Christmas. He'd been caught breaking into houses on Christmas Eve.

Another was a spoof of *MasterChef* presented by Loyd Grossman (I don't know what happened to him but I've just seen a jar of his jalfrezi in our pantry). I got some original footage from *MasterChef* and intercut myself with Loyd, so it looked as if I was actually on the show.

Loyd Grossman
What are you going to be making, Peter?

Me
Potato and leek Cup-a-Soup, Loyd. Followed by Smash, instant
mash potato with hot water, and I'll be adding in beans and
mini-meatballs with that, 5p a tin. For dessert, I'll be knocking
up some Elmlea rice pudding with a teaspoon of red jam for
added effect, stir it up, make it all pink

Saturday, we'd all meet up for a read-through of that week's script, and anything that needed changing at the last minute would be cut or added. A lot of the other cast would still be scrambling to put their sections together, but I'd already done mine well in advance. I wasn't a swot or anything, I just loved working and I'd always prefer to get it sorted.

I'd always pitch in and help the other cast if they needed it, we all got on very well. The main presenters were Jenny Ross and Paul Tonkinson. I got on with Jenny and knew her from doing stand-up around Manchester. Paul's a very funny comedian and a lovely man. Sadly, I never saw them much, as they had their own office and always had loads to do.

My World of Entertainment section was only originally allotted four minutes, but by the end of the series it had grown to over ten minutes. I was having a blast. One episode, I got three people out of the audience and tried to jump them with a toy Evel Knievel doll on a motorbike. I revved it up for ages and it failed, twice. So I ended up just throwing the toy over them as they lay on the studio floor.

Sunday morning, we'd all have to be in at eight for a run-through for the cameras. Then we'd be live at noon. The show lasted forty-five minutes and it'd whizz by. We found out towards the end of the run that this last series was to be axed.

I'd got on a sinking ship but who cared? I certainly didn't. It was nothing but experience, and I think I was indifferent about doing it all again, anyway. My World of Entertainment had a shelf life and even I could see that.

For the last episode, we decided to push the boat out, and we invited Jimmy Savile to make an appearance on my World of Entertainment to do a special mini *Jim'll Fix It*. The idea was that I'd written to him in 1980 asking if he could fix it for me to sing the *Jim'll Fix It* theme, only I never got a reply. Jimmy had found the letter down the side of his magic chair, and not being one to let a fix it go he chose to honour my request all those years later.

Jimmy said he'd do it for £500 cash and a box of his favourite cigars, which were £1,000. So the blond triangle rocked up in his shell suit and his bling for our last show. I found him to be a very eccentric character. You had no idea where you stood with him or quite what he was on about. From the moment he arrived he just talked utter nonsense, spouting weird quotes, crap jokes, limericks, anecdotes that didn't go anywhere or that he never finished. He also made a lot of noises, yodels, whines, whistles. 'Now then, now then.' Like so many, I'd grown up watching Jimmy Savile. He was a huge part of my life, almost an institution. He'd been on TV forever. Either doing *Jim'll Fix It* or telling us to 'Clunk Click Every Trip', 'Play It Safe' or that 'this is the age of the train'. We trusted him. He ran marathons for charity, for Christ's sake. How could we not?

On the day we rehearsed the segment to camera, I was to sing the *Jim'll Fix It* theme (a cracking theme, by the way, unfortunately now ruined forever). It had been specially re-arranged by Mike Flowers, who'd had a big hit with a cover a few years before of 'Wonderwall'. He arrived with his orchestra and his Pops' choir in tow. I'm telling you, the BBC spared no expense.

The only hint I got of Jimmy being immoral in any way was when he met our executive producer, Bridget Boseley. I remember she offered him her hand, which Jimmy took, then he flipped it round to kiss the back of it, but before his lips touched her skin I saw a quick flick of his tongue licking the back of her hand. Urgh! What was all that about? Bridget and I chatted about it later. She said, 'He licked the back of my hand.'

'I know, I saw him, the dirty old perv.'

Still, I got him to autograph my soap on a rope. Don't judge me, nobody suspected nothing at the time. I was counting on that signed soap on a rope paying for a kitchen extension one day. I'd be lucky if I could buy a fucking fish slice with it now. I might have to sell it on the dark web.

Years later I was invited to a showbiz soiree at the BBC, where it had recently relocated to Media City in Salford. I wasn't very keen, but Peter Salmon, the big cheese at the time, invited me and said I'd get to meet Mr Tumble from CBeebies, so I was in like Flynn.

Now, coincidentally, the night before, ITV had screened the now controversial episode of *Exposure*, *The Other Side of Jimmy Savile* presented by Mark Williams-Thomas. It broke the first revelations that Jimmy was not all that he seemed to be. Jimmy had died a few months before, and I remember watching it in bed with my wife, saying, 'Let the poor man rest in peace.' Ten minutes later I was aghast, shouting 'the dirty fucker', and I remembered him licking Bridget Boseley's hand all those years before.

Anyway, Guy Garvey from Elbow had also been invited to the BBC and I said I'd pick him up en route. I'll never forget his face when I pulled up outside his house playing the *Jim'll Fix It* theme full blast with my windows down.

The reason for the soiree was to meet George Entwistle, who was the new director-general of the BBC, but when we got there he offered us a quick handshake and said, 'I'm really sorry, I've got to dash back to London, it's all kicking off about Savile,' and off he went. I think he was director-general for about three weeks before throwing himself on his sword.

People wanted answers but, unfortunately, years had passed and a lot of people who'd been involved were dead, including Savile himself. It really was a terrible situation.

There were about fifteen of us for the soirée, including Mr Tumble (Justin Fletcher), Maxine Peake, Kay Mellor and a few heads of departments at the BBC, including the head of religious programming, who I finally apologised to for using his car parking space when I was doing *The Sunday Show*. We stood around awkwardly listening to a string quartet, then we had a lovely three-course meal and a chat about showbiz, and of course Savile.

I'll never forget how the night ended. Everybody had gone apart from Peter Salmon, Guy Garvey, Mr Tumble and me. The main corridor wall had a huge black and white mural featuring BBC icons from over the years. Michael Parkinson, *Only Fools and Horses*, *Dad's Army*, that sort of thing. Just like wallpaper, the images repeated along the length of the wall. I'll never forget Peter Salmon, he said, 'Here, could you do me a favour?' and he handed each of us a pile of big bright-yellow Children in Need Pudsey Bear stickers. 'Could you find Savile and cover him up?'

So there we were, up step ladders trying to find every image of Jimmy Savile so we could cover him up (ironically just what the BBC had reportedly been doing for years). It was like some depraved *Where's Wally?* or Where's Jimmy?

Coming in Your Ears

So, I went to London to meet up with the production company that was going to make the TV special for Channel 4. You know, the prize that I'd won at the Edinburgh Festival. The producer wanted me to do a stand-up special, thirty minutes in front of a studio audience. They were all the rage at the time. Being sat around a big table in this swanky London production office, I felt completely overwhelmed. Having my own TV special on a national television station was a huge deal, another one of my life's dreams, and so I found myself obliged to agree with them. I was kind of told that's what I was doing. It was all very quick and before I knew it I was back on the train home. In fact, I think it was the same train I'd come down on. I'm sure they'd just cleaned it.

On my way back I kept thinking about the idea of doing a stand-up special and something didn't sit right with me. It felt easy. It didn't feel like a challenge. I'd won an opportunity to make my own show on TV. I could do anything. This was a blank piece of paper. Doing stand-up just didn't feel like I was pushing myself.

I thought about what made me laugh, what inspired me comically. Victoria Wood's *As Seen on TV* had been a huge influence. Ahead of its time. I found Victoria Wood's writing extraordinarily funny, particularly when Julie Walters performed it.

When I was in third year at school it was on every Monday night on BBC2, and everybody in my class would watch it. We'd all gather first thing Tuesday morning in Miss Robson's English lesson and quote lines from the previous night's episode. It always made me laugh that all these burly teenage lads would be laughing and re-enacting lines from what was predominantly considered quite a feminine series. Quoting Patricia Routledge's Kitty monologues or Susie Blake's continuity announcer between the sketches. The sketch we all looked forward to the most was the weekly fly-on-the-wall documentary spoofs. 'Swim the Channel', 'Winnie's Lucky Day', 'Billy', 'Looking for Mr Right' ... they were all so funny and still are, the subtlety of the performances and the uneasy looks to camera. I can still quote so many of the lines word for word today.

Just on a side note, I was so shocked and devastated when Victoria Wood died. It still grieves me to even type those words. I still can't believe it and still can't face watching any of her series yet. It's too hard. Fucking cancer. I hope I live to see a cure for it in my lifetime.

Then, a few weeks after Victoria Wood, we lost Caroline Aherne, also to cancer. Awful, no other way to put it. Two hugely talented people that made so many of us laugh. I'm telling you, soak up the comedians while they're still here, these clowns that light up our lives, because when they're gone, they're gone. People are always surprised at the void they leave.

Cheery, but I wanted to say something about Victoria Wood and Caroline. I was lucky enough to meet Victoria Wood a few

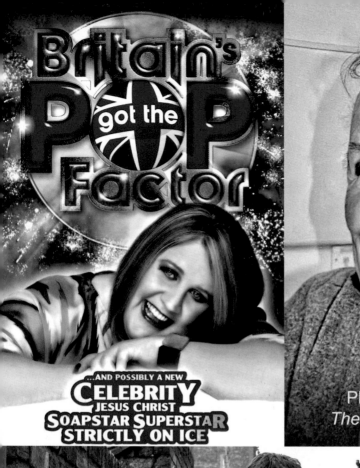

Playing a character in *The Catherine Tate Show.*

FROM THE MAKERS OF **PHOENIX NIGHTS**

MAX & PADDY'S
ROAD TO NOWHERE

'Peter Kay's comic masterpiece' - The Mirror

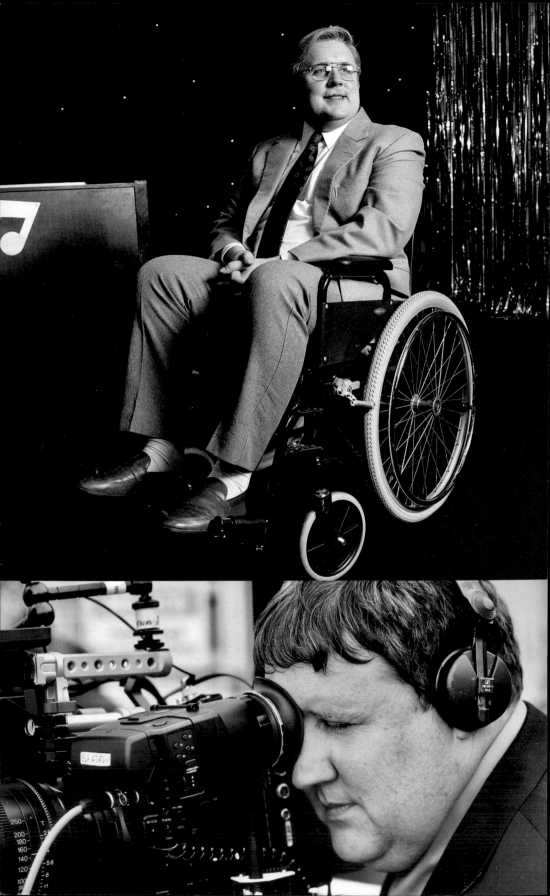

As the Abzorbaloff in *Doctor Who* – what a load of old bollocks

times. The first time I ever met her I plucked up some courage, went over and quoted some obscure line from *As Seen on TV*. It was so obscure that I'm not sure she even recognised it. She just nodded and smiled politely. I'm sure she must have been thinking, 'What a bell end' as the conversation grew stilted. I just wanted to try and convey to her how much she meant to me. It's difficult.

When I have had the good fortune to meet a few people that I admire, I always want to try and express to them how much they mean to me. I really want them to distinguish between me being just a passing fan as opposed to being an obsessive (and I don't mean in a tied-to-the-bed *Misery* kind of way). It's as if I want them to see inside my mind and understand what a huge impact they've had on my life. Fortunately for me, I've met all of my heroes. Ronnie Barker, Mel Brooks, Robin Williams, Billy Connolly, Victoria Wood and Billy Joel, and you'd be surprised how funny Billy Joel actually is.

I was lucky to meet Robin Williams for a few minutes after one of his rare stand-up performances in London. Nervously, the only way I could try and convey how much he meant to me was to tell him that I had every episode of *Mork & Mindy* taped off the TV. 'Wow! Really? That's dedication.' He was lovely, by the way, and exactly how I would have wanted him to be. God rest him.

I still haven't come to terms with his death, either. That really knocked me. It's the only time I've ever felt compelled to go on Twitter and pay tribute to somebody. I even wrote the tweet but then decided not to post it, as I find the whole social-media tribute thing a bit weird. Always the same 'celebrities' jumping on the bandwagon, saying the same things every time. It all feels shallow. I know what I thought of Robin Williams and my ninety-five episodes of *Mork & Mindy* on VHS say it all.

On *This Morning* once they said, 'And tomorrow we'll be joined by funnyman Robin Williams.' I did a double take towards the TV and spat out my Sugar Puffs. *This Morning* was filmed in Liverpool, which was less than an hour away. The next morning I was up early and off, on the train to the *This Morning* studios at Albert Dock in Liverpool to meet Robin Williams. I stood outside the studio for about an hour in that fine rain that soaks you through, only to be told by a Scouse security guard that Robin Williams wasn't even there. He'd filmed a pre-recorded interview in London a few days before. Crushed, I felt like flinging myself on Fred's weather map in despair.

Anyway, I've drifted again, but I think it was warranted. So, there I was on my way home from London thinking about the Channel 4 stand-up show proposal and what comedy most inspired me, the spoof documentaries on *As Seen on TV*. In 1998 there were a lot of half-hour documentaries on TV (or docusoaps as they were nicknamed). *Paddington Green*, *Hotel*, *Lakesiders*, *Driving School*, *The Cruise*, every channel was making them and the public loved the fact they were real. I thought they'd be great to parody. It'd be a challenge but one that excited me.

I needed a situation that'd make a good docusoap spoof. Definitely something that hadn't been done already. By the time I got to Rugby I'd come up with the idea of motorway services. I loved the idea because motorway services are such classless places. Everybody stops there, rich, poor, all walks of life, not to mention the staff who work there too. It felt like a winner.

Over the next few days, I wrote copious notes on characters and stories for the episode. Enthused by the idea I met up with a few of my friends from school and Dave Spikey. They all came round to our house to chat through ideas. A mate of mine who'd been working at Tesco told me about a DJ that turned up to try and promote a local radio station, only they put him at the far end of the car park and he was furious. We all thought this was very funny and so Chorley FM and the character Paul Le Roy was born. We needed a tagline for the station, 'Where the Listener Comes First', then my friend Paul added 'Coming in Your Ears', which we all thought was hilarious.

In fact, I've kept Chorley FM ever since. It's appeared as a fictitious sponsor on another series I made and I've even had merchandise made for tours, car stickers and contraceptive foam (that's a lie).

I felt the episode needed a linchpin, a main character that everything revolved around. A manager, or how about a manageress? I could play her, that certainly would be a challenge. Plus, the thought of it also scared me, which I always think is a good thing. Pearl Hardman is the services' lifeblood; she adores her position of authority and everything it entails.

I'd also started to consider playing multiple characters too. I thought, Why not? Have a go. I think you're a lot more fearless when you're starting out. The production only had a budget of £5,000, so at least me doubling up and playing some of the parts would only help with the cost.

I decided to go on a trip to a motorway services. It was there that I saw a roadside recovery man outside the main entrance in the rain, trying to flog cover to people as they walked past. He'd make a great tragic character. I doubted we'd get permission to use RAC, so I thought, What if he's been sacked and in his bitterness he's set up his own roadside recovery service, called ARC (Alan's Roadside Cover)? We could slowly discover that many other aspects of his life have gone wrong, leaving his mental health on the edge of a precipice. The documentary crew discovers that not only has he lost his job, but also his house, his wife and, by the end of the documentary, his mind. I couldn't write the ideas down quickly enough.

Staying true to the format of the docusoaps I thought it'd be good to have a 'next week' sequence at the end. It'd be a good chance to conclude storylines and perhaps in some cases offer a punchline. Using that method I was able to give Alan's ARC story a conclusion. At the end we see him losing the plot, smashing up his makeshift roadside recovery stall and staggering off down the motorway slip road with his trousers around his ankles, singing 'We Will Rock You'.

That was fun to film. However, some passing drivers weren't so chuffed, seeing a middle-aged man in his underpants staggering towards speeding traffic. Stunned by what they saw, a few of them rang the police, and when they arrived at the services a short time later, we had quite a lot of explaining to do.

Filled with ideas I headed back down to London again to meet up with the producer. Unfortunately, she wasn't as enthusiastic about the ideas as I was and still had her heart set on filming a stand-up special. I think it was because she'd been working on those types of series for the previous few years and obviously felt very comfortable, but I didn't. I told her that, on reflection, it didn't feel like stand-up was enough of a challenge for me. I just felt I wouldn't be pushing myself enough. She wasn't convinced and so I felt I had no choice but to stand my ground. I said I'd rather do nothing than do something I wasn't passionate about. That was a very hard thing for me to say. I mean there I was, on the brink of my own TV special, and I'm practically saying 'no, thanks'. Please don't get me wrong, I wasn't being arrogant or ungrateful, it just didn't feel right to just go with the flow.

As I was leaving, I walked past an office belonging to an executive producer I'd briefly met once before. He shouted me into his office. It was good to see him and we had a chat about the Channel 4 special. I told him about my predicament with the producer and my ideas for the spoof docusoap. Before I knew it, I was enthusiastically acting out scenes right there in his office, reciting lines and character voices. He laughed a lot and said he thought it was a great idea. He said he'd have a chat with the producer, as he could see how enthusiastic I was.

Thank the Lord he was true to his word, because a couple of days later I got a call from the producer telling me that my idea was officially a goer. The only problem now was finding a motorway services that would let us film there. They contacted them all, Welcome Break, Roadchef, Granada, but they all said no. The popularity of the docusoaps had scared them off. They were all nervous their brand would be damaged, especially it being a comedy too.

I understood that, but of course what I was planning wasn't going to be malicious at all. The production company still kept trying but to no avail. It even got to the point where I was asked to try and think of setting the episode somewhere else.

Perhaps a supermarket? That just felt like it'd been done already. A motorway services felt fresh and original.

Then we had an incredible bit of luck. I got a call from the producer telling me that we'd got permission to film at a motorway services. First Services, they were called, and they only had two service stations in the whole of Britain. One was in Swansea and the other one, you won't believe this, was on the outskirts of Bolton. What are the odds of that? I knew the services very well, as it was the only one on the M61, about three miles from home. It was a perfect location because it was a bit run-down at the time, which I loved, as it added to the comedy.

We had another production meeting in London where I decided to tell them I was taking the plunge and playing all the main characters myself. There were now five in total. Pearl Hardman, the manageress; Paul Le Roy, the DJ from Chorley FM; Alan, the angry ARC man, and two new characters: Utah, a coach driver who dressed like a cowboy, and Matthew Kelly, a customer care assistant who worked at the services and was also studying drama at college. I also decided that Matthew should be Northern Irish, as I could do the accent easily thanks to my mum.

Matthew is mopping the floor in the toilets.

Matthew

I hate it here. I'm sorry I'm ratty. I'm tired. I think I've got ME … and I was up all night learning my lines. We've got a big final production next week and I've got six monologues to learn. We're doing *Electra* by Sophocles, I'm playing Orestes the son of Agamemnon, that's a laugh, can you believe that? I've got to work up enough motivation to stab my own mother for three nights … and a matinee at a hospice

I know it was a tall order taking on so many characters, but I was so excited that the fear was measured. Plus, I also felt safe filming so close to home. I genuinely think if I'd been filming in another part of the country I'd have been a lot more nervous.

Now all I had to do was get my head down and write the actual script. The production company gave me a deadline. Slight problem, Susan and I had booked a fortnight in Las Vegas a few months before. I treated myself to a new-fangled laptop from Dixons with a floppy disc, no less. At least that meant I could take it on holiday and type on the go. I wrote everywhere, at the airport, on the plane, in the hotel room, by the pool with a towel on my head. The script poured out of me. I was completely consumed with ideas and it has been like that ever since. Whenever I write it takes over and I find it hard to switch off. It's as if some antennae have gone up and I find myself listening to everything around me for inspiration.

The production company needed the first draft of the script so they could start working on it back in the UK. I just had to figure out how to get what I'd written off my floppy disc and over to them. That's an absolute piece of piss in today's world. I could probably send it on my phone in a few seconds while simultaneously vaping, but in 1998 it was like pulling teeth, even in America.

The struggle I had trying to find a shop that could send my script to London was a nightmare. I finally found a printing shop that said they could fax it for $42, the robbing sods. Why they couldn't just email it, I still don't know. I was so desperate to get it sent I just paid the money and then waited over two hours for each page to be slowly faxed. Viva Las Vegas.

The production was assigned a director, Andrew Gillman. He'd worked on the trailblazing comedy series *The Day Today* so came with very strong credentials. I took to Andrew straight away. He was incredibly sardonic and very placid. He brought in two make-up and wardrobe crew, Sarah Jane Hills and Fiona Dealey. They took me to a place called Angels in Camden to basically play dress-up as we slowly created the five characters I was to play. We spent time with a very flamboyant wig designer called Brian Peters. As there wasn't much money in the budget we ploughed through Brian's cast-off wig box, with leftovers from other TV series like *Soldier Soldier*, *Cadfael* and *Robin of Sherwood* (that's where I found DJ Paul Le Roy's mullet). These wigs would then be styled to fit me. It was great fun playing dress-up (and let's be honest, that's basically what TV is). I tried on plenty of costumes too. It was a fascinating place, filled with over seven floors of film and TV memorabilia.

It was full steam ahead (whatever that means). We had another production meeting, this time at the actual services in Bolton with the crew. It was perfect, even more downtrodden than I remembered. It's not like that today, having had a complete revamp. It now has a Costa, Greggs and a Subway, but at the time it just had a granary-style café, a little shop and an arcade with driving games. Which is something I could never figure out. Who wants to pull in off the motorway and have a rest by going on a driving game?

There was also a footbridge that linked the north and south sides of the services. Most of the bridges that link motorway services are usually undercover, but this one wasn't. It was then I had the idea of Pearl the manageress getting a tip-off that a celebrity was going to be visiting the services. TV's own Bob Carolgees and Spit the Dog. You must remember Bob and Spit the Dog? They were on *Tiswas* and *Hold Tight!* They're still going. Bob sells Yankee Candles in Cheshire and I've no idea what Spit does. Spits, probably.

With the knowledge that Bob and Spit the Dog are en route, Pearl rolls out the red carpet, only to discover that Bob has arrived but he's on the opposite side of the motorway. Matthew, the customer care assistant, legs it across the footbridge clutching a red carpet. He's overtaken by a local photographer who tries to get a picture, but all he manages to get is a quick glimpse of Bob's car (registration Spit 1) as it pulls off down the slip road.

'Oh, what a bastard,' shouts Pearl over her walkie-talkie.

Just like Chorley FM, I've always tried to keep Bob Carolgees and Spit the Dog in everything I've made. I see it as a bit of a long-running game for fans. Try and find where or how Bob and Spit will pop up. Why not see if you can spot them? Answers on a postcard …

Another storyline that I enjoyed was with the character

Utah – the Wild West coach driver. Unfortunately, he parks his coach right in front of Paul Le Roy's DJ equipment, completely blocking his view of the services from the arse end of the car park. Paul is furious and goes off to complain to Pearl.

Utah tells his passengers, 'We're just stopping for a leg stretch and a toilet stop, it's just ten minutes so don't go getting a meal.' This message clearly falls on deaf ears, as a French couple never return and are last spotted queueing up in the granary. Utah drives off, leaving the French couple stranded at the services, but Paul Le Roy is finally out of obscurity.

Utah was based on a driver I met when I went on a coach holiday to Barmouth in Wales. He was dressed as a cowboy, in full Wild West regalia, but he never referred to it once. He even had a pistol on the belt, which I presumed was fake. He struggled to manoeuvre the coach through the tiny villages: 'Jesus wept, it's like threading the eye of a needle.' He also kept referring to the coach as a female, which was very funny: 'She's a thirsty girl, this one, she likes a drink.'

And so did the driver. 'I'm spitting feathers,' he said, parking up and flicking on his hazards outside a newsagent. He ran inside for a bottle of pop. Only to discover in his haste he'd bought a bottle of cordial by mistake, but he didn't realise it was undiluted orange until he poured it down his throat. Immediately, he spat it all back out over the windscreen and dashboard, coughing the word 'fucker' as he emergency stopped outside Woolworths.

Meanwhile, back in the episode, Pearl, the manageress, is in her office dealing with the aftermath of the missing French couple, who've apparently now got back on the wrong coach.

Narrator
It's one o'clock and there are clouds on Pearl's horizon

Pearl (on the phone)

Yes, well, there's going to be plenty of coaches coming into the car park, we're a motorway services. A French couple? No, not to my knowledge. I'm very busy and I've enough to be dealing with without dealing with people getting back on the wrong coach. What? … Well, that's NMP love, not my problem

She hangs up.

They've a damn cheek, National Express, phoning up here. Apparently a French couple has got on one of their coaches by mistake. I mean, what's that got to do with me? If had a pound for every person who got back on the wrong coach in this place I'd be a millionaire. I'd have four pounds for this week

Cut to later and Pearl's back on the phone.

Pearl

Well, it's not my problem, is it, Gavin?
(hand over mouthpiece – talks to camera)

This is this bloody French couple. They're up the M6 now having a ploughman's. Well, they want to try putting their clocks back an hour, they're in England now, we invented time. We're chock-a-block down here today, Gavin, yes, we're talking double figures. Well san fairie ann to you too an' all

She hangs up.

He's a cheeky get, that Gavin Allroyd. He used to work here, he used to mop toilets under me before he got lured over to Lancaster as lodge manager, all exotic

> The bloody French, you know, me and our Dean got caught up
> in Dieppe in '93 in one of those tractor and truck disputes.
> Eight hours, we were stuck … and nasty? They were setting fire
> to sheep at one point. It's a pity they weren't that bolshie in
> 1939 when we needed them

I used the 'next week' section at the end of the episode to get in another great line from Pearl, when she comes strolling out of the gents' toilets and shouts, 'I don't care whose it is or what it is, but it's floating.'

I thought it would be good to have a supporting cast in the episode, so I wrote a part for my friend Sian – a character called Alison who works in the granary. We catch up with her as she's doing prep.

Alison

> I'm not happy. I'm gonna kill Edina. She never does any prep
> and then she calls in sick with a water infection. Yeah, right,
> funny how it was her sister's hen night last night. She did this
> to me last week she called in sick, supposedly she had a bad
> leg. Anyway, I know for a fact she didn't because R Jason saw
> her that night in Club Excess off her face dancing on a podium
> doing the 'Macarena'

> Then she waltzes in the next day, reeking of Tia Maria, hands
> me a sick note and then buggers off. You know, I'm surprised
> she doesn't have that sick note laminated

It was so lovely working with Sian and in something that really was for TV. We both couldn't believe it. We still can't, after all these years. She's such a naturally funny person. In fact, I've just had a text off her about two minutes ago. She'll go mad but here's what it said:

'I went to HIIT Step this morning. Screwfix car park at 6. I felt like a new woman at 9 – now I'm not sure I'll make it to 5 p.m. I'm booked in again for tomorrow night but it's in Makro car park next door, as Screwfix is open late.'

Anyway, I'll get back to Sian later in the book. Another good friend who I've always believed is an absolute talent (and chancer) is Paddy McGuinness. We've known each other almost all of our lives, we actually met in nursery. Like Sian, Paddy is one of those special people who is naturally funny without trying. I asked Paddy if he fancied doing a cameo in the episode as a customer care assistant. He clocks Paul Le Roy spinning discs and dancing at the far end of the car park. He turns to the camera and says, 'Who's that dick?' Looking back, the only thing that's funnier than Paddy's line is his hair. I think he must have been going through a bit of a *Gladiators* phase at the time, as his hair resembles Wolf's.

Having friends and family in the episode and around during the filming made the whole thing even more special. My mum came down to the services with R Julie and my two nephews, who appear in a scene dancing in front of Paul Le Roy's disco equipment. They're mortified when they see themselves now, but it's great to look back on. Even my mate's dog Patch makes a cameo.

We filmed for four days in total, Monday to Thursday, and I don't recall there being any particular issues or stresses. In fact, I think everybody found the whole thing enjoyable.

The crew and Andrew the director headed back to London to work on the edit, which didn't take very long at all. I think it was completed within a week. I had to go down to record the narration for the episode. It was weird seeing it for the first time. I was very proud of it and so was the producer. I'm really glad I stuck to my guns and we went in that direction.

'The Services' was the first-ever episode of Channel 4's *Comedy Lab* series, which continued for a further 13 years. It gave new comedians a chance to have their own experimental half-hours. 'The Services' must have been well received because I was nominated for a Royal Television Society Award for best comedy newcomer at a big swish ceremony in London later that year. I found that more nerve-racking than filming. I didn't win.

I've never been a fan of awards. Of course it's great to be singled out and nominated, but there's suddenly so much pressure. Then, if you lose, you're a bit gutted. Please don't get me wrong, I'm not grumpy or ungrateful, I just find awards stressful to deal with.

Anyway, let's not end this chapter on a downer, as unbeknownst to me, 'The Services' was about to lead to bigger and better things.

'Have you ever thought about making a series?' asked the executive producer.

I stared blankly at my empty dessert plate at the awards ceremony. I hadn't, but it certainly sounded like an interesting idea.

The Big Sell

I was told the best way to write a series is to start with a thing called a treatment. This involves putting down all of your ideas and trying to come up with some sort of structure for each episode. That was the plan with my first series in 1999. Write a treatment then take it to Channel 4 to see if somebody fancied stumping up the money to get it made.

I was still very keen on the style of spoof documentaries that I'd used in 'The Services'. The standard template for a British comedy series has always been six episodes, but I was finding it difficult to come up with six different stories set in the motorway services. Then I had an idea to do a different story for each episode. I was inspired by a series that Ronnie Barker made in the early seventies called *Seven of One*, where each week he played a different character or characters.

Originally, it was to be called 'Six of One', with a planned sequel called '... And Half a Dozen of the Other', but then it was decided there would be seven episodes so that gag was ruined. In the end, the BBC chose two episodes to turn into a series: *Open All Hours* and *Porridge*. I wasn't aspiring to that level, I was just trying to find six good stories.

Somebody once said, 'Write about what you know.' I knew about my life in Bolton, my experiences with all of my part-time jobs and the people around me.

I also thought there could be a lot of comedy focusing on characters that are struggling in an ever-changing world. An ice-cream man, a bingo hall and a working men's club are three examples.

So, I started to write sat on the edge of my bed – I literally didn't have enough room for a chair. My laptop perched on the computer table I'd bought from Argos. I was self-conscious writing (I still am). My typing skills were crap and so was my grammar. Thank the Lord for spell check.

Scouring old notebooks for inspiration, I started to find ideas I'd written over the years. A treatment is like an extended synopsis. Each episode had a two- or three-page description of who the characters were and what might go on in the story. Slowly the episodes started taking shape. I just needed to put the hours in.

Which I did. I think the thing people never realise is how much time it takes. Nor should they, really, but it's all about the finer details. Writing and rewriting. A good tip is to step away from what you're writing, even if it's only for a few hours or overnight. When you read it again with fresh eyes you can immediately see what works and what doesn't. I'm sorry to say that the process never gets any easier and there's no simple way around it. Another good tip is recording your thoughts. It's easy now, having software like Voice Memos on your phone. I used to use cassettes and a tape recorder. There's usually always something you'll say out loud when you're rambling into a recording that'll be handier when transcribed.

After a few weeks, I felt happy with the treatment and sent it to the production company. They formatted it into a fancy binder with a picture of me on the front and a title: 'Peter

Kay and His Friends in the North'. This was a reference to a successful series called *Our Friends in the North*. I wasn't so keen on that title. It felt parochial and I felt it ran the risk of alienating people unless they were northern. But before I had a chance to say anything I was in a taxi on my way to Channel 4.

I never enjoy the big sell. It's tough pitching your ideas and never fails to feel awkward selling your dreams to somebody – hoping they'll understand what you're trying to pitch, and hopefully laugh. I met with a bigwig at Channel 4 called Kevin Lygo. He was actually really nice (and I'm not just saying that because he's now the head of ITV). We got on, and fortunately he laughed in all the right places and his laughs felt genuine. For some reason he was very keen on me playing a woman again. I've not got a clue why.

So right there in his office, he gave the series the go-ahead. Wow!

This was monumental. My own series. A television series that would be listed in the TV guides like *Look-in* (well, perhaps not *Look-in*, as it didn't exist anymore, but it'd still be in a TV guide somewhere and that was good enough for me). I celebrated on the train home with a Chicken Royale meal from Burger King and a can of Tizer.

Another huge bit of good fortune was that apparently Channel 4 had to redirect a portion of their annual budget towards regional programming. That meant filming in and around Bolton would meet that criteria. So we could film near home. Woo-hoo!

I've nothing against London but home is everything to me. I think that if I'd had to work in London or be away from home I would have given it all up. Seriously. Being near home is what keeps me sane. Now, don't get me wrong, I know Bolton. There's good and there's bad, but I love the fact that

I've lived there all of my life and almost everywhere is a memory. Being connected to real life is important. I still go to the same shops I've always gone to, and why wouldn't I? Sometimes people see me and say daft things like, 'What are you doing in here? I thought you'd be in London,' or, 'I thought you'd have a butler doing this for you.'

Anyway, I've gone off the point again. So, now, having the treatments for each episode was a huge leg-up. I asked Dave Spikey and Neil Fitzmaurice if they'd like to write the series with me, which ended up taking nine months. That was because we were all still doing stand-up gigs and Dave was also working full-time. Neil would come over to our house now and again to write, but what was weird was the three of us never once met up together. We wrote everything via email and over the phone.

My other friends also chipped in, Paul, Michael, Tomo and Paddy would all throw ideas in. In fact, anybody who met me over those nine months probably contributed something to the writing. As I said earlier in the book, my writing antennae were up.

The production office was in London. The idea was to prep two episodes down there and then come up north with the crew to film two episodes over a fortnight. So, I'd been down in London for a few weeks at a time to have production meetings and spend time with make-up and costume. I was back at Angels choosing character costumes and also back in Brian Peters' wig box.

I'd become good friends with Craig Cash and he let me stop at his flat in Covent Garden, which was extremely kind of him. I'd be prepping the episodes for my series and Craig was filming *The Royle Family*. We'd meet up back at his flat at night for tea and to watch a film. We were like *The Odd Couple*. I've fond memories of that time and it was much better than stopping in a hotel on my own.

Sometimes, when I didn't have much to do during the day, I'd stay in his flat and watch *The Sopranos*. It'd just come out on video at the time. So I went up to HMV in Trocadero and bought volume one (episodes one to three). I'd then go back to Craig's and watch them. Then I'd take them back to a different HMV in Oxford Street and swap the video for volume two (episodes four to five). What a tinker! This convoluted process continued for a whole month until some smart-arse staff member caught on and my ruse was thwarted. I've still never seen the end of series one.

Craig and I got on so well that he asked me if I'd like to help write a film version of *The Royle Family* called *The Royle Wedding*. I was over the moon, as I loved the series and, like Craig and Caroline, I had an infatuation with real-life dialogue. I was all set to write the film but Caroline changed her mind at the last minute and decided to make a Christmas special instead. Who knows what could've been? I've still got my writer's contract for the film.

Shame, as it's always been one of my big ambitions to make a film about a family wedding. Ever since I saw *Four Weddings and a Funeral*. I really enjoyed it but kept thinking to myself, I don't know anybody who has a wedding reception in a castle, marquee or stately home. My wedding experiences had always been upstairs in a pub function room or a working men's club, and always with a DJ, never a live band.

That's just reminded me of a DJ who used to work in Bolton. He was blind and luckily all of his records were in braille. I used to have visions of him trying to play an ashtray by mistake.

Anyway, so the first day of filming arrived, Monday, 12 July 1999. Orange Day, but I wasn't orange, I was red with embarrassment because I overslept. I was woken up by the sound of children walking to school. My alarm didn't go off. I was mortified. You are powerless when you oversleep. I stared at my clock in disbelief. Then leapt out of bed, threw my clothes on and legged it down to my Ford Fiesta.

It was my first day on my first ever series and I was bloody late. We were supposed to start filming at 8 a.m. It was 8.45 and I was forty-two miles away.

You see, I know I said the series would be filmed in and around Bolton, but the only location we could get for a bingo hall was in Blackpool.

I arrived around 10 a.m. and parked up on a side street. I turned the corner to find a whole load of big white filming trucks parked alongside the bingo hall. Wow! We never had trucks like this when we filmed 'The Services'. Now we'd gone up a gear. This was proper professional. Costume trucks, catering (still my fav), production trucks, make-up, generator trucks, lighting trucks and all of the cast and crew sat in the bingo hall waiting for me. They must have thought I was a right diva. I got a huge bollocking from the producers (quite rightfully so). Fortunately, as it was my series, they couldn't exactly fire me, but they certainly came close. I sheepishly and hungrily headed off to make-up. I'd missed breakfast too.

The first character I was playing was Tom Dale, the king of the bingo callers – a cross between snooker ace Ray Reardon and Dracula, with hair so black it was almost navy blue. I thought I'd play him with a very deep Scouse accent. To ease myself in, my first scene was with Sian. She'd been cast as Yvonne, a customer care assistant who's working at the bingo hall over the summer. Tom is giving her an appraisal in his office.

Tom
You seem to lack commitment

Yvonne

I wash pots

Tom

I know that, but I'm sure a pretty girl like you could be a bingo
caller if she wanted

Yvonne

But I don't want to be a caller

Tom

Have you no ambition? Have you no idea what you want to do
with your life?

Yvonne

I'm only here for the summer and then I'm back at uni

Tom

Uni? What are you studying there?

Yvonne

Advanced economics, politics and European law

Tom

That's all very well and good, but where's that gonna get you?

The scene was quick to film, as I was very comfortable with
Sian by my side (well, across a desk). It was also comfortable
with Andrew Gillman directing again. The next scene was Tom
Dale discussing working at the bingo hall.

Tom

I've given this club something it never had, class. I give the
billy bunters what they want. I've had all the top acts. I could
have got Shirley Bassey last year but her agent said she
wouldn't get changed in the toilets

After that scene, we moved inside the actual bingo hall itself.
Beautiful art deco design, as, like most traditional bingo halls,
it was once a theatre/cinema. I'm so glad we filmed at the
Apollo in Blackpool, as a lot of the other locations we saw
were modern and soulless.

We invited the real customers who played at the Apollo to
come down for filming. We supplied them with free drinks,
food and, most importantly, bingo tickets. They had a great
time. They were very giddy about being on camera, but they
were even more thrilled to be playing bingo all day for free.
The first scene we filmed was Tom coming on stage to 'Let's
Get Ready to Rhumble' by PJ & Duncan (well, Ant & Dec).
He then did some opening patter, not too dissimilar to what I
was used to hearing when I worked at the Top Rank Bingo a
few years before.

Tom

Hello, everybody, welcome to the Apollo. Good to see it so
busy this afternoon, was the cemetery shut? Just kidding.
Couple of hellos before we kick off. Sheila's in from Wigan.
Hello, big Sheila, you alright? Wigan is famous for two things,
rugby players and beautiful women. What position do
you play, Sheila? Just a bit of fun. Is Elsie Jackson with
us this afternoon?

Cheer.

There she is. Hello, Elsie, love. Seventy-eight years young
today, that's from your daughter Sandra and your sister-in-law
Sherise, many happy returns. I tell you, Elsie, if I was ten years
older … you'd be dead. Only kidding, love. Speaking of death,
the lady who collapsed at the back of the hall in the
wheelchair Tuesday afternoon sadly died this morning at
Bolton Royal Infirmary, but we've sent her a wreath of flowers
from the Apollo, so on with your blue kick-off flyer now, any
line, anyway, any four numbers across and let's tickle those
balls, eyes down for a full house

The idea was to film a different character each day, Monday to Friday. Even with the late start Tom's scenes didn't take all day, and by five o'clock we were done. I decided to stay over in Blackpool (I didn't want to risk being late again). That night all the cast and crew went out to the Pleasure Beach. It was good to see everybody relaxing. A bit like when you're with your teachers on a school trip. We went on all the rides, the big dipper, the log flume (twice) and the revolution (thrice). We all had a brilliant time and, of course, we all got fish and chips after, it's the law.

The next day I was back in make-up being made up into a character called Theresa, one of the female punters who played bingo. They did a great job of the make-up and costume, as I blended right into the crowd in my Princess Diana jumper. That jumper was specially made, we commissioned an artist to paint a portrait which we printed onto a light-blue sweater. We then added crystal beads onto the fabric to make it look even more tacky. Funny that this jumper would occasionally turn up in several series over the next twenty years. Lest we forget the Queen of Hearts.

I filmed all my scenes alongside another actress called Beatrice Kelley, who played Rose, Theresa's sister.

Narrator

As loyal followers of bingo at the Apollo, sisters Rose and
Theresa have been coming for twenty years and rarely
miss a session

Interviewer

What do you enjoy about bingo?

Rose

Oh, it's got it all, drama, glamour, tension, chips, fish, peas and
a drink for £2.49. I mean, what more do you want?

Interviewer

Let's say you're one number away from winning the jackpot.
All you need is a six and a nine, and Frank Sinatra suddenly
walks in and offers to make mad passionate love to you both.
What would you choose?

Theresa

There's no comparison. I'd say no, sorry Frank, thanks for the
offer of sex but I'd much rather have the sixty-nine

Rose

Too right. Anyway, when we were young we never had time for
sex, we were too busy having babies

Just like I was making 'The Services', I was in my absolute
element filming. It was everything I'd ever wanted it to be and
more. It felt as if we were getting funny stuff. The lighting
crew were laughing a lot so it must have been funny. I always
think if the lighting crew are laughing you must be doing
something right, because most of them don't give a monkey's
about what they're working on.

On the third day, I played another character, Patrick O'Neill, who was basically me playing me in a blond wig. Most of the episode was reminiscent of my time working as a customer care assistant at the Top Rank Bingo in Bolton. I worked there in 1994, the hottest summer for a hundred years, and I was collecting glasses in a room with no windows. It was without a doubt the worst job I ever had, and my clothes would stink of smoke every night when I got home, due to the amount of chain-smoking bingo players creating a thick fog that constantly hung in the air. I should sue Top Rank for passive smoking. I would cycle to work every day, just like in the first scene, where I ride into the bingo hall on a mountain bike.

Patrick
What's got ninety balls and screws old women?
Bingo. It's true

Old people, you can't beat them, pity. I tell you, they pour in the cast of *Cocoon* week in, week out, the same faces every time with their pensions burning a hole in their shoulder bags, spending every bit of money that they've got. Loose change, life savings, they won't even have enough left for a still orange. That's why most of them smuggle in their own drinks. I'm not kidding. Orange cordial in a bag for life

Funny but completely true. I eventually got sacked from my job at Top Rank but kept the manager talking for another twenty-five minutes just so I could get some extra wage before I clocked off. The manager in the scene is played by Pearce Quigley, who I'd worked with on my first ever job, 'Two Minutes' at Granada TV (remember, in Chapter 1?). It was so good to be able to work with him again and surround myself with friends. I was honestly having the time of my life.

Another funny actor I bumped into at the Edinburgh Festival was a man called Alex Lowe (who I'd also go on to work with many times). He too played a customer care assistant, called Sparky (because he got struck by lightning), in a scene along with Sian and me.

We're on our lunch break, sat in a small room in the back of the bingo hall, discussing why I won't attend a fire and safety meeting. It's because I don't want to spend my lunch break with a weirdo.

'Who's the weirdo?' asks Yvonne. I tell her it's a fire safety officer who has the nickname Dogtanian. Rumour has it that he has a fondness for dogs that far exceeds them being man's best friend. I think you know what I'm saying.

The entire scene was filmed in one take and I still don't know how, because we were laughing so much, even after they'd shouted cut. That scene was an introduction to the final character I was playing in the episode and one of the funniest characters I've ever created. With his basin haircut, seventies porn tash and tinted glasses, he looked the essence of the dodgy jobsworth. You basically wouldn't leave him alone with your kids, let alone a puppy.

Now, due to historic legal reasons I'm not permitted to reveal the character's name, which is crazy, especially as you can buy a DVD of the full series for a pound on eBay. I'll explain the reason why later in the book, but for now I'll just call the fire safety officer by his nickname, Dogtanian.

So Dogtanian is at the bingo hall to warn the staff about the dangers of fire safety. When we first meet him he's surrounded by staff and about to begin his talk. Sian's character, Yvonne, is flicking through a magazine. She reads the headline 'I snog my dog, says *Heartbeat* star Nick Berry'. Dogtanian yanks the magazine out of her hand and tells her to hand out some leaflets.

The magazine turns out to be his. 'Why have you coloured the dog's lips in red?' asks Yvonne. Embarrassed and flustered, he completely ignores her and starts his talk, which basically involves a lecture on fire safety.

I'll never forget filming this scene, as it was the first time I'd ever played two characters on screen at the same time. This involved quite a bit of precision. We filmed all the shots with me as Dogtanian, and then over the lunch break I transformed back into my Patrick character. Then we filmed all his reactions and interjections while somebody stood in and read Dogtanian's lines. It felt convoluted at the time, but I was impressed by how believable the scene looked when it was edited together and I think it's completely unnoticeable that I'm playing two characters.

Dogtanian reminds the staff that 'smoke kills in seconds and fire kills in minutes' and then he probes them on how to deal with a chip fire. Yvonne suggests putting water on it. Dogtanian is alarmed at the suggestion: 'Water?! If you do that then, Woof! The whole place will go up.'

Patrick interjects: 'What and the whole place will go up?'

'Woof!' replies Dogtanian (which is actually funnier now with that nickname). This causes the whole group to burst into hysterics. A very funny scene to film, made even funnier and more believable by using some of the actual staff who worked at the bingo hall.

Just like 'The Services', each episode was to end with a 'next week' scenario. We also managed to get Andrew Sachs to record all of the narration for the full series. Which was a big coup, as he did the voiceovers for a lot of the BBC docusoaps, so it brought a great authenticity. He said he was also happy to send them up.

In the 'Eyes Down' episode, Dogtanian is interrupted mid-safety briefing when the police turn up unannounced and want him to answer some questions.

Hesitantly, he gathers his things. We hear the squeak of what sounds like a dog toy when he picks up his bag. He is then led away down a staircase and that's where the scene ends. There was actually more filmed. I tripped and rolled down the staircase, dragging the two coppers with me. It was a very funny moment … In fact, it got a spontaneous round of applause from the cast and crew. But for some reason the sound man touched the camera and accidentally recorded over that footage, so unfortunately it was lost forever. Such a shame. The clumsy dickhead.

Mother Taught
Us to Hover

The following week, after filming in Blackpool, we were back in Bolton for the second episode, 'In the Club'. It was great to be on home turf and near to location (in case I overslept again, which I never did). Also to be filming a subject that was close to my heart, working men's clubs or social clubs. They'd always been a big part of my life. I'd been going to them since I was little. My dad used to take me to their Christmas parties. We'd go far and wide. I'd get left in a main function room for a few hours for party games while my dad would be in a games room sinking pints and playing snooker.

The Rumworth Labour Club was one. I used to get so excited because they always had pasties from Ye Olde Pastie Shoppe and had a fairly decent 'Father Christmas' (usually a committee member in a tatty old costume that spent its life stuck in a box under the stage). Their shoes were always the giveaway. I used to check all the committee members' shoes during the party and the ones that matched Father Christmas were the giveaway. Father Christmas wouldn't suit beige slip-ons. Well, not while he was working.

The thing I liked about the children's parties was that you'd always get a gift, and at the Rumworth Labour Club it was always a decent one. I got a toy car transporter one year, a decent set of felt tips another. Plus, you always got a selection box. My dad was still putting me down for the Christmas party when I was well into my teens. His twisted logic being it was well worth the price of a ticket in exchange for the present and selection box. I'd stop at home, he'd pop in for a pint and pick up my gifts. This continued until the committee got wise to our charade and I was nineteen.

The party always ended up in carnage, with seventy hyperactive kids from the neighbourhood throwing chunks of pasties and jelly at each other across the room. While a member of the committee tried showing cartoons on a projector. It was a thankless job. Lord knows why they did it.

A few nights later I'd be over the road at the Connie Club. Their party was always on a Wednesday night and would be much more sedate. I don't know if it was because they were Tories, but all the kids were a bit better behaved. For three years on the trot we had a magician. He'd do a card trick with a blindfolded wooden duck, and by the third year I knew it word for word.

I bumped into him in the toilets and casually said, 'You doing the duck routine again this year?' He wasn't amused as he zipped his flies and stormed out. The dirty pig didn't even wash his hands. Well, I wouldn't be picking a card from his duck's mouth for all the tea in China.

The year after, the Connie Club took us all on a coach trip to see a circus in Warrington. All I remember is puking up on the coach home after eating too much candy floss and watching John Carpenter's *The Fog* on BBC1 with my head in a washing-up bowl. Happy Christmas.

I had a party at St Williams Social Club in Great Lever with music from the resident DJ Jimmy Mack (real name Harold Fish; I could see why he changed it). He always used to end the party by playing the Motown song 'Jimmy Mack' by Martha Reeves & the Vandellas, but hilariously he'd interrupt after each line:

> *Jimmy Mack (singing)*
> What?
> *Jimmy*
> Yes?
> *Oh Jimmy Mack (singing)*
> What?
> *When are you coming back?*
> Next week

I was only eight, but I used to piss myself laughing.

Another annual Christmas party was at St Gregory's in Farnworth. This is the location I chose to film all of the exterior scenes for 'In the Club' and later for *Phoenix Nights*. Also, there was a party at the Anglers Club on Rishton Lane. Lord knows how my dad got me into that party, he'd never been angling in his life.

I was to get one of my first jobs at the Anglers Club years later, signing members in on the door and glass collecting on a Saturday night with my friend Paul Coleman. I also got to see all the acts in the main function suite. They were either fantastic or, more than usual, fantastically bad. It was the juxtaposition that I loved. Greengrocer by day, Neil Diamond by night.

Razor wire on the roof outside, car alarms going off, but inside a little Las Vegas. It spoke volumes to me. I even used to collect black and white photos of the club acts and hang them on my bedroom wall. Sad but true.

It was the naffness that I found both funny and fascinating. I wanted to emulate these club acts in the episode and so I came up with the storyline that the Neptune Club is hosting the grand final of a local talent competition. Park Avenue, a singing duo, had reached the grand final and the documentary catches up with them backstage for a chat. I played Marc Park.

Marc Park

I push Cheryl a lot but it's for the good of the band, and what she lacks in talent she makes up for in determination. She's a grafter, she's my bridge over troubled water, and she drives the van

We didn't even make it to the final of Talent Trek last year, we just did the heats. We did songs from the West End shows, Cheryl's idea, big mistake. We did *Cats*, *Starlight Express*, *Miss Saigon*, those people wouldn't know Miss Saigon if she was serving pastie and peas. It was on its arse and so was I, literally. I mean, you want to try playing bass on rollerblades dressed as a Persian. Crap. We came second to a plate spinner but not this year, this year I'm in charge and I've cooked up something special

I wanted the episode to be affectionate, never cruel. Marc Park was a self-absorbed idiot, with his long ginger hair (reminiscent of Mick Hucknall), huge nose and Bolton Wanderers top. Later replaced with a Manchester United one when he finds success.

The music for the series was composed by a fine musician called Tot Taylor who I'd met during my prep in London. He had a tiny budget but managed to create some fantastic music. We both worked hard on a medley for Park Avenue for the Talent Trek final. It featured 'Let Me (Us) Entertain You' by Robbie Williams into 'Nothing's Gonna Stop Us Now' by

Starship, where Cheryl briefly replicates a mannequin (from the film of the same name).

Marc Park
Ladies and gentlemen, I think you'll agree that the band behind me have both been … simply the best

Cue the Tina Turner classic painfully mashed up with 'I'm Horny, Horny, Horny' by Mousse T. Throw in a couple of badly timed flash-pot fireworks at the end and it wasn't a far cry from one of the acts at the Anglers Club.

Claire Rhodes (who played Cheryl Avenue) and I worked hard choreographing and rehearsing the medley at a dance studio in London a few weeks before, on my twenty-sixth birthday (it almost felt like my fiftieth birthday by the time we'd finished). It's hard to explain, but we're all familiar with the backstage footage from *Strictly Come Dancing* and just how much effort and time goes into learning all the routines. Fast-forward to a fortnight later and we were on stage at the Farnworth Veterans Club in Bolton in front of a real audience.

Just like at the Apollo bingo hall in 'Eyes Down', we used the venue's real punters, which gave the reactions authenticity. They genuinely didn't know what to expect when each act in the talent contest appeared on stage, as they thought it was all real. Maybe having free booze helped. I think some of them even tried voting.

Park Avenue were introduced on stage by Jerry 'The Saint' St Clair, real name Jerry Dignan (named after a very good friend of mine, Danny Dignan, who put in a good word for me doing warm-up on *Parkinson* a few years before). Jerry was played by Dave Spikey, his first time acting, I think, and he did a very believable job of capturing the essence of a club compere full time.

Jerry lives for his alternative life in clubland and the joy of performing. By day he's a bricklayer. 'When I was sixteen I fell into bricks and bricks get in your blood, but there are two halves to me. There's my work half, which is bricks, and there's my play half, which is what you'll see tonight.'

Jerry takes to the stage with his backing band Les Alanos. 'It's Les, Alan, Us, Les Alanos,' coughs Toby Foster before he shows off the new drum pads he's picked up at a car boot. 'There's not a noise I can't make on this set-up now.'

Like Dave, Toby was a stand-up comedian I'd known for a few years. He has a natural comic talent. Funny without doing very much. That was what I was after, and that is why I wanted to use a lot of stand-up comedians in the cast.

I thought they'd bring a realism to their performances. They also instinctively have great comic timing and can squeeze laughs out of each performance every time. The downside is they're usually crap at learning lines and their continuity can be dodgy. A cigarette or a pint of beer in a different hand for each take.

There were appearances from quite a few other stand-up comedians in this episode. A very funny comedian called Archie Kelly, who played Kenny Snr. Mark Jackson, a great stand-up who played Alan in Les Alanos. Another was a good friend I'd met at Salford College, Steve Edge. Now he is a funny man. I first saw him in *A Midsummer Night's Dream* at Salford University, and I hadn't got a clue what was going on in the story but Steve could make anything funny with just a look. I said to him that night after the show, 'If I ever get any work in TV I'd love you to be in it,' and four years later he was playing Alan in the series. The only character who turns up in four of the six episodes.

I was to play four characters again in this episode. Marc Park, Paul Le Roy (the Chorley FM DJ from 'The Services').

The third character was a doorman called Max. He'd been hired for the night alongside Paddy O'Shea – played by Paddy McGuinness.

I knew Paddy would be perfect for the part, so much so that I called the character Paddy, so as not to add to any additional nerves. It was basically just us together as we very much were in real life, only I had a deep voice.

Paddy was a bit nervous about taking on the part and that uncertainty grew when the producer insisted that he audition in London. I remember we spent a lot of time in my front room running the lines the night before. He gave a great audition. I mean, the part was literally written for him, and after I also gave the producer and director an impassioned plea Paddy got the part.

The scenes with Max and Paddy were a joy to film, as we were incredibly comfortable with each other. Having a close friend by my side really helped me, as the whole filming experience could be a bit overwhelming. We did our scenes in a few hours outside the club one night. One storyline was Paddy has some kind of sexually transmitted disease and insists on asking Max's advice, showing him his penis in between people arriving.

Paddy
Look at it, it's all, like, raw

Max
Put it away, man, I don't want to see that …

Paddy
Just take a look

Max

Is it weeping?

Paddy

Weeping? It's crying

Max

Well, what have you tried?

Paddy

I've been putting toothpaste on it

Max

Toothpaste? What have you put toothpaste on it for?

Paddy

Well, it's full of fluoride, isn't it?

Max

Bleach is full of hypochlorite, isn't it, but you wouldn't bathe it in that, would you? Would you? Yoghurt is what you need

Paddy

Yoghurt was the first thing I tried, but I kept getting pieces of fruit stuck behind my foreskin

Max

Live yoghurt, you tool, not fucking Müller Light

The fourth character I played was the club's owner, Brian Potter, who was named after and inspired by Mr Potter from *It's a Wonderful Life*, a wheelchair-bound cantankerous curmudgeon who rolls around Bedford Falls causing nothing but upset. I absolutely loved playing Brian, as he was such a grumpy old sod who just undermined everybody around him. In the episode, we discover how he lost the use of his legs in quite an intimate scene in his office, where he's checking the club's Christmas lights.

Brian

Christmas already, where does the year go to? I've never been a big fan of Christmas, very stressful time, very stressful if you work in clubland … *(pause)* … and it'll be four years this Christmas since the accident

Interviewer

Do you mind telling me what happened?

Brian

I was managing the Aquarius Club. We'd had a very ropey first year trying to keep our heads above the water, in a water full of sharks. We'd planned a big Christmas bash, fifteen quid a ticket, sell out, and then tragedy, there was a big freeze, pipes burst, water everywhere. Utter chaos, people running around getting electrocuted, it was like something out of *The Poseidon Adventure*. I was terrified. I had to swim to the safe for the night's takings and that's when I saw it coming towards me. Fruit machine. It pinned me up against a serving hatch. Then everything went black. Then all I can remember was this bright, warm, pulsating glow, drawing me towards it. The firemen said it was the fruit machine, but I've got my own beliefs. I was in a coma until the new year. When I woke up I'd lost my club, I'd lost my legs and I'd lost my will to live

Dave and I went out to do some research for the episode. We got permission to sit in on the quarterly general meeting of social clubs, which took place upstairs at the Rumworth Connie Club in Bolton. What a sight. It was full of Brian Potters, all clad in suits, shirts and slip-on shoes. Everything was discussed very seriously. New acts on the rota. The padlocking of fire doors. The much-debated controversy of female condom machines being installed in the ladies' toilets. My hand was aching, as I couldn't write it down quick enough. Then, to top it all, the meeting was brought to a close by a short talk from a lady from Rentokil. Talk about awkward in a room full of men.

She passed out some pamphlets and gave an update on 'the seat-wipe situation': 'It is a growing problem and, as most women know, sitting can cause infection and other discomforts. Mother always taught us to hover but that, I feel, does not promote feminine hygiene. We'll get there eventually, girls.' There was one barmaid at the back of the room. The Rentokil lady continued: '… speaking of toilets, we do know that a lot of clubs have problems with blockages, especially in the gents' urinals. This is caused by bacterial growth, which is brought on by uric salt.'

Bloke sat near me
Uric salt?

Bloke sat with him
Piss

She spent fifteen painful minutes talking about bogs, backsplash mats and channel blocks (those pineapple chunks that you often see sitting in the gents' urinals next to the used chewing gum and a few stray pubes): 'We can supply urinal cubes that come in a variety of scents, Calvin Klein's Obsession and Hugo Boss. Has anybody got any questions?'

Voice from the back
Yeah, where have you parked your van?

She ignored the comment and wrapped things up: 'Anyway, me and Janice will be lurking in the corner for the next half hour, but thanks very much for listening and enjoy your buffet.' Buffet! After all that? I grabbed a couple of whist pies as I legged it out of the door. I thought, That scene's got to go in the episode somewhere.

One of the scenes that I enjoyed the most was when Brian and Jerry are interviewed in Brian's office. They sift through some of the old club act photos and chat about the acts they've had over the years.

Brian
We've had some shit over the years

Jerry
Remember him?

Brian
Tommy Tanner

Jerry
'Crikey, not likely'

Brian
I gave him that catchphrase, he used it on the *Royal Command*, the thieving get

Do you recognise these two?

Jerry

Oh, don't tell me … The Tippet Twins

Brian

Correct … they weren't even twins

Jerry

They weren't sisters

Brian

They were lesbians before it was popular

Jerry

What was it they used to do?

Brian

'Swanee'

Jerry

That's it, a comedy minstrel act. They used to black up and go
on stage. Black up, can you believe it?

Brian

You couldn't do that now

Jerry

PC

Brian

If I went on stage tonight blacked up, they'd hang me
from a tree

Jerry
They'd take you out, it's mental

Brian
Crazy

Interviewer
Have you ever discovered any celebrities?

Brian
Oh aye, in my clubs … Bob Carolgees and Spit the Dog, the Krankies, T'Pau, Tom O'Connor. He started in one of my clubs, he got thirty-five quid. Then he got famous and when he came back he said he wanted forty-five. I said we'll give you forty but we'll let you win the raffle

Jerry
That's what you used to do in those days

Brian
Then next stop, *Name That Tune*. He didn't want to know us after that. I've always said it. The higher a monkey climbs the more you can see its arse

Jerry
But I thought he won *Opportunity Knocks*?

Brian
He was playing my clubs before he did *Opportunity Knocks*. Hughie Green, he were another one. I never liked that man. He wouldn't give a door a bang

Jerry
He had VD, didn't he?

Brian
Yeah, ninety-five on the clapometer every week

As usual, the episode ended with a 'next week' sequence.

'It's the children's Christmas party. Children are singing "Jingle Bells" loudly as Brian is being pushed into the main function room dressed as Father Christmas (in beige slip-ons). His wheelchair transformed into a temporary sleigh and Les Alanos dressed as oversized elves.'

In the next sequence we see Brian and the committee discussing booking an act for the children's Christmas party. Brian initially wants to book a local comedian called Nobby Allcock but they settle on Le Windy Dick, 'direct from the streets of gay Paree with his self-taught acrobatics and balloon sculpture, a pure flight of fantasy with a whole host of unforgettable characters, including Ricardo, his pet snake which erupts from his mouth'. Kenny Snr agrees 'the frog's a winner'.

Cut to the Christmas party and we see a scantily clad man on stage with his back to the camera gyrating provocatively in front of a crowd of hyperactive children. He's also holding and waving a very phallic-shaped balloon which is emanating from his genital region.

Narrator
Le Windy Dick is much more daring than Brian and the committee ever expected

Brian, Jerry, Les Alanos and Kenny Snr watch on in horror.

Le Windy Dick was played by another talented friend of mine from Salford College, Dave Galbraith. We filmed a second version from behind Le Windy, where he removed his sparkly robe to reveal a tight G-string perched between his bare arse cheeks. Unfortunately, Dave forgot he was practically naked and turned around to speak to the director, thus revealing his bare arse to the audience of children. They howled with laughter but their parents weren't amused at all. In fact, they were livid as they watched from the back of the function room. I immediately bolted from my wheelchair/sleigh and legged it out through the back fire-doors before the stampede ensued. The producer and director had a lot of explaining to do in order to calm the outraged parents.

The final scene of the 'next week' sequence was the biggest stunt of the series, when Brian's Christmas lights cause a fire at the club. The production department had done an amazing job building a prop façade. Full replica windows, pebble-dashed cladding, doors, and the whole thing went up in flames. We even had a fire engine putting out the fire.

Even before the series had finished filming I was getting an inkling that I might have found the episode that could possibly become a series, but in order to do that the club would one day need to rise from the ashes. See where I'm going?

Where There's Tragedy There's Trade

Narrator

An ice-cream van trundles its tuneful way along a British street.
Is this once-familiar sight in danger of extinction? Has the ice
age had its day? Are ice-cream men now dinosaurs roaming
desolate streets in search of man?

Robert Edge is Mr Softy Top. On the streets of Bolton, where
he's been dispensing ice cream for most of his life, he's known
as Softy

Mr Softy

The arse has fallen out of this business, nobody wants
ice-cream men anymore. Today it's Ben & Jerry and Häagen-
Dazs, and who in their right mind would want to queue for a
cornet in the piss rain when they can get one out of the SPAR
anytime they like?

The opening scene to 'The Ice Cream Man Cometh' was filmed
in the style of *Taxi Driver*. By attaching cameras to the side of
an ice-cream van we could replicate the taxi scenes when

Robert De Niro was driving. We even got permission to use the original Bernard Herrmann score from the film. I enjoyed hearing such dramatic sultry music playing over shots of a brightly coloured ice-cream van. The humour was in the contrast.

I wanted this character to be obsessed with movies and reference them a lot. Later in the episode he wears a T-shirt with Robert De Niro as Travis Bickle in *Taxi Driver* on, with his head shaved into a mohawk and holding two handguns. Mr Softy also re-enacts the famous 'Are you talking to me?' scene from *Taxi Driver*. Robert De Niro makes a contraption that triggers a gun down his arm straight into the palm of his hand. Mr Softy has a similar contraption, but this one sends an ice-cream scoop into his hand. We also shot a spoof of the opening scene from *Apocalypse Now* in Mr Softy's flat. We followed the shots of Martin Sheen getting drunk meticulously. He cuts himself and wipes his blood around a mirror. Only we used raspberry sauce. I like the detail.

Mr Softy's flat is over a takeaway called Kebabylon. The real flat belonged to Ibby, one of my mates I used to work with at the local cash and carry. That's why I love filming in Bolton. I had insider knowledge of so many locations and people, and I was slowly learning how it was possible to utilise places for many different purposes.

Being an ice-cream man is seasonal, that's why Mr Softy rents porn videos from his freezer for a bit of extra income. I really knew an ice-cream man who did a sideline in blueys. He'd always have two queues down at his van. One line of children, and one of blokes wanting porn. How could he?

Mr Softy is parked up and is talking to the interviewer. Darren, his young assistant, is also in the van.

Darren

It took me a while to get my head around it. I had customers coming up asking for big feasts, strawberry splits and screwballs. I didn't know if they wanted porn films or something to suck on …

Mr Softy

Or both. They're all good, though. They're always on loan. Look here, I've got *Beverly Hills Cock*, *Shaving Private Ryan*, *Schindler's Fist*, every one a winner and very popular with the gents. Hey, don't look so shocked, my friend. It's the real world out there

The episode needed something else, though. Another storyline. Years before I'd seen a film called *Comfort and Joy*, written by Bill Forsyth. If you've never seen it, I highly recommend it. It stars Bill Paterson as a radio DJ in Glasgow who somehow gets embroiled in a local ice-cream war between two families. I thought I'd take that idea and apply it to two rival ice-cream men who keep trading on each other's patch. One serves whipped ice cream, the other scooped.

Signor Whippy is the new kid on the block and Mr Softy isn't happy about it.

Mr Softy

That bastard's messing with tradition

Interviewer

Who, Signor Whippy?

Mr Softy

He'll not get a 'signor' from me, not while I draw breath

Mr Softy

Well, for a kick-off, he's not even been chiming for twelve months and I've already had reports that he's been trading on my patch. If I catch him I'll bite his fucking nose off. He's not even from here, he's not even Italian

In order to heighten the plot I wanted Mr Softy to catch Signor Whippy on his patch selling ice cream. I thought a housing estate would be a great location for a possible chase between the two ice-cream vans. I knew the perfect place in an area of Bolton called Great Lever. This is where my first girlfriend used to live. I'd sometimes catch a bus up to her house after school. I had to wear glasses when I was young, shitty NHS ones, and I badgered my mum and dad to buy me a snazzy private pair. Eventually, they caved in and bought me a big silver-rimmed pair like Deirdre Rachid-Langton-Barlow off *Corrie*. They were quite posh at the time. They must have cost a packet. Anyway, I took them up to my 'girl' friend's that night to show off, but when I got back home later I couldn't find them. I was in a right panic. I rang her to see if I'd left them at her house. She called me back a few minutes later.

'I've found them,' she said giggling.

'Oh, thank God. My mum would've lost her mind.'

Then she burst out laughing. 'I found them up at the bus stop and the bus had run over them.'

'SHIT!'

She was still laughing the next day when she brought them into school. I slowly prised my flat glasses case open to find shards of glass and my lovely silver frames now squashed beyond all recognition. Just like I'd be when my mum found out.

I was thinking of that moment when I floored the ice-cream van past the bus stop, chasing Signor Whippy's ice-cream van. Mr Softy is then thwarted by a lollipop lady stepping out to cross with some children. Beady-eyed viewers might spot the lollipop lady, Doreen Gash, turning up in another episode in the series where she wins a Bolton Community Award. I tried to cross-reference plenty of people and places throughout the series in an effort to create some sense of community. This particular episode even has a cameo from Alan the ARC man that I played in 'The Services'.

One of my favourite moments is when we discover Mr Softy has chained his bottle of raspberry sauce to the counter of his ice-cream van. Just like the banks used to do with their pens. He also drives to the scene of a road crash at one point to sell some ice cream to the onlookers gathered at the accident. 'Where there's tragedy there's trade.'

I was very fond of Mr Softy's macabre side and wrote a scene that was sadly cut where he's stooped so low as to sell ice cream in a cemetery. We see a group of mourners at a graveside all clad in black. One mourner casually joins the group licking an ice cream. The person next to him whispers, 'Where did you get that?' The person with the ice cream nods and we cut to reveal to Mr Softy selling ice cream from his van to a queue of mourners. Unfortunately, our series budget couldn't stretch to the funeral set-up.

We did film another scene where Mr Softy's young assistant Darren is forced to change all the prices on the side of the van before they drive on to a posh estate. That ended up in the deleted scenes section of the DVD.

Lots of footage was cut from the series simply because the scripts were massively overwritten. The cemetery scene was just too long to film and I was too naive to cut the scripts down. Problem was, each episode could only be a maximum of twenty-five minutes in length, so something had to go in order to get down to time.

Andrew the director was in the edit in London and he'd send me rough cuts on VHS every few days, but by the time the tape arrived it was already a couple of days out of date. It was so frustrating. I longed to be in the edit where I could time each laugh, but it was out of my hands.

So I'd flip out at what choices and cuts had been made. I'd write these long, impassioned emails back to Andrew, pleading with him to try and put footage back in. My text in block capitals, underlined: 'PLEASE COULD YOU PUT (SUCH AND SUCH) SCENE BACK IN, AS IT'S ONE OF THE FUNNIEST BITS IN THE EPISODE? YOU'RE CUTTING THE BALLS OUT OF IT.' Well, something like that, but probably with a lot more effing and blinding (I love that expression). On reflection, it must have been very hard for Andrew. Especially with me on his back all the time. I just wish I could have been in the edit with him.

Once I'd finished writing the entire episode of 'The Ice Cream Man Cometh', I accidentally deleted it. 'What did I just press??' Whatever it was, the whole script was gone. I just sat there staring at my screen. It was gone. All of it.

Such an awful feeling of despair. For some reason, I hadn't even backed it up. All I had was a load of notes in ink. I just had to try and remember it all. It was five o'clock in the morning by the time I finished rewriting. From that day to this I still press save every couple of minutes (he types as he saves).

A particular favourite scene from the episode is one where Mr Softy talks about his father.

Mr Softy

My father was a great ice-cream man. I'm good but he was great. He knew all about tradition and he'd be out in all weathers; rain, hail, snow, it never bothered him. Everybody loved him. Very sad when he died

Interviewer

What do you think made him so special?

Mr Softy

Well, for a kick-off he actually liked kids

Interviewer

... and you don't?

Mr Softy

No. They make this job a misery. The bane of my life. You know what they used to do to my dad? They used to slap the back of his ice-cream van and then lay down in the road. He'd brake, thinking he'd hit them. They'd be lying there pretending to be in agony and he'd be handing them free Mini Milks through the serving hatch. They did that to him for years and he fell for it every time. That was his problem. Lovely man, soft as shite. They won't do that to me, though. If I hear a bang on the back of the van and I see them lying in the street, well, they better get the power back in their legs before I reverse or it'll be bye-bye, Sunday football, bastards

Mr Softy was such a mean-spirited man. How could you serve ice cream and hate kids?

Some of the last scenes we filmed for the episode involved Mr Softy arriving late at the Bolton Show only to find his pitch has been nicked by Signor Whippy.

The Bolton Show takes place every August in Leverhulme Park, and fortunately for us the weather was glorious that weekend, which is a real rarity. The show features all sorts of archetypal stalls that you would expect at an event like this. Lots of competitions (best jams and cakes, etc.), army displays, dancing displays, lots of food on sale, bouncy castles, and Fred Dibnah always used to show up with his steamroller. Well, until he sadly died. We managed to capture all of the above and put it to an eighties soundtrack provided by DJ Paul Le Roy from Chorley FM, who also made another cameo.

Narrator
With very few customers Mr Softy has had to take action. The right publicity for his scooped ice cream could help him win the war with Signor Whippy

Paul Le Roy
That was Culture Club with 'Church of the Poison Mind', classic eighties on your classic radio station Chorley FM – Coming in Your Ears. We're down here at the Bolton Show, and if you're feeling hot and bothered in this glorious weather and you want some traditional ice cream from a traditional ice-cream retailer then go and see Mr Softy, located at the other side of the field. He's here all day and he won't try and fob you off with any of that foreign muck laced with chemicals

We then see Paul Le Roy surreptitiously reading the spines of some VHS videos; he's clearly been bribed by Mr Softy.

Mr Softy unleashes his secret weapon: 'Double cones – twice the ice for half the price'. Things are going very well for him until Darren notices they're running out of ice cream. Mr Softy has forgotten to remove his adult videos from the freezer.

'Oh, shit. What are we going to do?' Darren says in a panic.

'You're going to have to go to the SPAR quick and get some tubs of ice cream … and get some flakes too.'

In Darren's absence, Mr Softy is reduced to rationing ice cream on people's cones.

'I'd like some ice cream with my cornet,' says one angry customer.

'I've got more raspberry than ice cream.'

Darren eventually returns, but when Mr Softy opens up the tubs of ice cream it's melted. 'What's this? Milk? And what are these? I can't make 99s with fucking Crunchies.' A lady customer asks him to mind his language and that's when Mr Softy loses it.

That was the end of the scene in the script but I decided to go a step further. I had briefed Andrew the director and Ian the cameraman that I was going to go absolutely ballistic and that they should probably take cover. In a fit of rage Mr Softy throws melted ice cream all over the lady and her son. The actors never knew this was going to happen, so all of their reactions on camera are completely genuine. Then I continue to smash the contents of the ice-cream van, throwing everything in front of me – boxes of cones, chocolate flakes and whatever else I could get my hands on – towards the camera. Carnage. I still love it when I watch it now.

The episode ends with the habitual 'next week' section, and it's revealed that Mr Softy has given up his ice-cream business and is the new owner of Softy's Hard Stuff – an adult-themed establishment. He stands next to a sign outside of his shop: 'Ice Cream Available'. 'I've got to keep my hand in. I've still got four hundred litres to shift.'

The irony was that the location we used was in fact a real adult shop. It'd been there for a few years. We asked them if we could stick up a sign on the front of the shop saying 'Softy's

Hard Stuff'. They didn't mind. In fact, they kept the sign up for about ten years after, until it closed down. It sells Japanese sushi now.

'Leonard' was the next episode we filmed, and its pace was far more sedate. It was derived from the short monologue I wrote for the directors' training course that I filmed at Granada TV a few years before. It's the story of Britain's longest-serving paperboy, who's about to receive a special community award for delivering papers to the people of Bolton for over thirty years. The documentary follows Leonard on his special day.

I have to commend the art department for their detail in this episode. Leonard is a hoarder and when we first visit his bedroom it's filled with layer upon layer of miscellaneous arte-facts that he's gathered over the years. Empty biscuit tins, souvenir plates, walls full of pictures (a lot of which are my own family). A paint set, a half-open crossword book, a CB radio (without an aerial). A variety of model aeroplanes hanging from the ceiling. Cuttings from newspaper articles. Religious posters. Boxes of books and, on the wardrobe door, a small collection of signed celebrity autographs, including Denis Norden, Geoffrey Palmer, Colin Welland, Sandy Gall (the newsreader) and Ken Dodd. There's even one from Paul Le Roy. Leonard also has a punching nun doll that I bought on holiday in Las Vegas. Boo and Haydn Buckingham-Jones from the art department did an incredible job, again on a very low budget: they picked up a lot of Leonard's collection from jumble sales and car boot sales, but I have to confess most of it was mine, as I'm a bit of a hoarder too. Hence the forty years of Christmas TV guides sat in the attic.

Narrator
Leonard has lived on his own since his mother's death twenty-three years ago. He's officially unable to work, as he suffers from angina and is registered disabled, but he remains active by participating in numerous charity events and, of course, doing his paper round

Interviewer
How do you feel about tonight?

Leonard
Oh, I can't believe I'm getting an award. Me. I've never won anything before. Oh, I tell a lie and close one eye, I once won a paint-by-numbers set but the blue was missing …

He gestures to a painting of a ship on the wall where the sea is pink.

… and I once won a CB radio with muscular dystrophy

He picks up the mic.

'Ten-four, are you there, good buddy? Eyeball, this is Bernie's boy, do you copy?'

Silence.

It needs an aerial

Sarah Jane also did a brilliant job of my make-up. She spent hours adding prosthetics around my eyes to carefully age me, and with my white hair, beard and moustache I looked like Kenny Rogers. That's just how the real Leonard looked the last time I saw him. I'm not going to spend time talking about Leonard, as I wrote about him in my first book (don't forget, it's available for 75p now from most charity shops). Suffice to say, I knew Leonard very well and still have audio cassettes of interviews I did with him. I knew he was special even then, and this was years before I ever got into TV. He was eccentric, to say the least, but very kind and I really wanted to celebrate his story. I hope he would have been pleased with the end result.

I wanted this episode to have much more pathos than the others in the series. In one scene Leonard visits his mobile hairdresser (which completely defeats the object of her being mobile). In a poignant moment she says, 'Leonard's everybody's friend, but he's got no friends, his only real friend was his mother.'

We discover Leonard's lived alone since his mother's death and spends his time trying to befriend people, usually when he's on his paper round, which in the episode is exactly the same paper round that I used to do every night after school. We used a lot of locations that mean a lot to me.

In the opening titles of the episode we see Leonard kiss an old lady. That's Doris Bamford of 12 Glen Avenue. She's sadly passed now, but every night when I delivered her paper I'd always stop for a chat and a hug. I always remember she and her husband Charles had a black and white TV. They'd never pay the extra licence fee for colour because 'the programmes were crap'. Fair enough. Though I remember them both being very confused watching snooker.

Even Leonard's paper shop, Harry Haroon's, was the same shop I did my paper round. Ted Robbins plays the owner and he does a great job too. I'd bumped into him on a train back from London a few weeks before and he told me he'd just lost out on a part in *The Royle Family*, so I said I'd find him a part in the series.

A very funny stand-up called Janice Connolly also makes an appearance as a customer on Leonard's paper round. Janice and I would go on to work together for a very long time. Jayne Tunnicliffe, another fine stand-up, turns up as Leonard's love interest, Ruth, who works at the bus station café, and Catherine Tate makes an appearance as Valerie Sharples from the *Bolton Independent Leader*, the newspaper hosting the community awards. This was years before Catherine became a fully fledged comedy whirlwind in her own right.

Valerie

It's going to be a wonderful night and we've got a very special celebrity surprise guest handing out Leonard's award

Can you guess who the celebrity surprise guest was? Bob Carolgees and Spit the Dog. Finally, I got them both to appear in an episode. They were great fun. Though it came as a shock to find Spit was a puppet.

The hardest scene to film was when Leonard goes preaching in the town centre with the huge crucifix on his shoulder. I was wearing a radio mic and the camera crew were hidden upstairs in Clintons Cards, filming with a long lens. It was tough, I felt really uncomfortable, but I simply had to try and remember that it was the character doing this, not me, and just go for it. My arse tightened as I read as loud as I could from the Gideon Bible in my hand and sang hymns I'd learnt at school for about half an hour. I got some very strange looks and surprisingly quite a lot of support.

People gathered around, wanting to sing and pray with me. It was a real eye-opener. There's some footage on the DVD in the deleted scenes section where I'm chaining up my giant crucifix with a bicycle lock and a fella comes over and asks if I'd like to pray with him. He was giving it John, chapter two, verse twelve, and I'm ad-libbing, saying, 'I don't know that one, I'm sorry.' I thought he was going to make me kneel down with him outside the general post office.

The next episode was filmed at the Manchester Arena, where I re-enacted my real-life experiences working as a steward. Even down to the time they gave me the wrong name badge, Mohammed. Which I wore for two months.

I brought back some characters from 'The Services' – Matthew Kelly the drama student. He's now graduated and has a part in *Oliver!*, as well as working as a steward at Manchester Arena. Also, Utah the coach driver. He's driving a group of concertgoers to a seventies night at the arena that night. When he pulls the coach over to pick them up, he sees them waiting in their coloured afro wigs, block heels and flares.

'Jesus. What do you look like?' he says. 'You see some sights when you've not got your gun.'

Utah

My name is Utah. These are the rules. If you're going to be sick then you mop it up yourselves, there's a mop and bucket at the back and I don't want a repeat of *Gladiators*. We also have a chemical toilet on board. If you're going to use it, no solids

Passengers laughing.

I'm being serious, there are rules. No bottles, no food and no buggering about with the emergency exit, it's not a toy. I had one young lad bounce out en route to Torquay. He's now fed through a straw, so think on

I cast two other stand-ups in the episode. Jo Enright is one of the passengers on the seventies coach trip, and Daniel Kitson, who's hilarious as Duncan Beech, a St John Ambulance man working at the arena. I'd always talk to them when I was working as a steward so had a bit of an insight on the type of person required. Daniel Kitson is without a doubt one of the most gifted comedians I've ever met. He's definitely got very funny bones and can make you laugh without doing very much at all.

Neil Fitzmaurice (who co-wrote the series with me) also makes an appearance in this episode as Sean Bannon. With me alongside him as Chris Choi (practically unrecognisable with a bald head). We both work for Live Sec, a company that does security at the arena. They train Matthew Kelly for his new job as a steward, just as I was trained for my job as a steward (again, all in my first book, which has been reduced to 50p now in Marie Curie). Neil and I had a great laugh writing and filming those scenes, which were loosely based on courses I had to attend when I was training to be a steward at the Manchester Arena.

Sean
Chris came out of prison

Chris
Well, I didn't come out of prison. Sounds terrible, that. Well,
I did come out of prison but I hadn't done anything …
I was a prison officer

Sean
I used to box, flyweight, until I did my knee. What we do is
cover the first initial stages of training with the stewards, then
we up sticks to the next port of call. Next week we're in Berlin.
It's an international contract, we go all over, working with
many different acts, all the top names: Meatloaf, U2, Madonna,
Cast, we've worked with them all

Chris

I've seen Cher's arse

Sean

That was a dancer

Chris

No, it wasn't, it was Cher

Sean

Whatever

We filmed part of the episode during a real seventies night which was happening live at the arena. I'd seen it coming up in the schedules and so wrote part of the episode around this. It meant we could have real interactions with the public and also add our scripted characters into the crowd, which was quite a challenge, as we only had one night to film it. That created a lot of pressure, since if anything went wrong, we wouldn't be able to do it again.

There's one scene where Matthew gets asked by one of the backstage crew if he'll put a couple of bottles of water on stage for the main artist. Nervously I walk on stage in front of the arena crowd and get a huge cheer. That felt weird, and madly just a few years later I'd be performing at the arena for the first time myself. Crazy how things all work out.

'Lonely at the Top – The Marc Park Story' was the final episode of the series and the most ambitious of them all. In fact, most of our budget was allocated for this episode. I wanted to try and flip the series on its head with this story. At the time the docusoaps had created minor celebrities from the real people featured in their shows. Remember Mo from

Driving School? No, I didn't either, but she brought out a single, 'Driving in My Car'. And Jane McDonald found her fame on BBC1's *The Cruise*.

I wanted to send up those scenarios, the instant fame that appearing on TV can bring. In the club episode, Park Avenue had won Talent Trek and I wanted to show the viewers that Marc Park had gone on to have success. Making headlines, a song in the charts and all the trappings that fame can bring. Including a showbiz manager.

Narrator
Marc's new manager was local entrepreneur Bernie Santangilo, owner of BS Entertainments, a subsidiary of BS Taxis

Marc
I decided to go with Bernie because he was a lot like me in many ways, ambitious, successful and he'd also handled the Nolans

We meet Bernie for the first time sat behind an enormous office desk, which is the front half of a London taxi.

Bernie
The minute I clapped eyes on him I knew he had what it takes. He had an aura, a special kind of magic, and you can't buy that for love nor money

Interviewer
What is it?

Bernie

It is talent, my friend, and this lad shits it … and he better not
suffer from vertigo neither because he's going straight to the
top. The first thing I did was to get him in the papers. I've got a
mate of mine who runs a lap dancing bar, so we got a couple of
the girls to pose with their lallies out, so that sold quite a few
papers and kept things bubbling. We haven't got a contract,
I don't work like that, it's not my style. This lad's family,
he's like the nephew I never had. I made him a promise
and I've stuck to it

Interviewer

What is it?

Bernie

I'm gonna make him a star

Paul Mark Elliott did a blinding job playing Bernie with just the right amount of slime you'd expect from a manager like that. In the next scene we see Marc Park in a children's play area surrounded by three scantily clad girls in swimwear preening over Marc as he lip-syncs a cover of 'Gonna Make You a Star' by David Essex. The video is cheap crap and yet the record manages to reach number six in the charts.

Marc is then whisked off to a top London recording studio to make his 'much anticipated' first album.

Interviewer

This album sounds like it's come from your heart. What did you
want to say with the song 'African Tears'?

Marc

I've always been passionate about black music. That rural ethnic soulful sound, UB40, Eddy Grant, Aswad. This album has allowed me to work with some of the finest musicians in the world. The Samambi Singers, who are an incredible vocal trio that we flew over from South Africa. Don't worry, I'm not doing a bloody Paul Simon *Graceland* thing; he just exploited those people. As if they hadn't been through enough already. I saw that film the other night on Sky Premiere, *Amistad*. Those guys had a rough ride and that's why I wanted to say something about the turmoil the people of Africa have been through, but not just them, anybody who's ever had to experience any form of hatred and oppression. Anybody who's ever felt that fear of not knowing where your next meal is coming from, anybody who's had to struggle. I struggled for many years as a greengrocer in the fruit and veg business. There were times when I used to cry myself to sleep at night, and like so many others I found faith in the future through 'African Tears'

What a load of bollocks, but that was Marc Park. An absolute tool. I lifted a lot of dialogue word for word from a *South Bank Show* I'd seen about Sting. Marc then goes on to sing 'African Tears' and the lyrics are truly shocking:

> *African Tears for souvenirs and no one seems to*
> *care at all*
> *Down in Soweto, there's a child who thinks a*
> *landmine is a ball*
> *And at night I used to cry, at night I'd pray for*
> *peace*
> *I remember burning tyres and the riot police*

We filmed those scenes at Olympic Studios in London where Led Zeppelin recorded their albums, as well as The Who, David Bowie and Nick Knowles.

Marc buys a Tudor mansion (hence the budget). 'I think I might get it double glazed,' says Marc. 'I bet it's a bugger to heat in the winter.'

We also went to Elstree Studios to film Marc's video for 'Christmas 2000', his attempt to take a festive song to the top of the charts.

Interviewer

Christmas 2000? But this is Christmas 1999

Marc

What?

Interviewer

This is Christmas 1999. It won't be Christmas 2000
until next year

Marc

(shouting off)

Bernie?

Again, the art department outdid themselves, building an incredible North Pole set, complete with a mini-igloo. We even had a polar bear (well, an actor in a costume). There was plenty of snow falling throughout the scene, and at the end of one of the takes the dancers and I spontaneously started a snowball fight (in character, you understand).

One of the girl dancers accidentally threw a snowball at me, I turned to react, but another snowball hit me in the mouth and went straight down my throat. The fake snow was made from some kind of expanding substance (like Tampax) and when it mixed with the saliva in my mouth it started to expand. Flustered and a bit embarrassed, I began trying to clear my throat, but it was proving pointless as I staggered behind the igloo and fell to my knees choking. Everybody was busy, so it took a few seconds for anyone to notice me choking to death. It was very scary. They had to get an ambulance for me. The paramedics made me drink loads of water to flush out all the fake snow. It's a pity we didn't film any of that, as it would have made a great ending to the video.

My near-death experience was the last scene we filmed. When I look back now I can't believe how fearless I was playing fifteen characters, but that felt right at the time. The reason I took on so many characters was to challenge myself, but also to show my range to any casting agents watching. Perhaps I might get some other work. Fat chance. I've hardly done anything but my own stuff since. Life never turns out like you think it will.

When the series was finished I asked if the title could be changed to something else. As I said before, I wasn't very keen on 'Peter Kay and His Friends in the North'. I chose *That Peter Kay Thing*, simply because I thought whatever it's called, people will still say, 'Did you see that Peter Kay thing?' So I thought that fit the bill.

The series went out on Wednesday nights at 10.30 on Channel 4. It did quite well and I was happy with the reaction it got. Later that year it was nominated for Best New Comedy at the British Comedy Awards in London. I'd watched those awards for years, ever since they first started, when Michael Parkinson presented them from a theatre. I'd secretly dreamed of receiving an award and, in fact, it was seeing the quality of the comedies that had preceded me that inspired me to get off my arse and try my luck.

Dave, Neil and I went to the awards. It was definitely one of those 'pinch yourself' moments in life, as we sat alongside all of the top comedy talent at the time, and Freddie Starr. Our category was second to last on the night, so we had a very long wait. We were on a table next to the cast of *The Royle Family*, which was a thrill, especially as we knew them. Well, I knew Craig and it was great to see him. I always remember that Ricky Tomlinson had brought a carrier bag filled with cans of Special Brew with him and kept it under the table because he said he 'didn't like any of the shit they served at these things'.

Finally, we reached our category. We couldn't speak, we were so nervous, and were genuinely shocked when the series won. What an absolute bloody joy. Maybe because we felt like outsiders. A British Comedy Award. Wow! That was a huge deal, not just for me, but for everybody else involved in making the series. Though it left me with a 'burning' question, What to do next?

My Back Teeth
Were Floating

Just like Ronnie Barker had done with his *Seven of One* series, when I looked at all the episodes in *That Peter Kay Thing*, I thought 'In the Club' had the best potential to have its own series. There seemed to be endless possibilities. It was the slight naffness that appealed to me. Plus, the struggle of a social club trying to stay afloat in a modern world, with its dwindling attendance figures. They say the greatest comedy plays against the greatest tragedy (whoever 'they' are). This felt perfect. With all of its different club nights and acts playing each week, it all seemed colourful and ripe for the picking.

The other main thing that drew me to it was that the subject hadn't really been done before on TV. There had been *The Wheeltappers and Shunters Social Club* on ITV in the seventies but that was much more of a variety show.

That Peter Kay Thing was enough of a success for Channel 4 that they were happy to commission a new series for the new millennium. Four years in TV and I already felt like I'd achieved everything I'd ever desired. I'd been happy at every stage so far of my glittering showbiz career. Not that I was without ambitions, but I'd honestly been content performing stand-up at the weekends in comedy clubs up and down Britain.

I approached Dave and Neil to see if they fancied writing a series based on 'In the Club'. They did, but this time we agreed that we needed to meet up. I was fed up writing sat on the edge of my bed, so I decided to hire an office at Bolton Enterprise Centre. It was basic but it was perfect. Now we could all write together, full-time. Dave took a sabbatical from his job at the hospital and Neil drove over from Liverpool every day. Occasionally Paddy would call in on his way home from work at the local leisure centre. It was great when he called because it gave us a chance to read him what we'd written, which helped. He also gave us some great story ideas, like the idea of the club holding a *Robot Wars* night.

Writing every day felt exhilarating because it allowed us to become consumed with the scripts, to have the ability to analyse every aspect. Every line was meticulously written. Sure, we'd argue occasionally, but it was never personal, it was always about 'what's the funnier?' A funnier word, colour, even what's a funnier pie once. Chicken and mushroom or steak and kidney? Of course steak and kidney won.

The process was that we'd come up with an idea for a scene and then we'd all write our own individual versions of it. Then we'd edit the best versions together into the final script. It worked, and once we got our rhythm we were knocking out an episode or so a week.

Our golden rule was that we always strived to have as many *Only Fools and Horses* moments as we could. These were moments that we believed would have people talking the next day. Like the scene when a horse gets drunk during a Wild West night.

Kenny Snr

What's wrong with it?

Brian

It's pissed, that's what's wrong with it. Quick, get it a kebab

The horse drunkenly mounts a bucking bronco.

Oh my God, what's it doing now? Kenny, pull it off

Kenny Snr

I'm not pulling off a horse

Or another scene, where Max and Paddy are told to wear headsets and try to see just how far they can communicate with each other.

Max walking backwards across the car park away from Paddy.

Max

Can you hear me now?

Paddy

Hear you? I can see you, you dick

A few scenes later we see a double-decker bus drive past the club and hear:

Max

Paddy, I'm here. Look, I'm on the bus ... I'm on the bus!

We see Max upstairs on the bus waving frantically as it drives past the club.

When you're writing a comedy series I think you've got to try to make sure that each episode is as accessible as it can be to the viewers. Ideally, you never want them to feel alienated because they might not have seen any other episodes, but we did have a few story arcs across the series. One was Jerry's hypochondria. This begins in the first episode, when we find Jerry sat on the toilet reading a pamphlet about colon care (endorsed by Bob Carolgees).

In the following episode, the club holds the Wild West night and Jerry is punched in the stomach by a cowboy. Jerry believes the trauma to his gut has triggered a bigger problem. He visits several doctors and ends up having a colonoscopy. Finally, at the end of the series, Jerry gets an all-clear and he's overjoyed. Unfortunately, Brian has told the brewery that Jerry's dying so the club can get the grand final of Talent Trek out of sympathy.

Jerry

But I've got the all-clear

Brian

I know. Trust you to bloody ruin everything

Jerry

Ruin everything? But I'm all-clear

Brian

I know you're all-clear, but we're not, are we? We're in debt up to our eyeballs. In the red with the bills. We're in a catch-21 situation, Jerry, and only you can get us out of it

Jerry

Me? How?

Brian
Pretend you're dying?

Jerry
But I've told you I'm not

Brian
I know, you keep telling me. I know that and you know that,
but nobody else needs to know that. Not until after we've had
the grand final of Talent Trek
(winks at Jerry)

Brian manages to talk Jerry into pretending he's terminal just for the Talent Trek final. He even forces him to wear a baseball cap and sing 'Seasons in the Sun', with the lyrics 'goodbye, my friend, it's hard to die'.

From the side of the stage, Brian hands Jerry a piece of paper with the word 'collapse' written on it.

On reflection, *That Peter Kay Thing* was very restrictive with its mockumentary style. It meant the camera crew had to be privy to everything going on. Now that element had been removed, we had more freedom and flexibility to have characters on their own.

Like a scene in Brian's office where he's talking on the phone to a fella called Eric, who's sold him a wonky snooker table.

Eric
Hello, Game Sans Frontieres

Brian
Eric, Brian

Eric

Alright, Brian, how's it going?

Brian

It's not going. It's still here and it's as crooked as you

Eric

What d'you mean? What's up?

Brian

What's up? I've got a deformed snooker table and a flavoured-
condom machine that's ten years out of date

Eric

And?

Brian

And? Would you suck a ten-year-old banana?

Dave and I went out to several clubs to do more research. I even invested in a special recordable pen from The Spy Shop in Manchester. It looked like a generic Bic biro but had a microphone concealed inside, which I plugged into a Dictaphone in my pocket. We'd meet club owners and I'd secretly record them. I did this because I wanted them to be themselves and I thought they'd behave differently if they knew they were being recorded. I worried one of them would reach for the pen in my top pocket and drag me across the table.

Having a Dictaphone hidden in the inside pocket of my anorak did have its downside. It was July. I was roasting.

'Are you alright, son? Take your coat off.'

'I'm fine, there's a bit of a chill in the air,' I'd say with sweat rolling down my face.

The other problem with using a Dictaphone was it took cassettes. So I had to keep rushing to the toilet every so often so I could change the tape over. Fortunately, they were so busy bragging about their precious clubs they never took much notice of the lad in the anorak with cystitis.

One thing they did enjoy was slagging off their rivals.

'Which club are you visiting next?'

We'd tell them and then they'd start the bitching: 'I've heard they're on the verge of bankruptcy. That'll be their own fault for fiddling the books, and I wouldn't get on the bad side of the owner; he once stabbed a man up a back alley.'

I remember meeting the owner of the next club and he was about ninety. If he'd ever stabbed anybody it must have been a while back.

He took us on a tour of his club, boasting about his fog machine and his new cork dancefloor. The air conditioning was so loud I was conscious my spy pen might not record what he was saying, so I got as close to him as I could. He kept backing away as I invaded his space. Creeping towards him, sweating in my anorak. I thought he might whip out a knife and stab me.

We needed to get a director for the series. My first call was Andrew Gillman, who'd directed *That Peter Kay Thing*. He came up to Manchester and we had a meeting. I think I completely overloaded his head with all of my ideas, because he declined the job. His wife Ann had just had a baby and Andrew said he wanted to spend time with them both. Fair enough.

The only other director I'd worked with was Jonny Campbell, who directed 'Two Minutes', the first programme I'd made at Granada TV (where I illegally drove the getaway car). He was available and up for it. The only caveat being he already had a big holiday booked in December, but that didn't appear to be a problem, as we'd have finished filming by then.

Now we had a director on board we had to find the right location for the club. One idea the producers had was to build the interior of a club inside Granada TV. They reckoned it'd be more cost-effective, but we still needed a real club for any exterior scenes. After a lot of searching, we went full circle and ended up back at St Gregory's in Farnworth, Bolton, which we'd used for *That Peter Kay Thing*. It was perfect.

It always made me laugh when people would say what a good job the art department did making the club look so realistic. It was already like that. They hardly touched a thing.

The other dilemma was what to call the series. One idea was 'Out of Order', as I kept seeing that sign every time I went to a social club. It was usually written on a piece of white paper in black felt tip and stuck to a bog door or a fruit machine.

Though I thought 'Peter Kay's Out of Order' sounded like I was in a bad way or something. So that had to go.

Channel 4 was still hung up about having my name in the title. I understood why but felt awkward about it, especially as this series was much more of a team effort. I compromised and told them I'd only have my name in the TV listings but never before the title on screen.

But still, what to call it? Then it dawned on me. The Neptune Club had burnt down at the end of 'In the Club'. Brian Potter was re-opening a new club that's symbolically risen from the ashes, like a phoenix. Hence the Phoenix Club was born and, in return, *Phoenix Nights*.

Many of the cast from 'In the Club' were established in *That Peter Kay Thing*, so that made things a lot easier. I suggested more stand-up comedians for any remaining parts. Steve Edge replaced Mark Jackson, the original Alan in Les Alanos. Janice Connolly turned up as Holy Mary. Dave Galbraith returned as a brewery rep with a pop-up of 'Brain' Potter in the club's souvenir brochure. I even managed to write a part for my old pal Sian as Paddy's girlfriend Mary.

Neil Fitzmaurice was brilliant as a gypsy DJ and technical whizz called Ray Von. When the opening night is plunged into a power cut he saves the day by wiring the club to a lamppost in the front street. Daniel Kitson returned as Spencer, a hapless DJ from a local youth club, and Alex Lowe as Clinton Baptiste, a psychic who manages to upset just about everybody during his paranormal performance.

Clinton makes his way through the audience.

Clinton
What's your name, love? S-S-Sonia?

Debbie
No, it's Debbie

Clinton
I meant Debbie … and you've been ill, haven't you?

Debbie
Yes

Clinton
You have and it hasn't been easy, has it?

Debbie
No, it hasn't

Clinton
… and it is terminal, isn't it?

Debbie
No?

Clinton gives a look to Debbie as if to say 'think again'.

Clinton
Okay. Now, hands up who can't have children

The audience is restless. Brian mouths the words 'What the fuck?'

Clinton approaches a big bruiser of a fella sat with his wife. He looks him straight in the eye, clasps his hands and says:

Clinton
Now, I'm getting the word … nonce

There's an immediate shocked reaction from the audience and then the fella lunges straight at Clinton and grabs him around the neck. Pandemonium ensues.

When we wrote that moment we howled laughing. Luckily it came across on screen just as we'd imagined. Alex did a great job.

Jo Enright returned, this time as Brian Potter's love interest Beverly Hilscopto. The singles night is one of my favourite episodes. Brian bumps into Beverly, quite literally, and unexpectedly love blossoms. They go on dates together bowling, duck feeding, even paintballing, and then for a romantic meal where they're both approached by a woman selling roses.

Woman
Flower for the lady?

Brian
Fuck off

The woman leaves. Brian carries on eating.

My favourite scene is when Brian takes Beverly back to his house. I still find it excruciating to watch. The stilted conversation and the awkwardness.

Brian offers Beverly a piece of a massive Toblerone.

Brian
Toblerone?
(slapping it on the coffee table)

Beverly
Oh, no, thanks. If I eat anything else I'll burst

Brian
I hear you. Lovely meal that, weren't it? It's a cracker,
that burger bar

They do the lot, kee-babs, quarter pounders, all halal … do
you want a drop of Blue Nun?

Beverly
Er …

Brian
Top up? Go on

Beverly
I've got to go though soon, 'cause I've got an early
start in the morning

Brian
Have you? *(Deflated)* But you've not seen my jukebox yet. You
can't go without seeing this thing

*Brian wheels himself over to the corner and flicks a switch. A
huge classic jukebox taking up most of the corner of the room
lights up in an array of multi-colours.*

Brian
This is my Motown special. I got it from the States. America.
Do you like Motown?

Beverly
Lovely, yeah

Brian
Have you got any change? It's five for a pound

The other scene we cried laughing when we wrote it was when
Brian slowly travels on his stairlift holding Beverly's hand.
Silence, except for the sound of the stairlift motor. Then Brian
says:

Brian
Not long now. Just you wait. The things I'm
going to do to you

Oh, my God, I'm laughing now. 'The things I'm going to do to you'. What things?

We did have another line, 'I can feel it, Beverly, love. It's running down my leg,' but we thought that was one line too many.

A lot of the comedians I admired had worked clubs like the Phoenix throughout their careers. I thought this series would be a good opportunity to cast some of them, as they'd still got as much good timing as the new generation.

Roy Walker was one such comedian, but I wanted him to play himself, as the big celebrity opening the Phoenix Club. It's a mad dash to get the club finished in time. People cleaning and painting up to the last minute. Roy accidentally leans against a wet paint surface. He's completely unaware it's left a line of white paint down the back of his jacket. Brian almost chokes when he catches a glimpse of it and is desperate to get Roy to remove his jacket so that Holy Mary can try and clean the paint off. Eventually, she gets the jacket off Roy. She hurriedly takes it into the back kitchen, but she does a double-take when she sees the label on his collar: 'Property of Southern Television'. Roy's clearly nicked the jacket while filming *Catchphrase*. I loved detail like this, layering the comedy so you can laugh time and time again because you might have missed it the first time round.

When I got in touch with Roy he insisted that I visit him at his house in Lytham St Annes. It was a horrendously rainy night when I drove over to meet him. We sat in his lounge and chatted about all kinds of everything (not the Dana hit). Finally, we chatted about his part in the episode. I told him he really didn't have to worry, as he'd just be playing himself. But Roy had other ideas. He said he wanted to play the part like Joe Pesci in *Goodfellas*.

'Come again?' I said, spitting out my tea.

'I want to be a bit edgy,' he said. 'You know, like that scene in *Goodfellas* when they're in the bar and Ray Liotta says he thinks Joe Pesci is funny, and Joe Pesci says, "Funny how?" I'd like to play it like that. You could say, "I think you're funny, Roy," and I'd say, "Funny how?" We could have an exchange and I come across as really menacing. I could slap your face and say, "It's okay, I'm just busting your balls, Brian" … But am I?'

I didn't know what to say. Well, I did. I wanted to say, 'Have you had a drink?' and, 'Can you please just read the lines that we've written?' But Roy wasn't having any of it. In fact, he went on about it that much that I eventually caved and said I'd write a new *Goodfellas* scene just for him. Christ, as if I didn't have enough on my plate.

When he turned up for filming, he was so overwhelmed with everything and we were in such a rush that we only ended up filming the lines we needed and the whole *Goodfellas* idea went out the window. Unfortunately, we've run out of time, Roy, 'wink, wink'. Though, on reflection, I regret we didn't film it now, as it'd be hilarious seeing Roy Walker doing Tommy DeVito in *Phoenix Nights*. 'Funny how?' in his Northern Irish accent. Maybe he was right after all.

Another comedy stalwart everybody knew and loved was Jim Bowen. I'd grown up watching him on *Bullseye* every Sunday afternoon straight after *The Love Boat*. Jim made an appearance as Frank 'Hoss' Cartwright, owner of the Le Ponderosa Hotel in Blackpool. When he turned up, he assured me he'd learnt his lines, but clearly he hadn't got a bloody clue, and if you ever want proof just watch the outtakes on YouTube.

He was winging it. For a kick-off, he can't even remember my character's name and keeps calling *me* Frank. 'You're Frank! I'm Brian!'

Then he keeps looking straight down the camera. 'Stop looking down the camera! Ten years of *Bullseye*'s done that to you.'

My favourite bit is when he says 'cracker popper' instead of 'party popper': 'Hoswell Hornby died last week, he choked on a cracker popper.'

Then when the camera is turned round to film me as Brian, he still can't remember his lines. 'You're not even on camera and you still don't know them.' Jim also keeps saying things to himself like 'For fuck's sake, Jim, get your act together.' Which only makes me laugh even more. We eventually managed to get through the scene with me literally feeding him each line, one at a time.

Bernard Manning personified club land and he was one of the original presenters of *Wheeltappers and Shunters*. He was also one of the very rare comedians to be blessed with perfect comic timing. When he was on the hugely successful ITV series *The Comedians* he never swore or told blue jokes. He wasn't allowed to. But appearing on that show made him a household name. He told jokes. People don't tell jokes much anymore, now you get sent 'funny' clips and you either text back 'Ha-ha-ha' or send one of those laughing emojis. If it's very funny you can text back an even bigger laughing emoji (I'm shaking my head in despair as I type this).

Bernard was established as a very funny comedian but somewhere along the way he slowly got more blue and racist. Particularly with his club act. Times changed, but Bernard dug his heels in and refused to. 'What's funny is funny,' he'd say. 'I have a go at everybody. Never take a joke seriously.' The problem was his perfect timing had been completely over-looked when people started to label him a racist bigot.

There was a rival club owner in *Phoenix Nights*, Den Perry, and I thought it would be fantastic to have Bernard play him.

I thought it might be a chance for people to take note of his brilliant comic timing and perhaps restore a bit of his reputation. So I gave him a ring and asked if I could go to see him.

His Rolls-Royce, 1 Laf, was parked outside his big white detached house in Middleton. I knocked on the door. His housekeeper, Pat, let me in, and I went through to the front room to find Bernard sat in an armchair just wearing his vest and underpants. What a sight.

'How are you, Peter, my old son? Nice to see you. Quick, take a look at all my trophies, all my accolades.'

I turned round to see his mantlepiece overflowing with awards and framed pictures from over the years.

'See those silver hearts? I've just got another one of them last week from the Variety Club. Most people only get one, I've got fucking two. Services to charity. There's a picture of me shaking hands with Mrs Thatcher. There's me backstage at Royal Variety shaking hands with the Queen. I've met them all, Harold Wilson, Don Revie, I've met them all.'

I could have spent a few hours just studying his mantlepiece.

'There's photos of all my grandchildren there, light of my life, those kiddies.'

'What are their names?'

'Ben, Hayley and Chloe,' he said with immense pride.

'How old's Ben?'

'Ten or twelve, I don't fucking know.'

He was, without a doubt, a character, and what you saw was what you got.

I sat on the floor in front of him. With a stunning view of his piss-stained crotch. We chatted about everything and anything. It was a marvellous insight into not just the man, but also his mind. We talked a lot about old club acts, which I found fascinating. I asked what big acts he'd had on at his club, the World Famous Embassy, over the years.

'Every fucker. Marty Wilde, the rock'n'roller, he was ten quid. Terry Dene, eight quid. He sang "A White Sport Coat (and a Pink Carnation)", that was his big hit. The Beatles, seven quid. Freddie and the Dreamers, eight quid … er, who else … Vince Hill, John Barry Seven, Matt Monro, thirty quid for the week, the Merseybeats, you fucking name it.'

Then I asked him if he remembered any of the crap acts he'd had on at the Embassy.

'Oh, dozens. We had a couple of comedians once, the Two Bobs, they were called, and they were fucking awful. They were about as funny as a burning orphanage. Anyway, I paid them, fucked them off, but they nicked my keys off the side of the stage. I used to have this big bunch of keys for everything, house, burglar alarm, keys to the club, keys for the safe. I lost the lot. The Two Bobs? The Two Cunts more like. I never slept a wink that night.'

'Did you ever find the keys?'

'Never, but if I ever find the Two Bobs they'll get a fucking banjo-ing. I remember one bloke we had on, a fire-eater. He swallowed some petrol and he was supposed to blow it out his mouth and set fire to it, but when he blew it out it didn't fucking light. So the first six rows of people got covered in fucking petrol. It was pandemonium. The waiters were fetching trays of beer back full of fucking petrol. So he tried again, and the flame still didn't light, and the petrol went all over every fucker again. Ladies' dresses, the lot. All soaked in fucking petrol. Dizgrace.

'Then there was one act we had on, they were a couple, Little Beaver and Marie, they were called. They were dressed as Indians. Now, when we first opened the club, we bought the best fucking piano we ever had, a Blüthner. It was about a thousand pounds in those days, beautiful grand piano. And this Little Beaver was taking pot-shots at Marie on the other side of the stage. He was firing arrows, but he kept missing her and the arrows were going straight into the fucking piano. Then he pulled out a gun and started firing fucking bullets. They were knocking fuck out the piano. So, I ran up, grabbed him by the throat and said, "General Custer's here, now fuck off."'

I couldn't breathe for laughing. Such funny stories. At one point Bernard took me on a tour of his house. We went upstairs and he showed me his bedroom: 'I've got a colour telly in there.' Then he led me down the landing: 'Three guest bedrooms down there, each one's got a coloured telly.' Then we went back downstairs. It was surreal him leading me around in his vest and underpants.

Then he showed me his kitchen: 'That's a picture of me backstage at the Royal Variety shaking hands with the Queen.' It was exactly the same picture I'd seen earlier on his mantlepiece, but I didn't say anything.

'I shared a dressing room with Liza Minnelli that night and the Osmonds. They're Moomins, you know.' (He meant Mormons but I didn't say anything.)

When I looked around I got the shock of my life: Bernard was stood taking a piss out of the back of his kitchen door.

'What are you doing, man?!' I shouted.

'I'm having a slash!'

'But there's a toilet right there,' I said, pointing towards a downstairs loo.

'When you've got to go, you've got to go. My back teeth were floating.'

I thought, This is unbelievable. He's pissing on his own property.

We sat and chatted for a while longer, up until Bernard had to get ready. He had a gig that night in Surrey. An eight-hour round trip.

'What time are you on stage?' I asked.

'When I fucking get there. I'm usually still fastening my pants and shirt as I'm walking on stage or combing my hair. The band'll play "Simply the Best" and I'll give them the gear they all like. Then it's straight back in the car home. The audience'll be shouting for more and the compere'll say, "There's no use shouting for any more, he'll be halfway up the M6 by now." Always leave 'em wanting more, son.'

Bernard said he'd have a think about playing the part in *Phoenix Nights*, but after spending time with him I wasn't so sure. His mind was pin-sharp but physically his health was suffering, and from what little experience I had of filming I knew there'd be a lot of waiting around. The long hours would drive him crazy. Plus, I didn't want him pissing on everything.

So I did the next best thing. I just rang my old pal Ted Robbins and asked him if he fancied playing a part in the new series.

Ted said he'd be delighted.

'Er ... there's just one thing ... Is there any chance you could play it just like Bernard Manning?'

How Far Away
Are They?

The first scene we ever filmed for *Phoenix Nights* was Max and Paddy hanging a banner outside of the club advertising the opening night. Max is up a ladder with a hammer and he notices Paddy's hair is thinning.

Max
Are you going bald?

Paddy
No

Max
Well, I can see your head through your hair

Paddy
It's always been like that

Max
Since when?

Paddy

Since whenever. It's my hair, it's very fine

Max

I don't know about fine, but it's thin

Paddy

It's not thin

Max

Not thin? It's anorexic

Paddy

Alright, shut up, dickhead

Max

If it gets any thinner you'll be combing your arse

Paddy

Leave it

Max

Baldy bouncer

Paddy then shakes the ladder, which sends Max crashing through a window.

It was a thrill to be filming, especially with Paddy. It's like all my dreams come true being surrounded by friends. I've always tried to share all my experiences with everybody I know. It makes the atmosphere joyous and that's how it continued for the whole shoot. There was always plenty of banter too, which you would imagine, being surrounded by so many comedians.

I think I felt safe filming at St Gregory's too, and it had become a real home from home. Jonny the director and the crew laughed a lot (which I think is always a good sign). It felt as if we were getting some funny stuff, but you never actually know until it's on TV. And even though we'd worked hard on the scripts I encouraged the cast to feel free to improvise as and when they felt comfortable. Which a lot of them did.

We filmed the whole series chronologically, which really helped with the flow of the story and building up the characters. You don't normally do that much, but because so much of it was filmed in the club it was much easier to film in sequence.

On the advice of rival club owner Den Perry, a local folk band called Half a Shilling has been booked for the opening night, but Jerry's heard some bad reports about them. Brian catches up with Jerry in the toilets. Jerry is in a cubicle.

Brian
How long are you gonna be?

Jerry
How long's a piece of string?

Brian
What string?

Jerry
It's a saying

Brian
Well, balls to that. Have you phoned the band?

Jerry

No, not yet. Listen, John Picard had them on at the Vulcan last
week and there was almost a riot

Brian

A riot with Half a Shilling? They're a folk band, they're not
The Who. They had a song in the charts once. Flat caps
and clogs, this lot will lap 'em up. Anyway, they've
been booked for months

Jerry

I've got a bad feeling

Brian

It'll be your arse. Now, stop crappin' and get cracking.
We've work to do

When Half a Shilling finally take to the stage they turn out to
be racist.

Mike Fiddler

This song's about the time I asked my mum and dad for a pair
of white Holy Communion shoes. Times were hard and my dad
had to work extra shifts to buy those shoes. Anyroad up, when
they arrived they weren't white, they were black, and I said,
'Send the Buggers Back'

Mayhem ensues, a member of the local press points out to
Brian that the song is racist. Half a Shilling are forcibly
dragged from the stage and Jerry quickly launches into 'Dance
the Night Away' by the Mavericks.

Just like we did with the 'In the Club' episode of *That Peter
Kay Thing*, we used real audience members and regulars from

the club, so the reactions to Half a Shilling being ejected were real. Bear that in mind if you see this scene again: those shocked looks are genuine.

I also asked a lot of my family and friends. My mum, nana and sister are there, as well as most of my in-laws. I'll never forget going over to my father-in-law while I was dressed as Brian Potter. I stood in front of him and he just looked at me, bewildered. Politely he said, 'Hello,' and then, 'Do I know you?' Then I spoke and he recognised the voice instantly, but he just couldn't understand who he was looking at. I had to tell him, 'It's me, it's Peter.' He couldn't believe I was this older man stood in front of him.

Half a Shilling's members were made up of Tim Healy (star of *Auf Wiedersehen, Pet* and *Tickle on the Tum*), Buzz Hawkins (creator of *The Bradshaws* – a successful radio series about a northern family which is well worth checking out if you haven't heard it), Peter Hilton on bodhran and Toni Baker on accordion.

Peter and Toni had worked in the clubs for years, so I asked them if they'd like to record all of the music for the series. Nailing the club sound was really important. I think that's what made the whole thing work so well. Especially when they covered the more contemporary songs of the time.

Like the scene when Jerry sings 'Perfect 10' by the Beautiful South. It's so bad, it's hilarious. There are about seven pensioners in the audience who wouldn't have a clue what 'Perfect 10' was, but Jerry's singing it regardless, in a desperate attempt to be modern.

The song ends and there's a small smattering of applause.

147

Jerry

Thank you very much. That was 'Perfect 10' and we're ten perfect minutes away from tonight's 'Open the Box', where the jackpot still stands at a whopping thirty-three pounds. So, to take you there I'll leave you in the capable hands of your brand-new resident DJ, Mr Ray Von

Ray Von

Ta, Jezzer. That's right, my name's Ray Von, so let's rave on!

Ray Von plays extremely loud rave music, much too loud for the regular pensioners, who aren't happy. Ray has over-the-top DJ equipment, including two sets of actual traffic lights. He then fires up a smoke machine, which is just too much. Smoke fills the room, and the pensioners are left with no choice but to quickly leave the club, coughing their guts up. When the smoke eventually clears Paddy finds one of the regulars, the Captain, and he's dead.

The art department did a great job on the series. Especially the episode where the club holds a Wild West night. The whole main function room was done up like a saloon, with bales of hay and wagon wheels. They had a specially constructed scoreboard machine that tallied the results between Lancashire and Yorkshire during their shootout. We even had a horse in the club, Smokey Joe. I'd worked with Gerard Naprous and Smokey Joe at a corporate gig at Tankersley Manor in Barnsley a few years before. Gerard could get that horse to do anything, including shit on cue. Which it did, quite a few times on the dancefloor. We just added it into the script.

We contacted a few Wild West re-enactment groups when we filmed the Wild West night, as I thought they'd bring some authenticity. We weren't wrong. These people live and breathe the Wild West. I'll never forget the sight of them arriving in mass convoy one lunchtime. They proceeded to pitch up camp in a primary school playground across the road from the club. Luckily it was half-term.

They had actual horses, wagons, wigwam tents that they slept in over the two nights they were there. They even built a campfire on a bit of spare land just off the playground.

The big scene comes when all hell breaks loose during the gunslinging shootout. Jeremiah Jed from Yorkshire (who was quite small in height) takes umbrage at one too many of Jerry's insults and punches him in the stomach. The whole place erupts, fists are flying, guns are firing, chairs are thrown. We had plenty of stuntmen on hand and the whole thing looked glorious on camera. The Wild West re-enactment group were in their absolute element and loved playing their roles. At least I think they were playing roles. It was very hard to tell.

Another episode where the art department excelled themselves was when Brian hosts *Robot Wars* in the Pennine Suite. Tim Youngman, who was the props maker, built some incredible robots. Funny too. Including one made from a tin of Celebrations called Death by Chocolate. In the episode, Max and Paddy have secretly entered the competition and turn up with their own homemade robot called Ass Kicker. They then proceed to smash the other contestants' robots to smithereens. Max even resorts to holding the axe on the front of Ass Kicker and physically whacking a robot made out of a dustpan and brush to pieces.

I have to admit that, as much as I enjoyed the filming, I did feel like I had the weight of the world on my shoulders almost all of the time. I had a constant knot in my stomach, fretting that we were getting everything as good as it could be. As well as a lot of pressure to not let everybody down, including myself. Plus, I was also playing three parts in the series. Brian, Max and a small cameo from my fire safety officer character again, Dogtanian, who makes an appearance as a guest speaker at the monthly club affiliates meeting.

Den Perry, the rival owner of the Banana Grove, is already addressing the room, while Brian and Jerry are sat at the back, talking. Brian's handed a flyer and can't believe what he sees: today's guest speaker is the fire safety officer. Jerry has no idea who he's talking about, so Brian explains that he is the fire safety officer who got done for interfering with dogs: 'It was all over the papers.' This jogs Jerry's memory but he points out that Dogtanian was never charged with any offences. 'Aye,' says Brian. 'You wanna try getting an Alsatian to testify.'

Den Perry introduces Dogtanian and asks him to 'take the *lead*' on fire safety in the workplace. 'Don't worry,' says Den, 'his bark's worse than his bite.'

Dogtanian awkwardly walks centre stage and begins his talk: 'Do you want to know what my biggest fear is?'

'Rabies?' shouts Den Perry to a roar of laughter.

It was great to revive the Dogtanian character again for *Phoenix Nights*, but when marketing for the new series was released it was revealed that the character would be returning. The next thing I knew I got a call from Channel 4 (and you're not going to believe this, because I still can't) – they told me that there actually was a real fire safety officer with a very similar name and that he wasn't so chuffed with the return of Dogtanian (sounds like a bad musketeers film).

Channel 4 asked me if I'd ever met the man. I hadn't. It simply was a bizarre coincidence. This other fire safety fella was even Scottish. Channel 4 were concerned and asked if there was any chance I could remove the character from the episode. I said it wasn't really possible, as half the plot revolved around his appearance.

Channel 4 sent Iain Morris, a commissioner from the station, and a lawyer to meet this real fire safety officer and try to reach a compromise. Eventually they came up with a written statement that would appear on screen at the end of the episode explaining that any similarity with the character created in the episode may have led people to wrongly believe that it was based on this real person. I later found out that the fire safety officer made Iain Morris and the lawyer awkwardly sit through several fire safety videos in his front room.

I wasn't too happy with the result, as I've genuinely never met the man, a fact he publicly confirmed, but sadly it was all out of my hands. Channel 4 said that without an agreement the episode wouldn't be aired so I didn't have much choice. Hilariously, when the worded statement played at the end of the episode viewers just presumed that it was all part of the show. Then to top it all Channel 4 awarded the fella £10,000 compensation (I'm still shaking my head as I type this). The money was split between the fella and several other organisations. I did try to insist that one might be the local dogs' home but I don't think they ever saw any money.

All in all it was a real shame, as I had lots of other ideas for Dogtanian. Including a Live Fire Safety Bonfire Night Special where Dogtanian cruises the streets in his Rover (get it?), encouraging people to keep their pets indoors, especially their dogs. Ah, well.

One of my favourite scenes in the whole of *Phoenix Nights* is when a minibus pulls up outside of the club and seven dwarves get out.

'Oh, no,' says Paddy. 'I hate match days.'

The seven drunken dwarves stagger towards the club in their Bolton Wanderers tops: 'We're Bolton, we're barmy, we're on the march tonight, we're Bolton, we're barmy, we're on the piss tonight.'

'How far away are they?' says Max (which was actually an improvised line).

'Get back on your bus, you're not coming in.'

'Come on, let us in. It's his stag night.'

The dwarves then proceed to overpower Max and Paddy (the crappest doormen), pushing them out of the way, a few of them even walking through their legs. There's then a lot of violence, with bottles being smashed over Max and Paddy's heads as they're both dragged to the floor and kicked. Max manages to get one in a headlock: 'Come here, you little bastard.'

Brian hears the disturbance and wheels over. He opens the door, takes a glance at the carnage in front of him, shuts the door and wheels himself off.

We did some laughing filming that scene but not as much laughing as we did on the dining bus when we had lunch with the dwarves. I remember Justin Moorhouse asking one of them what he was up to after filming.

'I'm straight back into rehearsals for panto.'

'What panto is it?'

'Take a fucking wild guess,' he said, without missing a beat.

We were all still crying laughing during dessert.

One of the sequences that we all loved filming was the weekly auditions which featured at the end of each episode. They were filmed on the last day in the main function room at the club, and what a way to end. We did some laughing, especially when we auditioned The Rumburgers, a real-life husband-and-wife act of two pensioners dancing badly to ballroom. We couldn't believe our eyes and were all cracking up so much that it ended up in the final scene.

Another auditioning act was Steve Royle, a very funny comedian – and juggler. He manages to drop everything. First balls, then plates, smashing them all over the stage. He then turns his back and when he spins around he's holding three lit torches. The regulars all run in fear. Apart from Brian, who's wedged in between two tables shouting, 'Next!' and trying to blow the torches out from a distance.

It's quite common now to see crap and weird acts because of *Britain's Got Talent*, but this was years before that, and we loved celebrating them. We had a one-legged Elvis singing 'Blue Suede Shoe'. An escapologist trapped in a sack on stage who realises he's left the keys to his padlock on the outside of his sack. A pervy-looking bloke leaping around the stage to 'Nellie the Elephant' with nothing but a stuffed elephant's head covering his genitals.

The female magician with doves was one of the best. She's prancing around the stage to a bad version of 'Every Little Thing She Does Is Magic' when she motions to her doves to fly. That's just what they do, straight up into an extractor fan that's directly above Brian and co.'s heads. They're minced to pieces, and we see bits of feathers and blood sprayed all over the regulars. Marvellous.

The first series finished filming on Saturday, 2 December 2000. Then it was off to the edit, but there was a snag. Channel 4 had decided that they'd like to start showing *Phoenix Nights* in early January. It was originally scheduled for the summer. The problem was that Jonny the director had stated that he was going away for quite a long holiday over Christmas when he got the job. There was no other choice but for me to go into the edit and work on the series.

It was a daunting task, but also a dream come true, and I loved every second. I worked alongside an editor called Pete Hallworth. He'd been working at Granada TV since the late seventies and he certainly knew his stuff. We hit it off immediately and have stayed good friends ever since. The other joy was that all of the editing took place in Granada TV. This iconic place that I'd been in awe of my whole life.

So, there I was, officially at the one place I'd always dreamed of working. I was even given a staff pass, which allowed me to spend time wandering around the corridors soaking in memories. There was so much history. Lunchtime in the canteen was always an eye-opener. You'd find yourself queueing up with stars from *Coronation Street*. Bob Monkhouse was often in there if he was filming a quiz show. I even remember eating my Christmas dinner once sat next to Richard Harris. I wanted to say hello and how sad I was when he got shot at the end of *The Wild Geese*, but I didn't have the bottle.

There also used to be a drama called *Medics* that was filmed at Granada. Several of the cast would come for their lunch and it could be quite gross. Eating while facing a burns victim or someone with half their head cut off. Nice.

Working at Granada TV also came in handy if you ever just wanted to name-drop. I once skidded on some black ice on my way into work and bumped into another car. I rang my insurance company and, even though I was entitled to a courtesy car, they fobbed me off like they often do. So I gave them a phone number with an extension to call me back. When they did, they would have heard 'Hello, Granada television' from the switchboard operator, and when they asked for the extension they got me answering the phone saying, 'Hello, *Garages from Hell*.' They must have shit themselves because I had a courtesy car dropped off about two hours later, the bloody charlatans.

I tried it again when my mum was having her bungalow done up. I'd bought her a free-standing bath from a showroom in Leigh and the legs started to rust a few months later. So I got the showroom to ring me at Granada. 'Hello, *Builders from Hell 3*,' I said as I answered the phone. I told them that my mum's bungalow refurbishment was actually being secretly filmed for a series on ITV exposing dodgy trades and my mum had a full camera crew in her loft, 24/7. It worked a treat and my mum had fresh legs for her bath the following day.

Meanwhile, back in the edit, I was working my arse off and really enjoying seeing everything slowly come together. I'd edit during the day and spend my nights watching through the footage we'd filmed, logging it all in a notebook, choosing which scene had the funniest performance. I'd be up until two or three in the morning so I could be prepared for the edit the following day with all of my notes. I've still got countless ledgers of notes from all the edits I've done over the years.

I've always worked in this way. Leaving no stone unturned. For me, it's what I've got to do to get the very best out of what's been filmed. There might be a take that was abandoned due to something being wrong, but when you watch it you might find it's actually fine. It might be possible to save a portion of it and edit it together with the rest of the scene. Sifting for gold. It takes time but knowing that I've done my best is all that matters.

Working on the post-production element of *Phoenix Nights* was a huge education. I'd no idea of the process involved. After the edit was complete the episodes would then get a sound mix. That really brings them up to a whole new level of quality. I was introduced to John 'Fingers' Wood (as he's known), a legendary sound producer who'd worked on a lot over the years, from *Bob the Builder* to the Beatles' *Magical Mystery Tour*. Even *The Royle Family*. Literally a giant of a man in both stature and reputation. Like George Martin and Dwayne Johnson with the ears of a bat.

We got on great and he taught me a lot. I was fascinated with his knowledge, and fortunately I'd go on to work with him for many more years to come.

Pete Hallworth and I worked on *Phoenix Nights* until Christmas Eve and were both back in after Boxing Day. It had to be a quick turnaround in order to get the series ready for its broadcast on Sunday, 14 January 2001 at 9 p.m. on Channel 4. Right up against a new series of *A Touch of Frost*. We didn't stand a chance, but despite the poor ratings Channel 4 showed great faith and commissioned a second series. My mind was already swirling with ideas.

The first series ended with Den Perry setting fire to the club, disposing of his cigar in a wastepaper basket in the toilets. So, the new series started with Brian Potter having lost everything, his club, his licence and his will to live.

When Dave, Neil and I returned to our office at Bolton Enterprise Centre we all had plenty of ideas. I arrived with the full story arc for the second series, with the Phoenix Club literally rising from the ashes a second time. Brian is given an idea by Frank (Jim Bowen), who suggests asking Jerry to be the new licensee, but it'll be Brian who's actually manipulating things.

Dave, Neil and I never lost our meticulous method of working and any disagreements were still always about the quality of the scripts. Sometimes I'd say that something was 'too funny'. Dave and Neil would both look at me incredulously: 'Too funny?' But for me, everything always had to be rooted in reality.

Channel 4 had asked if I'd like the opportunity to direct the new series. Wow! That was a big step, but it felt like a natural progression that I was ready to take, as I already had the series filmed in my head. Logistically, I just needed to figure out how every scene could be filmed. I spent a lot of time drawing up storyboards in felt tip. Was I out of my depth taking so much on? I still can't decide after directing for years whether having more control is less stressful or not.

We wrote through the summer and then, when we'd finished, we had a read-through at the club with the cast and crew. It was great to see everybody again and the laughter was loud. We all sat around tables in the main function room with episode one, which was actually a secret dummy script. Everybody knew except Justin Moorhouse. In this version, we killed off his character in the first scene. We couldn't wait to see his face when he found out he'd been bumped off. His face was ashen. We all just carried on reading for a few pages and then when we couldn't contain our laughter anymore, we pulled out the real version of episode one's script. Lordy, was *he* relieved.

I wanted series two to be reminiscent of one of my favourite films, *The Blues Brothers*, where Jake and Elwood are on a mission to get their band back together. Brian knows he can't raise the Phoenix without everybody else and so he sets about trying to recruit everybody.

First, Brian tracks down Jerry, who's now resorted to singing in Asda. Flogging black bin bags at the front of the store, he's accompanied by Alan from Les Alanos. His lyrics are adapted from Will Smith's 'Men in Black' (originally 'Forget Me Nots' by Patrice Rushen, for the music trivia fans among you).

Jerry
(singing)
Come and get your black bin bags, they're on offer till
December

Come and get your black bin bags, they're long and black
and slender

Brian can't believe what he's seeing.

Next, Brian calls Holy Mary, who just happens to be queueing for Holy Communion when her mobile goes off. Her ringtone, 'Hot Stuff' by Donna Summer. She's mortified.

Then Brian calls Les from Les Alanos. When we catch up with him, he's selling meat from the back of a wagon on a local market. Luckily, the local market was only a few hundred yards from the actual club we were filming at in Farnworth.

Toby Foster was brilliant as Les, stood behind the van counter, holding a carrier bag full of meat and wearing a radio mic headset: 'It's BSE day, bit of something extra, and I'm not asking eight quid, I'm not even asking seven quid – six quid for this lot and I'll chuck in a pig's dick for the dog.'

Brian calls the rest of the *Phoenix Nights* gang, including Kenny Snr, who's working as a lollipop man – lying to some school kids as he helps them cross the road – and Ray Von, who's back working on a funfair: 'The louder you scream the faster the ride, but please stay seated at all times or you may die.' Then the camera cuts to a wide shot to reveal Ray over-seeing a kiddies' ladybird ride with only three small children on it. Meanwhile, Max and Paddy are driving a minibus of Asian Elders around Bolton. There is, in fact, a minibus that drives Asian Elders around Bolton. Well, there used to be.

We got supporting Asian Elders actors from Huddersfield. I'd seen their pictures beforehand and they all looked perfect; all they had to do was look confused. There was a problem, though, when we arrived to film. There'd been a misunder-standing with the art department and they'd got a small passenger bus instead of a minibus.

I didn't want to seem pedantic, but it just wasn't as funny as a minibus. What to do? I remembered that my old school Mount St Joseph had a red school minibus. I rang Mrs Walker, the headmistress (thankfully all the nuns had left by now otherwise I doubt I would have got anything).

I told her our emergency and she said the minibus was there if we needed to borrow it for a few hours. The art department raced across town to pick it up. Another reason we were rushing was because we only had the Asian Elders until noon, as it was Eid and they had to get into the nearest mosque to pray.

The Asian Elders were patiently waiting on the passenger bus, so I decided to explain why we had a hold up. 'I'm really sorry, but we got the wrong bus. We've now got a new bus on its way from the other side of town,' etc.

Just as I was finishing explaining, a chaperone who had arrived with the Asian Elders climbed on board and said, 'They can't speak a word of English. Let me know if you want me to translate.'

I felt like a right dick. They'd just been staring at me.

Eventually, the school minibus turned up, but I'd forgotten it had Mount St Joseph Secondary School written down the side in big white letters. So everybody had to individually peel the letters off and quickly replace them with 'Asian Elders'.

Finally, we set off. We filmed Max and Paddy singing a few songs, but we couldn't decide which song to use. We filmed 'Green Door' by Shakin' Stevens, 'Rhinestone Cowboy' by Glen Campbell, 'I Could Be So Good for You' by Dennis Waterman (which we ended up using) and '(Is This the Way to) Amarillo' by Tony Christie. The Asian Elders did a brilliant job of doing what they seemed to do best, looking baffled.

We then dropped them off at the mosque right on time. In fact, when you see them getting off the minibus and going into the mosque, that was for real. The minibus had the correct lettering reinstated and was dropped back off at school. They were none the wiser until they saw the episode on TV.

I don't know if you remember, but Brian had a model of a disabled boy in the entrance of the Phoenix Club. It was the type you'd often see outside high street shops years ago, a little boy sporting a caliper and holding a collection box – with Brian secretly putting any funds towards his holidays.

When the club burns down at the end of the first series we catch a creepy glimpse of the disabled boy burning through the flames. Luckily the firemen manage to save him, but unfortunately his face has melted. Anyway, one night when we were filming, some cheeky bastards stole him from the club. They walked in and took him. When we discovered he was missing there was a big palaver. 'Someone's taken the disabled boy. He's gone!' There were a few gasps from the extras in the club, who, completely unaware of any context, thought a disabled child had been kidnapped.

It transpired the disabled boy had been stolen by taxi. Can you believe it? Who steals anything by taxi? So it didn't take long for us to get him back. We just rang a few local taxi firms and asked if they'd had a booking for the club in the last hour. We found them. Our useless security team went round to the address, rescued our disabled boy and gave the culprits a slap. You couldn't write it.

The Phoenix fun day episode was a challenge to make. In order to try and raise funds for the club, Brian and co. host a charity fun day in the car park. With mobility scooters for dodgems, a soft-play area for children made from a converted portable toilet with bubble-wrap wrapped around scaffolding, and a ball pool with manky odd balls from off the club roof. It also has a condom machine that's been converted to sell penny chews at 10p each.

There's a jumble sale. Face painting with indelible spray paint, hence Young Kenny sporting a tiger's face for the remainder of the series.

Holy Mary even does fortune-telling in a tent in the car park.

A woman enters her tent, sits down and asks how much it is. Holy Mary tells her that 'it's a pound for two questions'. The woman's shocked. 'A pound for two questions? That's a bit expensive, isn't it?' 'It is,' says Holy Mary, '… and your second question?'

We also had an obligatory fun-day inflatable. Only this one was a bit unorthodox, Brian having booked the inflatable with Eric, a local entrepreneur who runs Game Sans Frontieres. When Eric pumps up the inflatable it has a giant penis at the front of it with two testicles on either side. When Brian sees it he nearly has a heart attack.

Everybody gathered around the inflatable outside.

Jerry
We're not having that

Brian
You're damn right we're not having it, Jerry – it's going back.
Go on, take it!

Eric
But Brian …

Brian
It's a family fun day

Eric
Yeah!

Brian
There's kiddies around, they can't be jumping up and down
on a love length

Muffled laugh from everybody around.

Eric
A what?

Young Kenny
Can we not disguise it?

Brian
Yeah … we'll stick a woolly hat on it and say it's you

Eric
But it's not how it looks, Brian

Brian
Not how it looks? It's a twenty-foot cock and balls. It doesn't
look like nothing else

Eric shows Brian that the penis can easily be strapped down
and disguised with some camouflage tarpaulin and two big
eyes stuck on the side. 'Hey, presto, Sammy Snake! Kids love
reptiles, Brian.'

'And what about the balls?' Brian says suspiciously.

'Snakes' eggs?'

We had some very surreal phone conversations with companies that made inflatables, which usually ended with them
hanging up. We eventually found a company in Bury and the
production crew and I went to visit them.

I'll never forget what the owner, Barry, said as he led us to
his workshop. 'I'm in showbiz myself,' he said. I thought, That's
a bit tenuous, you hire out inflatables for kids' parties. People
do love to be associated with telly, no matter what the capacity.
A woman once told me her husband worked in television.

'What does he do?' I said.

'He fits the set-top boxes for Virgin.'

I thought, Fuck me, he's hardly a cameraman on *Strictly*, is he?

So we were stood in this huge workshop/storage unit surrounded by inflatables, having one of the strangest conversations I've ever had as I basically asked 'Showbiz' Barry if there was any chance he could attach a giant penis and testicles onto a bouncy castle.

'Is this a wind-up?' said Barry.

'No. I'm deadly serious.'

I told him the story of the Phoenix fun day and eventually (and thankfully) he understood. He did us proud and the final inflatable looked fantastic.

In fact, Showbiz Barry even threw in a second, slightly bigger penis for free. That was for the final scene, when the penis overinflates and explodes over the audience of families.

After filming I hung on to the inflatable for a while but ended up donating it to the Manchester Pride festival. I didn't have any use for it at home. I mean, I couldn't exactly put it up in the garden. How sus would that have looked sticking up over the hedge?

So with the second series complete, all we needed was a date for it to be on telly. But Channel 4 just sat on it for months. There'd been a big staff shake-up and I think it just got forgotten about. As the months passed by, I started to wonder if Channel 4 were arsed about it at all. Whenever I got in touch, they just fobbed me off. So, I resorted to writing to the *What's on TV* letters page under a pseudonym to try and find out. They printed my letter and told me that it'd be on at the end of the summer. They were right, it was, plus I got the £5 letter of the week. It was crazy I had to write to a TV magazine to find out.

Viewers seemed to enjoy the second series as much as the first, but I don't think *Phoenix Nights* really caught on until both series came out on video/DVD. That's when people really started to get into it. It won the People's Choice award that year at the British Comedy Awards, which was a huge thrill, as that was voted for by the public.

I truly loved and still love *Phoenix Nights*, but after two years of solidly being in clubland, I felt that it was time for a change. We all agreed that we didn't want any future scripts to be patchy or weak in any way. I think with a third series there might have been a strong possibility of that happening. As Bernard Manning said, 'Leave them wanting more.'

Brian and co. made a few appearances over the next two decades. In *Max & Paddy's Road to Nowhere*, which is coming up in the next chapter, and once in a sequence for *Sport Relief* on BBC1, Brian performs a fitness workout live from the Phoenix Club.

It only took a few hours to film back at the club and so we didn't bother getting an audience. I thought we'd use some old audience stock footage we had from the series. Shots of the regulars clapping, etc., which when edited looked like they were in the audience for Brian's live *Sport Relief* workout.

On the night Davina McCall introduced the sequence and said, 'Now, we're going to go LIVE to the Phoenix Club in Bolton.' Then we saw Brian on stage wearing a shell suit, with Les Alanos behind him. Brian launches into 'Tubthumping' by Chumbawamba, lifting cans of WD-40 as weights while the audience in the club cheer and clap along.

The only snag was, it'd now been four years since the audience footage had originally been filmed, and unbeknownst to me some of the audience members had since died.

It came as a huge shock to their family and friends watching. Davina goes live to the Phoenix Club in Bolton and there's some poor bloke's dead mum on the front row clapping along. The next I knew it was all over social media and then the press. All quite funny on reflection but not so funny at the time.

I always liked to support Comic Relief over the years. I even filmed some intros once for Comic Relief as Brian Potter, rolling around a basketball court with Ade Adepitan and some other Paralympian guys in a parody of a genuine BBC trailer that was being shown at the time. They were all very athletic, doing choreographed wheelies in unison. Then I rolled through them as Brian saying, 'I can't do that, no chance, these lads are clearly blessed.' I try to do a wheelie but my wheelchair tips back too far. I crack my head on the floor and can't get myself up. 'Help! Somebody help me. I can't get up. I'm like a ladybird.'

Fifteen years after the last series of *Phoenix Nights*, I had an idea to reunite the cast for a special stage show that could raise a lot of money for Comic Relief. The venue was to be the Manchester Arena. I rang the cast a year in advance to see if they'd all be up for it. It was a very big ask, as we'd all be giving our time and effort for free. They all unanimously agreed it'd be great to work together again. Then I got a call back from Archie Kelly (Kenny Snr) about ten minutes later. 'When you say for free do you really mean for free?'

I had to laugh. 'Yes, I do, it's all or nothing.'

'Okay,' he said. 'Let's do it.'

Incredibly, we sold out sixteen shows to over a quarter of a million people and raised over five million pounds for Comic Relief. I'm still proud to say that's the largest amount of money raised by any comedic endeavour for the charity, but was it the end for *Phoenix Nights*?

It's been over twenty years since the first series, and I still write down ideas. I had an idea only today of Brian getting Young Kenny to paint an enormous letter 'H' on the roof of the club so he can advertise they've got a helicopter pad. The chance of a helicopter ever landing is, of course, zero.

As the years pass, I'm becoming more like Brian, but if *Phoenix Nights* rose again it'd have to be for something very special, maybe a film? Perhaps Brian could get visited by three ghosts. Now, wouldn't that be an idea?

The Thinnest of Thin Ice

Everybody did very well off the back of *Phoenix Nights'* success. Mostly, all of the cast went on to do great things. Neil went on to star alongside Paul O'Grady and Sheridan Smith in a BBC sitcom set in a bingo hall called *Eyes Down*. Dave dusted off our old *Fogborough* scripts about the local newspaper and got his own series on ITV, *Dead Man Weds*.

I'd been writing a lot with Paddy during the second series of *Phoenix Nights*. He was and is naturally very funny, and we had a rapport that came from years of knowing each other, right back to school. I was thinking about when we used to record our own plays in my bedroom. He'd come round for his tea after school and we'd record scripts I'd written, both doing voices and adding sound effects and music. We used to laugh a lot then too. You get that synchronicity with friends. So close that you know what the other one is thinking. Just with a look.

Max and Paddy were part of *Phoenix Nights* but they were also in their own little world. Slightly separate, fixed on the front door of the club. I was curious to see if they could exist within their own separate storyline. So in the second series of

Phoenix Nights, Max dreams of owning a motorhome and heading off for a life on the road.

Then, when a woman asks him if he can bump off her husband for money, Max spies an opportunity to make his dreams come true. He enlists the help of Paddy (for a smaller fee) and buys himself a motorhome. The series ended with Max and Paddy heading off for pastures new, but what I was really doing was setting up the possibility of a spin-off series.

There hadn't been a comedy series spin-off for years on British TV. Not unless you count *Porkpie*, the spin-off series from *Desmond's*, and I don't because it was piss poor. It'd be a challenge. Would people care enough about Max and Paddy to watch them in their own series?

Like directing, it felt like the next natural step. I was going on tour at the time and Paddy came on the road with me. We wrote as we travelled across Britain, mirroring what our characters would be doing. When I look back that whole period was one of the happiest times of my life. What was there not to love? Driving around with one of my best friends, coming up with ideas. We'd stay in Holiday Inn Expresses ('cause they did duvets) and write when we got back from my gigs at night.

Paddy met a girl once (well, I say once), and he ended up back in her room for the night. I woke the next morning with him knocking on my door.

'Did you have a good night?' I said, letting him in.

'It was shit. I never got a sniff. I ended up sleeping on that tiny couch in her room,' he said, motioning towards my room. 'My neck's fucking killing me.'

'That's not just a couch, you tool. It's a pull-out bed.'

'You're joking? I've been twisted up like a cripple.'

One night, driving back from a gig in Newcastle, we were absolutely starving but nothing was open. We got a glimmer of hope when we saw the neon lights of a Little Chef on the A1, but as we drove in closer we could see a waitress putting chairs on top of the tables. I said, 'Wouldn't it be funny if someone was so hungry they held up a Little Chef at gunpoint just so they could get a meal?'

This later became a scene in the series where one of Max's old doormen buddies, Billy (Craig Cheetham), holds up a Little Chef at gunpoint.

Billy
Leave it to me, Max. Let's see if she'll succumb to Billy's charms

He then flicks his tongue out several times.

If you've ever seen the outtakes to this scene it's probably the worst I've ever been for laughing. We were filming for over an hour. The whole crew stood freezing outside the motorhome at two o'clock in the morning and we just couldn't get it right for laughing. Paddy even had a handkerchief stuffed into his mouth to try to stifle his laughing, but it was useless.

Anyway, Billy walks to the Little Chef and taps on the glass.

'We're shut, pet,' the waitress tells him.

Billy pulls out a gun and holds it up to the window.

Billy
No, you're not. Get that fucking cooker on

Next thing, they're all sat inside the Little Chef waiting for their meals.

Max
I was just saying to Paddy she's got a heart of gold cooking after hours like this

We see the waitress delicately walking towards them with two big plates of full English. She looks petrified. Billy discreetly raises his napkin off his knee and lets her see his gun. Max and Paddy are completely oblivious to what's happening.

Max
Here she is

The waitress brings the plates of food but she's trembling with fear.

Paddy
Whoa, steady, cockle! Hey, she's shaking like a shitting dog, this girl

Max
I'm not surprised, the hours they have them working in these places, it's disgusting. I bet she's knackered, the poor cow, and judging by her age the menopause won't be helping either

Paddy
Meno what?

Max
The menopause

Paddy
I've never heard of it

Max
The menopause? The change? Hot sweats? Vaginal dryness?

Paddy
Hey! There might be hot sweats when Paddy's in town but
there's certainly no dryness

Billy
(to Max)
Who's got this, you?

Max
How? How have I got vaginal dryness?

We once got stuck in a traffic jam near Salisbury. Apparently, somebody had knocked down a cow. This gave us another idea. What if we accidentally knocked a stray cow down? Then try to get some money from the farmer for damage to the motorhome. Maybe he could offer us a pig as compensation. It seemed funny, driving around with a pig in a motorhome. The thought of it shitting and farting all the time. Max being forced to wear swimming goggles as the smell is burning his eyes.

Paddy
Urrgh! It's dropped its back again

Max
My eyes are burning. How dare you! You dirty pig. This is our
home! We live here

The pig farts again.

I don't want to ruin the magic but we had to react as if the pig had farted. The fart sounds were conjured up later in the sound mix. John 'Fingers' Wood got a big bucket of soapy water and some Fairy Liquid. He positioned a microphone, pressed record, and then we spent the next half hour making fart noises with our soapy hands. What a job. I'll tell you, though, we got some amazing fart sounds, and they went straight into the episode. You can't tell they're not real.

It was during filming with the pig that I appreciated the old adage 'never work with children and animals'. The pig was a bloody nightmare. It weighed a ton and did whatever it wanted. Squealing all the time, pissing, shitting and dragging the pair of us every which way but loose. We spent most of our time trying to catch it with the rest of the crew, as it was forever running off. There's a great outtake with Graham Walker (from the Grumbleweeds), who played the farmer. God knows how, but he ends up backwards on the pig, being bucked around like he's on a rodeo. It's very funny, if you ever get a chance to see it.

The series was to be set in different parts of Britain, though we never really say where. Mainly because most of the filming was done in and around Bolton. I learnt a lot about how you could cheat a location and then bolster the believability by casting actors with different accents. There's a shot at the end of episode one where the motorhome drives off towards the sea. The image of the sea was actually a picture I'd taken on holiday in Ireland. We magically inserted it into the scene and added some sound effects of seagulls squawking. It worked a treat, and suddenly we're at the seaside and not on a main road in Bolton.

We were incredibly fortunate with the weather that summer. It made a big difference to the look of the series and also to everybody's moods. Sure, there were plenty of ups and downs, but all I can remember is a lot of laughter. Especially from Paddy and me. That's when he managed to turn up for filming. He was a bugger for being late in the mornings. I know I was late on the first day filming *That Peter Kay Thing*, but Paddy slept in all the time. We'd get a message from his driver picking him up: 'He's not answering the door.' Eventually, he'd get to us, and we'd all be sat waiting because we couldn't film anything without him. We were in every scene together. A right pain in the arse.

The only other thing I struggled with was driving the motorhome. It was a huge beast of a thing and I'd no sense of spatial awareness. There were no rear parking screens, they hadn't been invented when 'she' was built. I was forever hitting walls and clipping other vehicles as we drove past, leaving the art department with their heads in their hands. They spent a lot of time leaving notes under people's windscreen wipers with our insurance details or knocking on residents' doors, apologising and advising that someone would be calling round to fix their wall or fence.

We did travel for a few scenes. Up to Newcastle for a few nights and one in London. In the London scene, Max and Paddy are both asleep. Max wakes and staggers to the toilet for a very loud wee. When he's finished, he staggers back out of the toilet carrying a bucket filled with urine that we can hear slopping about. He opens the door of the motorhome and chucks out his piss without even opening his eyes. Then he climbs back into bed.

We then hear the sound of some very loud chimes. Cut outside to reveal the motorhome parked directly under Big Ben. There's a traffic cop knocking on the motorhome covered in piss. Max opens the door, stares at him, confused, then puts his hand out to see if it's raining.

We had to film this at half four on a Sunday morning so there was no traffic. The permit to film cost a fortune too, but it was worth it for the comedy reveal. Pity I clipped the side of a wall as we were driving off. Though we didn't stop to leave a note, as it was the Houses of Parliament and I didn't fancy spending a night in the cells.

The majority of the episodes were stand-alone storylines so they could be accessible to the viewers, like the episodes about the pig, Billy the doorman and the first episode, where Max and Paddy steal a plasma TV from a local shopping centre dressed as giant teddy bears. But across the rest of the series, we developed a subtle story arc about a historic love interest of Max's. He discovers that his ex-girlfriend Tina had his baby after they split up. This rocks his world. So he decides to find his son, Daniel. He's desperate to get to know him and parks the motorhome outside the school. Paddy wakes and climbs into the passenger seat in his dressing gown.

Paddy
(yawning)
Where are we?

Max
School

Paddy
I can see that. Why?

Max
I've got a son

Paddy
I know, you've said, you had me up half the night.
Look, are you sure he's yours?

Max
Oh, I'm sure, don't you worry

Paddy

It's just, you know, I thought …

Max

Thought what?

Paddy

Well, aren't you supposed to have sex with someone first?

Max

The thinnest of thin ice. Look at them, playing. He could be one
of them there right now

Cut to shot of kids playing in the schoolyard.

Paddy

(looks)

I can't see any bald kids with beards, although that dinner
lady's a dead ringer for you

Max

(looks at watch)

They'll be coming out soon

Paddy

And?

Max

I want to see him

Paddy

You're better off staying away

Max

And how would you like it if you had a son that
you'd never seen?

Paddy

Might have, you know the kind of lifestyle I lead. There could
be a squadron of little Paddys running around as we speak. So,
have you got a plan?

A yellow school bus pulls up in front of the school.

Max

I have now. Quick, get some clothes on

They steal a school bus thinking Max's son is on board, but this goes horribly wrong when they discover he's on a different bus. The police soon catch up with them, and before you can say 'filthy screws' Max and Paddy are tossed in prison. Where they remain on remand until a trial date's set.

We filmed at Her Majesty's Prison in Preston. That was an eye-opener. Due to it being high-security, all of the cast and crew were pitched up about half a mile down the road, in the car park of Homebase. We all had to walk up to the prison. I'll never forget the reactions on the motorists' faces when they saw eighty blokes dressed as convicts strolling through the rush-hour traffic towards the prison. It even made the news on the local radio station.

We were given permission to film inside the prison because D Wing was having a refurb. I met one or two prisoners while we were in there. Mainly trustees serving us dinner. Which was bloody gorgeous by the way. Better than our own caterers on the outside. To this day I still fantasise about the spotted dick I had in there.

Being back in the role of director allowed me to experience some new challenges. This series was very different to *Phoenix Nights* in the fact that there wasn't a central location. If we ever had any bad weather on *Phoenix Nights* we'd go inside the club to film, but the majority of this series was set outside. We did have some scenes in the motorhome but everything else was on location, which meant we had to find everything in advance. If we were shooting any controlled driving shots, roads had to be closed, and we even had to bring in a stuntman for some particular shots. Like Roy Alon from Leeds. He'd worked on some Bond films and *Howards' Way*. He came to help us knock down the cow.

We had to try and manoeuvre the cow into the middle of a country lane then drive towards it without actually hitting it, but as I've said, my driving skills left a lot to be desired and it was almost corned beef on the first take. Mooing all over the road as I thundered around the bend, it literally shit itself as I slammed on the brakes.

Luckily, Roy Alon jumped out of a bush and I hit him instead. He was alright. Well, he said he was, but I'm sure he was concussed when we had lunch later. His eyes were slightly crossed when he was bragging about doubling up for Tom Hanks in *The Da Vinci Code*. I thought we'd have to run a disclaimer at the end of the episode: 'No animals were harmed during the making of this programme but Roy Alon got twatted in the head with a motorhome.'

There was also some flashback footage in this series, which was a first for me. One of these scenes took place at the Aquarius Club, a precursor to the Phoenix. This was Brian Potter's first club before it flooded and he lost his legs to a floating fruit machine.

In the flashback, Brian is holding a New Year's Eve party, and at the end of the countdown to midnight Young Kenny's job is to pull a rope, releasing a net filled with balloons from the ceiling. Young Kenny pulls the rope on the stroke of midnight, but when the net falls the balloons remain on the ceiling.

Brian
(to Young Kenny)
What did I tell you? I said don't use helium, you big tit

Brian Potter turns up again in the series when he visits Max and Paddy in prison. That was a complicated scene to film, as I was playing two parts. I had to film Max's shots and make sure I had got everything, because I then had to shave my beard and moustache off in order to film Brian's lines. That was a shock, seeing myself without a beard after having one for a few months.

Max
(on prison phone)
What are you doing here?

Brian
I've come to get you out

Brian slams a petition down on the ledge in front of the glass.

Max
What's that?

Brian
It's a petition, I've over four hundred signatures here.
I'm hoping to have you out for Christmas

Paddy

It's August!

Brian

Sweet Jesus and Mary Chain, I'm doing my best

He pulls a pink box out of his bag.

Here, and I've got a cake for you. Holy Mary's made it

Max

A cake?

Brian

A cake? You know, a cake?

Max

I know what a cake is

Paddy

(taps his nose)

He means a cake, Max. You mean a cake, don't you? I know
what he means

Brian

(taps his nose)

That's right, a cake

Max

(realising)

Oh, a cake. *(Whispering)* Is there something in the cake?

Brian
(whispering)
Yeah, sponge and a bit of jam. What did you want? This is real
life, son, not the friggin' *Shawshank Redemption*, and if you
hadn't stolen a bus full of kiddies in the first place you
wouldn't be here

*Max shushes him. Brian takes the lid off the box, revealing the
cake. 'Happy 60th Birthday Jerry' is written on the top of it.*

Paddy
It's not even our cake

Brian
You're a pair of ungrateful gets, aren't you? There's me rolling
around like a blue-arsed fly, getting T-shirts printed, and this is
all the thanks I get

Max
T-shirts?

*Brian proudly rips open his coat, revealing a T-shirt that reads
'Free the Phoenix Two'.*

Brian
It worked for Deirdre Rachid

Max
Oh, my God

Brian
Nine pound a throw, I've raised nearly three
grand in bail money

Max
There's no bail

Brian
Is there not? I'll use it on the website, then

Paddy
Website?

Brian
www.freemax&paddy.com. It's big business, this amnesty lark

Paddy
Yeah, for you and the Phoenix. You're a selfish arsehole

Brian
Selfish? I wasn't selfish at half six this morning when I was sat in the back of a Jumbulance with a puncture, freezing my tits off. Six hours it took me to get here, you wanna get sent down nearer to home next time

Paddy
Unbelievable!

We had a great cast for this series and because a few of the episodes were stand-alone it allowed us to get actors in for just a few days. Brendan O'Carroll turned up as Gypsy Joe. This was a few years before *Mrs Brown's Boys* had arrived on TV. Brendan was effortlessly funny.

I'd always been a big fan of Reece Shearsmith from *The League of Gentlemen*. He played a character called Bobster, who turns up at a fortieth birthday party. He's full of regret, everything is bitter and negative. His divorce, his vasectomy.

He ends up on stage singing 'The First Cut Is the Deepest' before holding a banana skin at the front of his crotch. Then, drunkenly re-enacting his vasectomy, he peels it open in the faces of some party guests, shouting, 'I'm half a man.' I'd known Reece for a few years and it was great finally working with him. As a favour to him, I filmed a cameo a few months later in the movie version of *The League of Gentlemen* alongside Simon Pegg.

Somebody else we cast in the series was Paddy's older brother Tony. He'd been angling for a part for months. Recently returned from New Zealand where he'd been living for years, he was constantly spouting stories about his TV work while living over there. So we wrote a part specially for him. He was in the prison playing one of Raymond the Bastard's bitches. Raymond is a hardened prisoner who secretly runs things.

Tony was mortified. 'I'm what?!'

I'll never forget his face when he had to soap up Raymond in the showers. We were crying laughing behind the camera. 'Go on, Tony, be a bit more erotic, rub the shower gel into his chest. Don't be shy, get a good lather going.'

He was glaring at us both.

'For fuck's sake, Tony, do you want a part or not?'

He didn't speak to either of us for the rest of the year, and when the episode went on TV he flew back to New Zealand for a few months.

We wrote an episode where the motorhome breaks down and, as luck would have it, a tow truck soon turns up by the side of the road offering assistance. The owner was a character called Mick Bustin, and while writing it we both kept picturing Noddy Holder playing the part. So we asked him and he said he'd be delighted to do it.

What a lovely fella he was. We spent a lot of time together and he gave me some advice that literally changed my life forever. I was talking about the tour I'd done the previous year and that I'd made some money from it. He said you want to use that money to buy yourself some time with your family. Susan and I had just had our first child, and all I wanted to do now was be with them both. Noddy said that he was from working-class roots and spent most of his early career chasing the money. He ended up being estranged from his children and deeply regretted his decisions. Fortunately, he said that he'd been able to put things right and now had a great relationship with his children. 'So think on it and don't miss out like I did,' he said. 'They grow up so quickly and you really don't want to miss it.' I'm not being over-sentimental, but that conversation did change my outlook on everything. I'd been grabbing every opportunity with both hands in an effort to get my foot in the door, going from job to job for years and not considering what really mattered.

Max & Paddy's Road to Nowhere premiered in November 2004. Surprisingly, the series got twice as many viewers as *Phoenix Nights*, and I was delighted to win a prestigious Rose d'Or Award for Best Comedy Performance. If there's anybody who knows a thing or two about comedy, it's the Swiss.

One of the most exciting moments of *Max & Paddy* was creating the artwork for the series. I wanted it to resemble the film posters I loved as a child. Especially James Bond. I managed to find an artist to draw Paddy and me in character, as well as various scenes from the series, and carefully we put them together. With the cast and crew added at the bottom, it looked nothing short of spectacular, and I was thrilled when I saw it on billboards as I drove around. I just wish I'd got a picture of myself standing underneath one at the end of the street where I used to live.

The series did incredibly well, but despite having so much fun I decided to heed Noddy Holder's advice. Perhaps it was time to get my priorities right. Maybe that's why we never did a second series. We did film a fitness DVD the following year, *Max & Paddy's The Power of Two*, which I'm proud to say remains the UK's biggest-selling fitness DVD. That does make me chuckle. I can't speak for Paddy, but just look at me. I'm hardly Davina McCall.

We did write a Christmas special of *Max & Paddy*, with the pair of them working as doormen on a Christmas grotto in a shopping centre. Dressed as elves with rosy-red cheeks and green tights, they're both overly aggressive with the children as they go inside.

Just reminiscing about it again makes me realise how much of a joy it might be to film it one day and work with Paddy again. I just hope he'd manage to get out of bed on time.

Lizard Head

Funny TV ads can be worth their weight in gold. I'd been offered a few over the years but they just weren't funny. Then John Smith's got in touch to ask if I'd like to front their new beer campaign. I didn't have the heart to tell them that I didn't drink (well, apart from the occasional glass of Baileys).

They sent some scripts and what I loved the most about them was that I didn't have to say anything condescending like, 'Wow! That tastes good.' In fact, the ideas for the adverts were just a series of funny sketches that had nothing much to do with John Smith's bitter. The theme of which was 'no nonsense'. A character who tells it like it is. They'd seen my stand-up and saw me as that person, straight to the point. Saying whatever's on his mind whether it's appropriate or not. Which, in truth, is my personality completely nailed. Though that's not necessarily a good thing, having spent a big part of my life often wondering, Why did I say that?

The money was fantastic, which I'll not lie, was a bit of a head-turner, but I never would've agreed to do them if they weren't funny. They even let me rewrite the scripts and improvise, so it was a win-win.

The first two adverts were set in an Indian restaurant. I even brought Paddy along for company and he ended up appearing in those two ads with me. The set-up was two couples eating a meal and my mobile rings.

Me
Hello, Britney

My wife
What's up?

Me
It's Daddy ... you what?
(to others)
She's having nightmares ... about the wardrobe monsters
(to Britney)
There's no such thing as wardrobe monsters, it's the burglars that break in through the window that you want to be worried about. Sweet dreams
(ends call)
She's gone. Two more lamb bhunas over here

He looks around at everybody's astonished faces.

... what?

The next one was the same set-up in the restaurant.

My wife
Kids grow up so quick these days, don't they?

Me

Hey, you're not wrong there. I didn't tell you, did I? Our Britney,
she's only four, mind, she comes up to me the other day, she
says where do babies come from?

My wife

What did you tell her?

Me

I said, well, when a daddy loves a mummy very much he
inserts his erect penis inside her vagina …

*I say this while holding a long thin phallic-shaped piece of
Indian meat.*

He then ejaculates sperm, which travels to the womb,
which fertilises the egg and develops into a baby
over nine months

Then I bite into the meat.

What? What have I said now?

All good, but I just wish I hadn't decided to bite into that
meat. It tasted horrible and what's worse, we had to do ten
takes of the same scene. So I had to bite into the meat each
time for continuity. Urrrgh! I can still taste it now. Like a burnt
dog's cock. Not that I know, you understand.

Apparently, that particular advert was banned because it
was discussing the facts of life. I think that was just some
clever PR stunt, as I was always under the impression that it
was filmed exclusively to be shown in cinemas. Alongside
certificate 15 or 18 films.

I'm still thinking about that meat. The whole dog wouldn't have been burnt, you understand. Just its cock.

We filmed the adverts over four days in London. I was surprised by how quickly and smoothly everything went. The director was Danny Kleinman, who designed the opening title sequences for the James Bond films. The creative director was a lovely man called Paul Silburn. They were good fun to work with and I relished the freedom they gave me, particularly in the advert where I was football training in a park alongside some highly skilled players. We were all in a semi-circle performing skills with the ball. Circling it with their feet, rolling it around their neck then flipping it in the air before passing it to me. I just booted it and said, ''Ave it!' We cut to see the ball bouncing off somebody's garage roof at the back of a house before disappearing into a back garden.

It only took two takes. The first one, I tried to kick the ball and missed. The second time I kicked it and shouted, ''Ave it!' for some reason. The one and only time.

We watched it back and they were so happy with that version that we finished filming for the day. The crew couldn't believe their luck and appreciated an early dart on a weekday. When the advert was shown on TV later that year ''Ave it' became a huge catchphrase. Really powerful, the old adverts. Just one moment captured and a national catchphrase born. Funny, you spend all your time working your arse off making a series then you film a few adverts over four days and they catapult you into the national consciousness.

I suggested my friend Beatrice Kelley for the next advert. She'd played Rose in the 'Eyes Down' episode of *That Peter Kay Thing*, as well as Marion in *Phoenix Nights*. She was perfect playing my mum, who I wanted to move out. I casually walk into the front room carrying her suitcase and pull the plug out of her hoover.

Me

Come on, Mum, it's time to go

Mum

Go? Go where?

Me

The old people's home. They'll look after you now,
it's for the best

Mum

Are you mad? I'm fifty-five

Me

I know, but I've had a word with them and they'll
take you. Come on

Mum

Get off! Why should I go and live in an old people's home?

Me

Because I want to put a snooker table in your bedroom and the
kids are frightened of your moustache. Now come on. Avanti!

I'm still laughing and wonder if you'd be allowed to get away with an advert like that today. Probably not.

I filmed ten John Smith's bitter adverts over the next few years. One was at Crufts, which was filmed at Wembley Arena during the actual competition. Danny Baker made an appearance in another ad, which was a parody of the Daz doorstep challenge.

Danny knocks on a front door. I open it and Danny says, 'Would you swap these two large packets of ordinary washing powder for your one packet of biological powder?' I think for a second and say, 'Yes.' Then I take the two large packets from him, give him my smaller packet and close the door. Leaving him flabbergasted.

It was so good to finally meet Danny. I'd been a fan of his for years and think he's one of the best broadcasters that Britain has ever produced. His inventiveness, his sense of comedy and his choice of music is second to none. And boy, could we talk. We were at it non-stop all day long and became firm friends quite fast.

Other adverts included a spoof of *Antiques Roadshow*. One as me playing a controversial DJ at a family wedding, while another was set in Las Vegas (actually Surrey) watching Engelbert Humperdinck performing 'Please Release Me' on stage. He's singing as I'm walking back from the bar with a tray of drinks.

'Please release me, let me –'

Then I interrupt him by shouting out, 'GO!'

It was based on a time when my dad did the same thing in a nightclub in Blackpool. He shouted out the last line of a song, leaving the artist on stage horrified and embarrassed. Though my dad said, 'There were no hard feelings, and I got a signed photo with him backstage after the show.'

We filmed the Las Vegas ad at a place called the Lakeside in Surrey, which is famous for hosting world championship darts. I was introduced to the venue's owner, Bob Potter, who accused me of basing *Phoenix Nights'* Brian Potter on him. I was flummoxed and couldn't tell if he was being serious or not.

It turns out that Bob Potter actually had a fire at the Lakeside which burnt it down. Then he was fined for breaking health and safety violations. It was a bit eerie, I must admit. I'd never heard of him or the place.

For a moment I panicked and thought I might have another situation like the one I had with Dogtanian, the fire safety officer, on my hands and I'd have to go back and add *another* disclaimer to the end of *Phoenix Nights*.

Paddy was also in the Las Vegas advert with me, recreating the same character he'd played in the earlier ads. Beatrice Kelley also reprised her role as my mum, which suggested a family trip to Vegas. After filming was complete me and Paddy were offered a driver home. It was a hell of a drive from Surrey to Bolton. I had a portable DVD player with me, so we thought we'd settle back with a few films and enjoy the long journey home. Magic.

The driver was very professional, opening both of our doors, calling us both 'sir'. We chatted for a little while when we got in the car.

'It's gonna be quite a long drive for you, this,' I said.

'Oh, it's okay, sir. Coincidentally, I've got a family christening in Bolton this weekend, so I won't have to drive back, sir.'

Then Paddy chirped up: 'I've got a christening this weekend too. It's a mate of mine, Del.'

'Black Del?' said the driver (that made me laugh, as he was also black).

'Yes,' said Paddy, surprised.

'He's my cousin, sir!'

And that was the last 'sir' we got, as all professionalism flew straight out the window. Suddenly it was like a family reunion. Paddy and the driver were now thick as thieves and my portable DVD player never even got switched on for the next seven hours.

The next thing I knew we were doing ninety up the motorway, the driver chain-smoking and playing the loudest fucking rap music I've ever heard in my life. My ears were throbbing with the bass. It was 'motherfucker' this and 'motherfucker' that.

I was texting Paddy, who was sat right next to me: 'What the fuck is going on? Motherfucker?'

Paddy texted back: 'What can I do, motherfucker? He's Del's mate.'

When we drove into the services I almost pulled a muscle in my chest trying to reach over the front seat, to turn the bass down on the motherfucking stereo.

When I finally got in at four in the morning Susan said, 'Have you been to a nightclub?' I stunk of smoke that bad.

My favourite of all the John Smith's adverts was set during a diving heat at the Commonwealth Games. We filmed it using the diving boards at the Olympic pool in Crystal Palace. It looked so realistic when it was edited together. In fact, they cleverly scheduled it right in the middle of the Commonwealth Games, so it felt as if you could've accidentally switched channels on your remote, with the same commentators and graphics, etc. There are two professional divers up first. They each do incredible dives, triple somersaults, hitting the water with grace. Then the commentator says, 'Now John Smith of Great Britain, what's he going to do?'

It then cuts to me standing on a very high diving board wearing a very loud pair of Bermuda shorts. Turquoise with palm trees on. We hear the commentator announce, '... a running bomb'.

Then I charge down the diving board, bounce straight off the edge, pull my knees up to my chest in mid-air, and hit the water with an enormous splash, spraying the judging panel and some of the audience. Great fun.

'Oh, that's terrific,' says the commentator. The judges, drenched, hold up tens on their scorecards. 'The crowd love it and so do the judges ... top bombing!'

I have to confess, I didn't actually jump off the diving board. They got a stuntman in to double for me. I climbed up to the diving board to consider it, but when I saw how high it was I thought, Bugger that.

Though I can proudly say it was actually my backside that you see when I'm climbing out of the pool at the end. They didn't need a stunt arse.

After making a few series back to back for the past few years, I decided to take some time out from filming my own work. I started to get invites from my peers to play characters in their shows, which was really lovely. Matt Lucas and David Walliams asked me if I'd like to appear in a *Little Britain* special they were filming called *Little Britain Abroad*.

I was to play the younger brother of Dudley Punt (David Walliams). He's just married his Thai bride, Ting Tong Macadangdang (Matt Lucas), in order to make an honest man/woman of her. They go on their honeymoon to Belgium, where they meet up with my character. I live in a caravan park with my new eighteen-year-old virgin wife Ivanka (Julia Davis), 'who's set me back two hundred quid'.

It was all very far from being politically correct but that's what made it funny. It probably wouldn't get made now. Sadly, Matt and David have taken a lot of flak in the past few years for the work they did. I think that's a shame. Comedy is such a minefield, with political correctness changing it all the time. Sometimes for the greater good, most of the time not.

Everybody's a critic on social media. Something or somebody gets 'slammed on Twitter' (which might only be by a handful of people) and the press jump all over it. They sensationalise a story in order to generate clickbait for themselves and their websites. It can really damage or destroy somebody's career.

I fall for clickbait all the time and spend countless hours on the bog swiping to see 'how much weight Susan Boyle has lost' or 'what the cast of *The Goonies* look like today'. My arse is numb and I'm still clicking 'next'.

Another show I made a cameo appearance in was Catherine Tate's. I'd kept in touch with her since she'd appeared in *That Peter Kay Thing*. Her first series was a great success, deservedly so, as she's so talented. I remember texting her when the first episode went out on BBC3. We were back and forth commenting on her sketches. I was chuffed for her. Then she invited me to play a cameo alongside her legendary Nan character.

I was to play an old man called Young Tommy Upson, a friend of Nan's who she brings back to her flat. Halfway through the sketch Nan and her grandson, Jamie (Mathew Horne), hear a toilet flush and I slowly walk into the room.

Tommy

Aye, aye

Nan

Here he is. Is that better, sweetheart?

Tommy

Oh, I'm about a stone lighter now. It flushed itself

(pointing over shoulder)

I tell you something, it's good to see you got plenty of loo
rolls in there. Thirty-six I counted. I don't understand it,
you go to someone's house for a pony and you've got
to ration your wipes

It was the first time I'd ever used prosthetics. It took hours in make-up, but the end result was incredible. In fact, I've put a photo in one of the picture sections of this book. I'd also never filmed a sketch in front of a studio audience before. They'd built the interior set of Nan's flat in the studio at BBC

Television Centre. It looked amazing. I loved the detail, just like with Leonard's bedroom when we filmed *That Peter Kay Thing*. You'd think you were inside an actual old person's front room. Well, until you turned around and saw a full studio audience sat watching. I relished the opportunity.

Nan
Here you are, Tom. This is my Diane's boy, Jamie

Tommy
Hello, son

Jamie
Nice to meet you

Tommy
He's home early, hasn't he got a job?

Jamie
I'm at university

Tommy
Oh, that's right. Your nan said something about you being gay

Jamie
I'm not gay, I've got a girlfriend

Tommy
My brother, he had a gay dog

Nan
Who, your Billy?

Tommy
Yeah, that's right. It cost him a fortune in vets' bills

Jamie
A gay dog?

Tommy
No, not gay. Diabetic. Some kind of disability

It took about an hour to film, as there was a lot of laughing, and we ended with an impromptu singalong of 'Bridge Over Troubled Water', with the audience joining in.

Tommy
Right, I better love you and leave you

Nan
Well, you know where I am. Ta-ra, Tommy, sweetheart, mind how you go

Tommy
(to Jamie)
Look after her, gay boy

I leave. Nan comes back in and takes a breath.

Nan
What a fucking liberty! He's used all my fucking lavatory paper. What was he fucking doing in there? Making fucking flags?!

A few months later I got a call from *Coronation Street*, inviting me to appear again. This time I was to have a much bigger part, playing Eric Gartside, a drayman who delivers beer to the Rovers Return. Eric's asked Shelley (Sally Lindsay) out on a date. I'd met Sally when she appeared in *Phoenix Nights* as Ray Von's girlfriend. She's a great actress and had gone from strength to strength over the years, but will always be remembered for marrying the bigamist Peter Barlow.

My character had been created to add a little light relief to *Corrie*, as it had been a very heavy year for Sally's character. I was to appear in two episodes, both to be screened on the same night. The script was in great shape but they allowed me to rewrite it. This was a great honour and it meant I was able to hopefully add a few more laughs.

In the first scene, Eric picks Shelley up from the Rovers. That was surreal, being on such an iconic set in Granada. This was the Rovers Return pub! I'd grown up with it my whole life, filled with unforgettable characters like Bet Lynch, Hilda Ogden, Elsie Tanner. Mike Baldwin and Ken Barlow even had a fight in there, and now I was in it. It was also really weird seeing the cameras and crew where you imagined another wall in the Rovers to be. For each take I just kept coming through the tiny pub door and thinking, I'm in the bloody Rovers, acting with Jack Duckworth.

What also freaked me out was how quiet it was. There were plenty of regulars in the background, but they were all miming chatting in silence. Obviously all of their chatter would be added later, as well as the jukebox, but the quietness was really odd.

Eric takes Shelley for a posh meal at a restaurant and he's disgusted by the size of the food portions. Over the duration of the night Eric begins to reveal a little more of his personality, which slowly leads Shelley to realise that sadly he's not the man for her. His heart is in the right place but he's just a bit of a soft sod.

Eric takes Shelley back to his house, which he's expecting to be empty, but unfortunately his mum's home.

Eric
Aren't you supposed to be at jazzercise?

Mum
I was but Marlene had a groin strain. Stick the kettle on.
Eric's not brought a girl home in … in fact, he's never brought
a girl home

Eric's mum was played by Janice Connolly (who also played Holy Mary in *Phoenix Nights*). I'd suggested her for the part, as I knew she'd be perfect, and as usual, her comic timing was spot on.

Meanwhile, Shelley, Eric and his mum sit in awkward silence as
Eric's mum insists on joining them for a cup of tea.

Mum
Do you keep fit, Sonia?

Eric
It's Shelley, Mum

Mum
(snapping)
I know

Shelley
Er … no, not really

Mum

I didn't think so. I do. I'm very active. Always keep busy, that's
my motto. I go to bingo a lot. Eric comes with me. He's very
quick with his dabber. He can do four books at once. I like him
coming with me. I find it hard to concentrate. Mind you,
I always did. Hey, have you told Sandra what your
father used to call me?

Shelley

It's Shelley

Mum

(ignores her)
Dolly Daydream. You see, that's my name, Dolly … and he used
to call me Dolly Daydream

She laughs just too much.

Dolly Daydream

Shelley laughs awkwardly. Eric just smiles. Silence.

Shelley

What did he call you?

Eric

Eric

*The scene ends with Shelley calling for a taxi on the home
phone. 'Tell her to put the money in the box,' says Mum. Eric asks
if they could go out on another date but Shelley politely says no.
She gives Eric a gentle kiss on the cheek and leaves.*

Mum
You better get off to bed, Eric. Your electric blanket's been
on for over an hour

Eric
Yes, Mum

It was a thrill to have a proper go in *Corrie* again. The longest-running TV soap in the world. Although, to be honest, I haven't watched it since the tram crash. It was also good to give Mr Softy's teeth an airing again, as they'd been sitting in my underpants drawer since I'd last used them.

Knock, knock.
Who's there?
Doctor …
Doctor Who was brought back to our TV screens in 2005 to much success and critical acclaim. He was revived by Christopher Eccleston and then played by David Tennant.

I'd always been a fan of *Doctor Who*. Not a geeky fan who could tell you some obscure fact like what the Doctor was wearing in series 12, episode 6. Like my friend Ian Savage, who could tell you the names of every alien in every *Doctor Who* episode. Ian even has a full-size Dalek in his vestibule.

Doctor Who was a series I grew up with. It always reminds me of eating a full English breakfast at Saturday teatime, listening to the *Final Score* results while my dad filled in his coupon.

Tom Baker was my Doctor. He was irreverent, witty, had a great stare in his eyes and he enjoyed offering Jelly Babies to baddies at inappropriate moments. *Doctor Who* also used to scare me on the odd occasion, though not so much as I got older, when Peter Davison and Colin Baker took over. It started to look a bit cheap, with lots of filming in quarries doubling as alien planets. Then when it moved to Monday nights I knew it was doomed, and it was axed in 1989.

It always bugs me when the BBC says, 'It's been going for over sixty years,' when it was off-air for sixteen years (well, apart from a one-off, lacklustre Canadian TV film with Paul McGann. Now who's the geek?).

I got a few *Doctor Who* annuals from Father Christmas. I also got a 7-inch single of the *Doctor Who* theme, but I spent more time playing the B-side, a catchy little number called 'Reg', composed and played by the BBC Radiophonic Workshop. Look it up on YouTube.

My mum and dad bought me the single from a *Doctor Who* exhibition in Blackpool. I used to love going there and would mither my mum and dad to take me all the time. It was a replica TARDIS on the side of a café facing the central pier, but when you walked through the doors and down some stairs it was enormous. Just like the TARDIS. It was filled with Daleks, Cybermen and other aliens. K-9 was there (Doctor Who's robot dog) and it had the actual controls from the TARDIS that you could fiddle with to your heart's content. I loved it.

So you can imagine my delight when I was offered a part in the real *Doctor Who*. It was 2006 when I received a lovely handwritten letter from the series writer, Russell T Davies. I went to visit him at his house in Manchester where we had tea and biscuits. Lovely man.

He wanted me to play the part of Elton Pope, a man who'd accidentally met Doctor Who when he was a child and had been obsessed with tracking him down ever since. Every month Elton met up with people who'd also met the Doctor and they discussed how they could possibly track him down.

Then a mysterious man called Victor Kennedy arrives at their monthly meeting and manages to manipulate the group.

One by one the members mysteriously disappear. Eventually, we discover that Victor is absorbing them into his body and he's really a big green alien called the Abzorbaloff. Classic *Doctor Who* bollocks.

I was well up for it until I found out that I'd be filming in Cardiff for three weeks. I've nothing against Cardiff, it's just that Susan was pregnant and I didn't want to be away for that length of time. I asked Russell if I could swap my character from Elton to Victor Kennedy/the Abzorbaloff. It was only four days of filming, plus I'd always fancied being an alien. Who wouldn't?

Russell was fine about it and so I drove to Oxford to have a cast made of my body. That was an experience. I had to strip down to my underpants. In fact, they gave me some of their own special non-stick underpants. Then about twelve people stood around and smeared me in this weird white plaster of Paris. I felt like I'd joined some religious cult.

When they covered my face I began to freak out. They said it wouldn't take long, then they covered my eyes and stuck two straws up my nose so I could breathe. Suddenly three weeks in Cardiff seemed preferable. Everything was black. I couldn't really hear anymore. I felt trapped and paralysed from the plaster of Paris that had now set. Now I was literally freaking out with claustrophobia and about to scream the place down (though nobody would have heard me), when they cracked me open, splitting my hardened outer shell in two. They were then left examining these two full-size body casts as I went off for some fresh air and a much-needed shower.

When I arrived in Cardiff a few weeks later I was to be in make-up at four on a Sunday morning (actually it was three, as, unfortunately, the clocks had gone back an hour). It would take four hours in make-up to turn me into the Abzorbaloff.

I sat in the make-up chair slowly nodding off, listening to music while the make-up designer applied layer upon layer of make-up and prosthetics. When I woke up and saw my reflection in the mirror, I shit myself. I was a big fucking lizard. Oh, my God. The make-up was astonishing and I still had two hours to go.

I had to wear a full lizard-type bodysuit. The interior was lined with thin plastic tubing so cold water could be pumped around the suit at various intervals throughout the day and stop me from overheating. It felt lovely but a bit like I was pissing myself. Which proved to be extremely frustrating when I was bursting for a wee, as I was sealed into the bodysuit. There were a few times when I was literally begging them to get the suit off as quick as they could before I pissed myself. Then I'd run to the bog in my lizard head.

A producer came into make-up once and told me that the *Blue Peter* competition winner was here and they wanted to film him meeting the Abzorbaloff. *Blue Peter* had run a 'design a *Doctor Who* alien' competition a few months before and a nine-year-old boy had designed the Abzorbaloff. I was intrigued to meet this disturbed child with such a vivid imagination.

Konnie Huq brought him in and I spun around in the make-up chair, revealing the Abzorbaloff in all its glory. The boy's face was aghast.

'Wow! That's absolutely AMAZING!' he screamed in a high-pitched voice, '... but you're supposed to be the size of a London bus?'

'Can we cut?' said Konnie Huq. Then the boy and his parents were quickly bundled off the make-up truck. Apparently, he wasn't supposed to reveal that fact, as the BBC didn't have enough money in the budget to have me stomping around London the size of a bus.

Another thing I discovered about this episode was that it was specially conceived to allow David Tennant extra time in the schedule to film more *Doctor Who* twenty miles up the coast in a quarry (not again). Disappointingly, David Tennant only ended up being in the episode I was in for about five minutes at the end. In fact, I think they should have renamed it Doctor Where that week instead.

Later that year my family came round to our house for the big premiere, when it went out live on BBC1. We even had a full English breakfast for tea and did our coupons, just for old times' sake. I hadn't seen the finished episode and we all sat in silence as we watched it. Then it ended and everybody still sat in silence, until my nan said, 'What a load of crap.' She wasn't wrong. There was no denying it, and it's since gone on to be voted the worst *Doctor Who* episode of all time. Well, at least that's something to be proud of, in a perverse sort of way.

We went to New York about ten years later and I found a plastic figure of the Abzorbaloff in a sci-fi shop. I was tempted to buy it but never did. It then became clear to me how brilliant it was to be part of *Doctor Who*. Crap or not, if everything ever goes tits up in the world of showbiz you'll probably find me at one of those sci-fi conventions. Sat between K-9 and an Ewok, signing pictures of the Abzorbaloff for a tenner each. Ka-ching!

Die Well Hard

The only problem I've ever had with talk shows is the talking bit. I just never want to sit and talk. I understand that the host has an agenda, to probe, to discover light and shade within their guests, but at the end of the day it's light entertainment, not a therapist's couch. I never set out to be subversive, it always just happens. It's a combination of nerves and adrenalin. When they fuse together all hell breaks loose and I literally do not know what I'm going to do next, never mind the host.

Appearing on Jonathan Ross's shows has always been the worst for that. Before I realise it I'm climbing around the set and generally misbehaving. I think I do it more on his shows because I never know what he's going to say. That's why I try and get in first.

The first time I ever did his show it was at short notice. Sir John Mills had dropped out at the last minute and I got a call asking did I want to do it?

'It's tonight?! But I'm in a garden centre in Leigh ... HOW MUCH MONEY???!!! I'll be on the next plane.' Normally you never get paid for appearing on talk shows because usually you're promoting something, but it's different when somebody drops out.

I'll not tell you how much it was, but it'd have bought a lot at the garden centre. Some top-notch patio furniture, a couple of barbecues and lunch from the granary, and I'd still have change.

Before you could say Four Poofs and a Piano (which you probably can't anymore), I was walking onto *Friday Night with Jonathan Ross* at BBC Television Centre. Straight away the nerves and adrenalin kicked in, and instead of going over to Jonathan I went straight over to the piano for an impromptu singalong. I wanted to do 'Starmaker' by The Kids from 'Fame', but they didn't know it. Call themselves 'Poofs'?

I was so nervous that I told him, 'I'm nervous. I wasn't expecting this tonight. I was in a garden centre in Leigh four hours ago eyeing up begonias.'

On my second appearance on *Jonathan Ross* I sang 'I Love to Love' by Tina Charles with the Four Poofs and their piano. Jonathan asked me what I was up to next and I said, 'I'm going to remake *Die Hard*. It's going to be called "Die Well Hard".' It got a big laugh from the audience, but the truth is, it wasn't a joke.

It'd been a dream of mine for years. So much so that a good friend of mine who had a contact at 20th Century Fox in London got me a meeting so I could pitch the idea. He came with me and we ended up in this swanky office with all these bigwig Brits and Yanks, all sat around a big glass table.

This Yank started: 'So, Peter, it's such a pleasure to meet you [not a clue who I was]. I've been told that your career trajectory has been phenomenal over the last few years, so I'm keen to hear your idea. How would you like to work with us?'

I dived straight in, as I'd been rehearsing it on the train.

'I'd like to remake *Die Hard*.'

The whole room erupted in laughter for a good minute or so and then I added, '... with me playing the John McClane role.'

Then off they went, laughing again. 'That's funny. No, seriously, how would you like to work with us?'

Fucking hell, how embarrassing. They thought it was a joke.

I gulped then just carried on regardless: 'I arrive at the airport on Christmas Eve to meet my wife. She's at a staff party at Beetham Tower in Manchester ...'

I waffled on for a while. They all nodded politely, smiles stuck on their faces. Then this one guy closed things down by telling me that, unfortunately, the *Die Hard* franchise was still very active. In fact, Bruce Willis had plans to make a fourth film the following year. The selfish bastard. Did he not think for one second that somebody else might fancy having a go?

The only other time I was paid to be on a talk show was when somebody pulled out of Paul O'Grady's show on ITV. I got a call asking if I'd go on and they offered a lot of money. Again, I'll not telling you how much, but I could have gone back to said garden centre and bought a few swing chairs, a couple of those massive umbrellas for your garden and probably half their Christmas decorations too.

I liked Paul O'Grady. He told it like it was. I did his teatime chat show a few times and I always liked to dress up. No real reason other than it's fun.

The first time I dressed up as a snowman. The following year, a Christmas tree. The next, a big yellow chicken. So when I got the last-minute call to appear on his big new Friday night chat show, my first thought (other than the money and the garden centre) was what could I dress up as?

I fancied dressing as a big beer bottle. I thought it might be funny to see my face painted green poking through a hole in the bottle. So I told them and they said fine.

Then I got a call back: 'The producers don't want you to be a bottle. They're worried it could encourage drinking.'

'I'm dressing as a beer bottle, not drinking it.'

'They said they'll offer you more money not to dress as a beer bottle.'

I said, 'Fine, then. I'll take the extra money. Forget the beer bottle,' and that was that. Sometimes the business of show can be completely crazy. I wasn't even that arsed about being a beer bottle.

Then some cheeky sod producer got in touch to say because of the amount of money I was now getting (not to be a bottle), would I stand in the middle of a wall of death, live, while a motorbike rode around me at the end of the show.

I just said I was packing my beer bottle costume and they quickly backed down.

John Daly is an Irish presenter who had his own talk show in Belfast. I appeared on it quite a few times, mainly because it was an opportunity for a lovely weekend in my favourite part of the world, plus I got to see my family in Coalisland. Sometimes I'd take my mum with me, or my cousins would travel up to see the show and sit in the audience. One night John came into my dressing room to tell me that Eamonn Holmes'd had to pull out at the last minute, but they'd got a replacement. He said I wasn't to tell a soul, as it was a big surprise. It was George Best.

Now, George Best was a legend, everybody knows that. He's even got an airport named after him. At the time he'd been back in the media due to his ongoing battle with alcoholism and had just received a controversial liver transplant. I was shocked that he was well enough to come to the studio, but he did.

John and I finished our interview and then he told the audience that, regrettably, Eamonn Holmes had had to pull out at the last minute, but he had a replacement: 'Ladies and gentle-men, George Best.'

Well, the place just erupted. The whole audience immedi-ately stood to its feet at the very mention of his name. I've never experienced such a reaction. As soon as he walked on set you could feel the love for him. It was palpable. He didn't look too great as he walked down the studio steps. He actually looked nervous. George hugged John and then he hugged me (though I'm sure he hadn't a clue who I was). He had this sweet smell I'll never forget and his skin tone was faintly yellow. As were his eyes. Everybody seemed to be crying. Even I was filling up. It was very hard not to.

I can't remember much of his interview. They did discuss his recent liver transplant and he stated that he was going to start a new life, but sadly it had all come too late and he died within twelve months of recording that show.

It's tragic for anybody to pass, but for somebody who was so loved like he was, well, the loss is still immeasurable.

Without a doubt, the greatest British talk show host was Sir Michael Parkinson. He was in a class of his own. His journal-istic training gave his interviews a great foundation and he was always well researched when it came to his guests. He also knew how to listen and, more importantly, when to interject.

His show had been off air for a while but returned in 1998. I was fortunate to get the job of warm-up in the studio each week. It was a great honour to sit on the front row and listen to these interviews first-hand. I also got to know Michael and his wife Mary. So you can imagine how utterly surreal it was to be invited on as a proper guest in 2002.

As overwhelming as it was, in many ways I felt comfortable because I was so familiar with the crew, the set and Michael himself. He wanted funny stories about real life and he was happy to steer me that way.

It was a perfect partnership. He knew just when to nudge me in a different direction without ruining a punchline. I felt safe every time I appeared on his show. Which ended up being five times over the next six years, alongside guests including Dame Judi Dench, Sandra Bullock, Take That and Morgan Freeman. I was scheduled to appear with Daniel Craig once, but he got a head cold and bailed. James Bond with the flu. So I had to cover for him by doing an extended interview, which actually turned out to be one of the best I ever gave, especially considering it was all last minute.

The first time I was a guest on *Parkinson* it was alongside Lulu and Bob Monkhouse. I remember arriving on my own at the BBC and going to the door of my dressing room, when I heard a commotion in the corridor. Lulu arriving with an entourage: eight people, including Lulu with her dog on a lead. I shook my head and chuckled. All I had was a rucksack and a portable CD player.

I'd written to Bob Monkhouse in 1995 when I was at college. I'd always been a great fan of his stand-up. I was delighted when he wrote back and I stuck his letter in the front of his autobiography. I decided to bring the book with me and I showed it to Michael Parkinson before the show. He thought my letter to Bob was fascinating and said it'd be a good opportunity for 'a bit of business', revealing to Bob that he wrote to me and maybe getting him to read his letter during the show. I said it was fine with me and handed him the book.

When Bob came on, Lulu and I moved up a couple of seats so he had the chair nearest to Michael. Bob's whole routine had been written in advance. All Michael had to do was ask him a few prompted questions and Bob did the rest. That's how Bob wanted it, as this was probably going to be his last ever interview. Bob had been diagnosed with cancer, which he discussed openly on the show. He made light of a very grave situation. Personally, I found it a bit uncomfortable laughing. Not because it wasn't funny but because it was sad. He wasn't even well enough to walk down the stairs for his introduction. When the camera cut to him, he was already standing at the bottom.

So, it came to the bit when Michael brought up the subject of my book. He carefully waited for a gap in Bob's conversation and said, 'Do you remember writing to this young man?'

Bob, slightly flustered by Michael's deviation, said, 'Pardon?'

'You might not remember, but Peter wrote a fan letter to you quite a number of years back and you wrote him a rather lovely reply.'

'Did I really?'

'Well, I have it right here,' said Michael as he lifted Bob's autobiography from his side table.

'How marvellous,' said Bob.

'Peter stuck your letter in the front of your book …' Michael handed him the book.

'Did he really? How lovely of you.'

Then Michael said, 'Why don't you read to us?'

There was an awkward pause then Bob said, 'I'm sorry, I haven't got my reading glasses.'

There was another awkward pause then Michael simply lifted the book from Bob's hands and, without missing a beat, said, 'So, working in the clubs in the 1970s, you must have …'

Ouch! That died on its arse, I thought as I sat there grinning.

The painful moment was cut out in the edit later, but if you ever get a chance to see the interview you might notice Bob Monkhouse's autobiography on the table by the side of Michael Parkinson. For no reason whatsoever.

One of the biggest honours of my career was being asked as a guest on the last ever episode of *Parkinson* – 'The Final Conversation'. Just before he retired. Well, I say retire. He went on to flog Sun Life insurance in the afternoons. 'Just £6 a month could help towards funeral costs and you get a free Parker pen just for enquiring.' Mother of God.

Immediately I said yes (to his show, not the free Parker pen), then I panicked when they told me who the line-up was going to be. David Beckham, Sir Michael Caine, Sir David Attenborough and Sir Billy Connolly. How could I be on with Billy Connolly? It's Billy Connolly, he's one of the best comedians there's ever been. Our styles aren't that far apart. What to do? I'd have to try and think of some other way of being funny that didn't tread on Billy's toes.

As it was Parkinson's last show, maybe I could bring some things with me to celebrate. Like on the last day of school, to have a party. I packed a big holdall with a selection of things and headed off to the show.

I never told the producers what I intended to do. It would only have caused aggro. Everybody would be getting involved, discussing if I could or couldn't, so I just didn't tell anybody. In fact, I blatantly walked around with my holdall, and nobody even quizzed me about why or what it was. It's a good job I wasn't a terrorist.

A funny thing happened when I went into make-up. I'd dressed in my shirt and suit, but I'd had a bit of trouble with my tie. I always do. The knot never looks right. Perhaps because I had an elastic tie until I was in the fifth year.

I was discussing it with the make-up lady when Michael Parkinson overheard my conversation. The next thing I knew I had Sir Michael Parkinson, Sir Michael Caine and Sir David Attenborough stood round, all having a go at fastening my tie. 'No, that's not it,' said Michael Caine. 'Give it here,' said David

Attenborough. 'He needs a Windsor knot.' I just sat and watched this surreal reflection. Can you believe this? Three knights of the realm flapping over my tie.

Billy Connolly was completely lovely and very funny as usual. Talking about the health benefits of eating brown bread versus white bread: 'Health-wise,' he said, 'eating brown bread adds about a fortnight to your life. But this isn't a fortnight when you're eighteen, shagging everything in sight. This is a fortnight when you're sat in a nursing home being spoon-fed, with food from a blender.'

I was stood backstage laughing, watching on a monitor. Clutching my holdall. Getting more nervous by the second. I was to be on last, no pressure whatsoever. Finally, my time arrived and a producer led me to the top of the stairs. A make-up lady gave me a quick check. 'How's my tie look?' I whispered. We both laughed.

Parky

Our next guest used to be my warm-up man and he used to say to me, 'One day I'm gonna walk down those stairs and be a guest on your show.' [I didn't] He's now one of Britain's funniest comedians, would you welcome please, Peter Kay

Laurie Holloway struck up the band and out I walked. Well, here goes, I thought to myself as I walked down the staircase, holdall in hand. It never gets any easier. I shook hands/hugged the other guests. That took a while and then Mr Adrenalin took over and so did I. I began by emptying my holdall. I pulled out the board games, Buckaroo! and Twister. I got out some party hats and handed them to the guests.

Parky asked, 'What's all this?' I told him that it was a bag of treats I'd brought, as it was his last show and I thought we could have a bit of a party. I got out a cake tin and took the lid off – 'Victoria Sandwich'. Then I turned to David Beckham and said, 'I bet you've said that a few times, haven't you?' This brought the house down and I knew I was in.

I stood up and fired a party popper over Sir David Attenborough (it's not often you can write a line like that). Then I got out some French fancies and a bottle of orange cordial.

Me
I've got some paper plates an' all. I've got cordial

Parky
(laughing)
He's got cordial

Me
I can't believe this is your last show. You've had them all on here, haven't you? Fred Astaire

Parky
Yeah

Me
Bette Davis

Parky
Yeah

Me
Morecambe and Wise. You're the kiss of death, when you think about it

How long have we all got? We're not on because we're good,
we're on because we're alive
(turns to David Beckham)
Thank God you're on. I thought I was the youngest.
It's like *Cocoon*, this

Parky asked after my Nana – he knew she was a big fan of his. I told him she was doing well and that she'd got him a present. Then I handed him a small parcel which he unwrapped to reveal a white plastic fob with a big red button on it. The fob was attached to a piece of black cord. I gestured to Parky to place it around his neck and he obliged, asking, 'What is it?'

'It's for when you're in your warden-controlled flat. You put it around your neck and if you're having any trouble, you push the button. Say if Mary's in the garden and you keel over watching *Cash in the Attic*. You push that and she'll come running.'

I then told him that now he was retiring I didn't want him going stiff, so I'd got him a job. Out of my holdall I pulled a big luminous-yellow coat and a hat, basically a lollipop lady's outfit (I think they're called crossing guards now). I handed him a collapsible lollipop stick and said, 'It's twenty minutes outside a primary school – morning and evening.' Then Parky and I acted out a little scene in front of the other guests where I pretended I was crossing a road while he pretended to hold back traffic.

The audience seemed to love it and the whole idea came off much better than I ever imagined it would.

I was just relieved my tie looked alright.

Little Crazy
Bastard Frog

'(Is This the Way to) Amarillo' had gained a lot of popularity since Max and Paddy sang it to the Asian Elders in *Phoenix Nights*. On my tour, I was playing it every night before I went on stage.

When the DVD of my *Mum Wants a Bungalow Tour* (which, incidentally, she got) was released, I wanted a special treat at the start. Something jolly and rousing. So I filmed myself marching to 'Amarillo' along the corridors of the Manchester Arena dressed as a steward. I mimed along to Tony Christie and was flanked on either side by my friends Karl and Gordon – who'd worked on the tour. It was nothing but a bit of fun.

The following year, 2005, I received my usual email from Richard Curtis asking if I'd like to get involved with that year's Comic Relief. I'd always supported Comic Relief ever since it began, when I was at school. I remember wearing my red nose to assembly, only to have it swiftly confiscated by Sister Actoo. She was having 'nun' of it.

I'd filmed a sketch for Comic Relief a few years before with Steve Coogan (as Alan Partridge) when I played an irate boxing trainer with one lung. The following year I filmed a special BBC trailer for Comic Relief night as Brian Potter, which I mentioned earlier in the book.

But this time I really fancied doing something musical. I showed Richard Curtis the opening to my stand-up DVD with the 'Amarillo' footage. 'How about doing something like this, but instead of my friends I could add random celebrities every few seconds?' There was no rhyme or reason to it, it was just fun. Richard really liked the idea. Initially, it was just to be a sketch on the night. None of us had any idea about the phenomenon it would eventually become.

I drew up a wish list of people to appear in the sketch. I didn't want the usual suspects, the ones you always see in charity videos. I wanted people you hadn't seen for years, but unfortunately a lot of them were either unavailable or dead. My list was dwindling, fast.

A director was appointed to film the video, David Mallet. I'd never heard of him and remember speaking to him on the phone, asking him if he knew what he was doing. That night there was a programme on Channel 4 called *50 Greatest Pop Videos of All Time* and David Mallet had directed about twenty of them. I was mortified. He'd worked on some of the most influential music videos of all time. 'Ashes to Ashes' by David Bowie, 'I Want to Break Free' by Queen, 'I Don't Like Mondays' by the Boomtown Rats, 'Chain Reaction' by Diana Ross, Mr Blobby … that was a joke. Although he did end up being in our 'Amarillo' video.

Our main location was good old Granada TV. There were plenty of corridors to walk down and it was a regular home from home for me now. So it was planned that we'd film there for two days in February.

The first day got off to a great start with Ken and Deirdre from *Coronation Street*. They were already in Granada TV filming so just had to nip across. I'd met William Roache once before, having been asked to compere a charity testimonial dinner for him. I remember asking, 'Is William Roache's agent in the room?' There was a shout from the audience and a man stood up and waved. 'That fella is one of the luckiest men in the world. He got William Roache one job on *Coronation Street* in 1960 and he's been on a commission ever since.'

I'd met Anne Kirkbride briefly before, too, when I first appeared in *Corrie* and I bumped into her love rat Jon Lindsay (remember that? Way back in Chapter 1).

This was to be the opening shot of the video. I stood behind some double doors at the end of a corridor. 'Amarillo' played and I pushed the doors open and mimed as I started to march towards Ken and Deirdre. I still don't know why I marched. It just seemed to fit the music. I obviously never imagined people would be marching along to 'Amarillo' at family weddings, children's parties and wakes forever and a day.

Ken and Deirdre threw themselves right into it, Ken being very animated, wobbling his head. They did it in two takes and I think they were both a bit gutted it was all over so quickly.

Next up, Keith Harris and Orville alongside Bernie Clifton with his big yellow ostrich. Again, it was all over for them in a couple of takes. In fact, they were in and out like a duck mating. A big green one.

I kept getting messages throughout filming from celebs who couldn't make it. Anne Robinson and Terry Wogan pulled out and so did the Chuckle Brothers. That was a kick in the balls, but onwards and upwards.

Then it was the turn of local lads Shaun Ryder and Bez from Happy Mondays (just in case you've been living on the moon for the last thirty years). They're hilarious without even trying. If you ever want proof, listen to the commentary on the DVD for *Max & Paddy's Road to Nowhere* – episode two.

Shaun and Bez both turned up pissed at the recording studio with a carrier bag full of lager. At one point the sound recordist John 'Fingers' Wood called me in a panic and said he was worried, as 'they're both rather inebriated'. I said, 'Don't worry, John. Keep recording.' I knew they'd be giving gold.

Funnily enough, they still had cans of lager when they turned up to film 'Amarillo' and it was only half ten on a Monday morning. There was a big discussion with some BBC bigwig who wouldn't let Shaun march while holding a can of Red Stripe. So as a compromise (and before Shaun headbutted him), we filmed two versions. One with the Red Stripe and one without. All Bez had was his maracas (that man has stolen a living).

Next up it was my old friend Sally Lindsay – and Sir Jimmy Savile. I know, I know! But like I said earlier in the book, I didn't know about his notoriety at the time, nobody did (well, apart from half the BBC, by the sound of things). If I'd known at the time, I would have made him wear a giant Pudsey Bear costume, the dirty bastard (Jimmy, not Pudsey). I also wouldn't have asked him. Then maybe the video to 'Amarillo' wouldn't have ended up on YouTube years later with the warning 'Beware: This video contains a paedophile'.

As usual, Jimmy wouldn't take a fee but said he'd do it for his usual box of cigars. The price of which had risen to £1,500 since his appearance on *The Sunday Show*.

When Jimmy arrived I threw my arms around him, to give him a hug for old times' sake. Immediately, he recoiled. 'Do not hug me. The last person who hugged me is now in traction.'

On reflection I thought, Now then, now then, calm down, Jim, that's a bit hypocritical coming from a prolific sexual predator.

Then we had my height-disadvantaged comrades (dwarves) from *Phoenix Nights*. Seven of them, of course. All in Bolton

Wanderers tops. For a bit of variation, we sneaked over to the set of *Corrie* and quickly filmed in the backstreet behind the Rovers. Two takes and we were done before anybody even noticed.

It was going great, but we were running out of celebrities. We were that desperate Max and Paddy even turned up in the next sequence, but sadly we had no choice but to stop filming, our two days in Granada TV reduced to just one half-day.

We decided to relocate filming to London, the logic being we might entice more celebrities. We used a little studio in Covent Garden and swapped the corridors to a green screen so we could add in backdrops later in the edit. That worked a treat and made the video much more colourful in the second half. We also used treadmills for everybody to walk on. The only problem being that they were out of the ark. I'm sure they'd been condemned after an old episode of *Swap Shop*. They didn't even run at the same speed and had to be adjusted manually with a screwdriver. Death traps, as Ronnie Corbett would later find out.

We got a much better response from turns down in the smoke. First up we had Geoffrey Hayes and Bungle from *Rainbow*. I did want Zippy and George, but they didn't have any legs.

Geoffrey was looking his age and was now earning a crust as a taxi driver in Stockport. I asked him if he'd 'been busy' but he didn't get the reference. Bungle, on the other hand, hadn't aged at all. Geoffrey struggled with the unstable treadmill and I thought he was going to go arse over tit, but they both found their rhythm.

Then we had the Welsh Elvis himself, Shakin' Stevens. That was a stroke of luck, that was. He was actually quite conservative and flatly refused to sport any denim, shake his legs or walk on the treadmill. Instead, we had to just have Shakin' clicking his fingers towards the camera in a close-up. Ah, well, at least he turned up and gave his time. We were still struggling a bit for celebrities, though. So much so that someone went off to Hamleys toy shop to buy the puppets of Sooty and Sweep. We also got in 'lookalikes' of Gandhi and Cliff Richard. The whole video was turning into a surreal mishmash of whatever we could lay our hands on, but miraculously it all worked in the end.

I got in touch with my old pal Danny Baker. He said he could get Chris Evans and Gazza, but neither of them turned up … though Danny Baker did. Ted Robbins got in touch to say he'd ask his cousin (surely everybody must know by now that Ted's cousin is Paul McCartney?). That would be amazing. Then we got a call saying Paul couldn't make it, but did we want Heather (Mills-McCartney at the time)? I mean, what can you say? Next thing I knew Heather was in the studio dressed as Dorothy from *The Wizard of Oz*, Danny Baker as the scarecrow, and me? Why, the lion, of course. Luckily, my costume from school still fit me. Well, just.

Tony Christie also appeared in the video. I thought it'd be funny to see Tony miming along to his own vocals. I was in the background alongside a guy who makes a living performing as a tribute to me. Madness. He basically goes on stage, does his own act and shouts out 'Garlic? Bread?' every ten minutes. He charges more than me too, £39.95! (But you do get a three-course meal thrown in for that.) Well, that's what I read on a banner at the turn-off for Huddersfield. I nearly ended up in a farmer's field.

I also thought it'd be funny if Tony Christie wore my purple suit and shirt. The only problem was, they were about three sizes too big for him and had to be tightened at the back with four big bulldog clips.

I'd met Tony the year before, when he recorded the theme to *Max & Paddy's Road to Nowhere*. His manager (his son) had previously been in touch asking if I wanted to re-release 'Amarillo' as some kind of mega mix after it'd been used in *Phoenix Nights*. He wanted to make a video with Paddy and me, but as it wasn't for charity (and sounded shite) I politely declined.

So you can imagine how chuffed Tony was when Comic Relief said they wanted to use 'Amarillo'. I'd always preferred Tony's original recording of the song. He was in his prime and it sounds like he's got three throats, his voice is that strong. You could never top that, which is why I decided to mime it.

Next on the list of celebs was Jim Bowen. He travelled all the way down to London, God love him. He'd wanted to come to Granada TV but he couldn't make the date. Fortunately, he didn't have any lines to learn this time. All he had to do was walk on one of the wobbly treadmills with Mr Blobby. When I told him that he said he would have preferred to recite *Hamlet*.

Now that was a pairing, Jim Bowen and Mr Blobby. Blobby was a headcase. He also smelled of wet dog and an inflatable at the end of a kids' party. I should have led him out to the car park and sprayed him with a fire hose.

Miraculously, we got two genuine superstars, Brian May and Roger Taylor. David Mallet pulled in a favour from his Queen video days. They were both good as gold (I love that expression), but surprisingly they were piss-poor at clapping to the beat. Which shocked me, especially as Roger Taylor is considered to be one of the best drummers in the world.

It was a long but great day filming 'Amarillo'. But of all of the contributors, Michael Parkinson and Ronnie Corbett were easily the most memorable.

I knew Michael Parkinson, of course. Ronnie Corbett, I'd met a couple of times. So I was delighted when they both turned up. Especially Ronnie. He couldn't wait to get on his treadmill and was stomping away as soon as the music started, his little legs going ten to the dozen. He was waving his arms around and pulling faces, and then he fell off. Oh, my God! He'd caught his foot on the bit that didn't revolve and flew past me horizontally, landing on the floor with a wallop.

There was poor Ronnie rolling around on the floor. David Mallet ran over to pick him up. Unfortunately, David had broken his shoulder and couldn't do anything except stand over him helplessly. Ronnie pleaded, 'Pick me up! Pick me up!'

'I can't,' said David, 'I've broken my shoulder.'

Michael Parkinson and I were still walking. We had no choice. Quickly, some other crew members ran in and yanked Ronnie up like an elf on the shelf, or the floor, in his case.

The treadmills slowly stopped. There was a lot of concern for Ronnie. He was seventy-five, after all. I hoped he was alright but was struggling to stifle my laughter, which was building up inside like a geyser.

Ronnie was fine. Just flustered. All he wanted to do was watch his fall. We all gathered around a monitor. The footage was played back. It got to the moment Ronnie fell over and the whole room exploded with laughter. What a relief, as I don't think I could have kept it in much longer.

I honestly don't think I've ever experienced such a perpetual moment of laughter. I even woke myself up at four the next morning, still laughing. I think it was because he was messing around so much before he fell – acting pompous as he walked, which was then undermined by his literal fall. Maybe it was because he was so small. Either way, I knew we'd mined a beautiful block of comedy gold.

Filming was complete and it was off into the edit. We cut two versions, one with Ronnie's fall and one without. I would never have released Ronnie's fall without his consent. I sent him a copy and he watched it with his family. Fortunately, they all laughed as much as we did, so Ronnie gave that version his blessing. Thank the Lord. I would have been gutted if nobody had ever got to see it.

Once the finished product was complete the wheels began to turn incredibly fast. Comic Relief loved the video. Suddenly it was all change and they wanted to release it as their official single that year, as well as a DVD.

When it premiered on Comic Relief night it got a huge reaction. What really surprised me was that children seemed to love it. I found that odd, as they didn't really know anybody in the video. I think they latched on to all the puppets: Orville, Bernie Clifton's ostrich, Bungle, and Sooty and Sweep. They also liked the song, and it went down a bomb at children's parties.

The single went straight to number one. I was at Alton Towers when I found out. Richard Curtis called when I was queueing up for the log flume.

Who'd have thought it? Number one in the charts. Absolutely unbelievable.

And it stayed at number one for the next seven weeks until that little Crazy bastard Frog knocked it off the top spot. I couldn't complain, it raised over one and a half million pounds for Comic Relief.

YouTube had recently been launched and that pushed 'Amarillo''s success even further, as people now had the ability to watch it over and over again. Also, they could film their own versions. The best was yet to come, and I was completely blown away when 'Amarillo' made the TV news. It seemed British soldiers had re-enacted the video in Iraq. They'd filmed themselves marching to it in the desert. Wow! Now that really was wonderful and I was so happy it'd brought them some joy.

Tony Christie was well chuffed. A CD of his greatest hits was released and also went to number one, in the album charts, alongside the single. The next I heard he was performing at the Albert Hall in London. Quite an achievement for somebody who was semi-retired twelve months before, settled on sun-drenched shores playing golf.

'Amarillo' changed my life and will probably be my legacy. It'll no doubt get played at my funeral. I just hope the congregation all march in unison. That'd be hilarious. Perhaps the pallbearers could march in with my coffin on their shoulders.

A spring night in May 1989 and I'm walking home from High Street Library in Bolton listening to my Walkman. The library hired cassettes out and I'd just landed lucky, hiring the debut album by a new Scottish band called Texas. The slide guitar chords of the opening track 'I Don't Want a Lover' (their recent hit) sent shivers down my spine. Then the drums hit hard. The pounding beat fit perfectly with my strides up Goldsmith Street. I've never stopped playing that album in all the years since.

Fast-forward to July 2005. I was backstage at a concert in Edinburgh and I bumped into Sharleen Spiteri. In fact, I went to kiss her but awkwardly completely missed her mouth and hit her nose with my teeth. We've been good friends ever since.

As promised, she sent me a copy of the new Texas album *Red Book*. I liked it; pretty easy, already being a fan. Then one day, when we were chatting on the phone, she asked if I'd ever consider directing a video to one of their new songs or just maybe appearing in a video. I was extremely flattered and also thrilled. I knew I'd worked on the 'Amarillo' video, but this would be something different. A chance to work with a band that I really loved and also create something with them. It felt a bit more next level.

This was a real dream come true for me. I'd been brought up on music videos in the eighties and would often drift off to sleep fantasising about ideas to the music I was listening to. Now I was making a pop video, and with a band I really liked. I just didn't want to let them down.

I picked 'Sleep'. It was a beautiful song where Sharleen duetted with Paul Buchanan. I definitely wanted it to be funny. Sharleen had enjoyed Park Avenue in *That Peter Kay Thing* and so I thought it'd be fun to resurrect Marc Park and perhaps we could both play a duetting club act. Sharleen loved the idea.

We filmed at Farnworth Veterans Club in Bolton, where we'd filmed the original Park Avenue scene, and I recruited a lot of the crew I usually work with. The club audience was made up of regulars (only these ones were actually alive). My mum also appears in the audience with her friend Kathleen and her brother Joe.

We filmed the sequences of us as a club act performing and these were to be intercut with spoofs from other famous films and music videos. We did a parody of 'Hello' by Lionel Richie. Marc Park plays a maths teacher and he's called to the art room. There he finds Sharleen, and she's made a clay model of Marc's head. Just like the blind girl in the original Lionel Richie video. Bashfully, Sharleen slowly rotates her model, revealing a slightly grotesque (but hilarious) bust of Marc's head. His nose is massive. After filming, the model was fired in a kiln and auctioned off for charity. Whoever's got that in their house, good luck to them.

Next, we set up in the gym of a local secondary school to re-enact the famous scene from *Ghost*. The one where Demi Moore's working at a potter's wheel when Patrick Swayze appears behind her. In order to recreate the scene we needed candles, but unfortunately the art department forgot to get some. So I nipped to the church over the road, Our Lady of Lourdes. Father Brian got a shock to find me wearing a false nose, a long ginger wig and a white vest. 'Peter, is that you?' he said through a crack in the presbytery door. It was pitch black.

God love him, he let us borrow two huge racks of candles out of the church, the ones where the parishioners donate. Just like the Asian Elders minibus in *Phoenix Nights*, filming in your home town certainly has its benefits.

It was only a two-day shoot for the music video, and the last scene was a spoof of the climactic scene from *An Officer and a Gentleman*. We filmed at a factory in Farnworth on Saturday night, with all of the workers playing extras. They were fantastic and stayed until well after midnight in order to get the last scene finished. Sharing a love of pop videos, Sian Gibson even made an appearance as a factory worker.

In *An Officer and a Gentleman*, Richard Gere turns up at a factory in his naval uniform having just graduated. He goes to pick up his girlfriend Paula (quite literally) and whisk her away. In our version, Sharleen was wearing the naval uniform and she'd come to pick up Marc Park. But she had a bit of a job lifting me. The scene ended with me carrying Sharleen as we walked off into the sunset. Well, it was actually a big white screen at the end of the factory loading bay, lit by the cameraman and director of photography Jeremy Hewson. He'd worked on 'Amarillo' and did a brilliant job of the Texas video. I was so proud of the end product. It looked gorgeous.

We were going to recreate a sequence from *Flashdance* but Sharleen couldn't weld.

'Sleep' was released a few weeks later and reached the top five in the charts. I was so delighted, as it was the first music video I'd ever directed.

It's a real shame music videos have faded, as I'd have loved to direct/produce many more. Especially at their lavish peak in the eighties. They were a huge part of my life growing up. I used to have VHS tapes filled with pop videos, taped from *Top of the Pops*, *The Chart Show*, *No Limits*, and I'd watch those tapes constantly. So working on the Texas video finally allowed me to fulfil a dream I'd had for a very long time.

January 2007 and Richard Curtis is back on the phone. Comic Relief time again, and after the success of 'Amarillo' he asked if I'd like to produce something else. I'd already been thinking of ideas (I never stop). One song, 'I'm Gonna Be (500 Miles)' by the Proclaimers had always been popular, and I'd noticed the reaction it got at family gatherings over the years. It was up there with 'Come on Eileen' for multi-generational foot stomping. It certainly felt like a worthy and uplifting follow-up to 'Amarillo'.

The concept for the video was to be a celebrity karaoke session for Comic Relief. That meant we could pack the place out with famous faces and make it look like a real event on the night. As you know, we'd struggled to get celebrities for 'Amarillo', but this time we were inundated with responses. It was like *Field of Dreams*. If we build it, they will come – and come they certainly did. Here's the line-up in alphabetical order. Cut and pasted from Wikipedia, of course.

Johnny Ball, David Beckham (lookalike; well, he said he was), David Bellamy, Dusty Bin, Tony Blackburn, Stan Boardman, Basil Brush, Bob the Builder, Bucks Fizz, Tommy Cannon and Bobby Ball, Bob Carolgees and Spit the Dog (of course), Jasper Carrott, Keith Chegwin, Jimmy Cricket, Mark Curry, Tess Daly, Bobby Davro, Carol Decker, Sally Dynevor, Lesley Garrett, Clare Grogan, Paul Henry (Benny from *Crossroads*), Elton John (lookalike), The Krankies, Burt Kwouk, Bonnie Langford, Eddie Large, Michael Le Vell, Limahl, Mad Lizzie, Des Lynam, Kenny Lynch, Timmy Mallett, Jennie McAlpine, Amanda Mealing, Terry Nutkins, Bill Oddie, Paul O'Grady,

Postman Pat, Wendi Peters, Robert Powell, Rod, Jane and Freddy, Showaddywaddy, Frank Sidebottom, Sonia, Kathy Staff, Status Quo, Dennis Taylor, David Tennant, Willie Thorne, Roy Walker, Louis Walsh, Pete Waterman, June Whitfield and Gary Wilmot.

Christ! I didn't realise how many until I read that. It was like *Look-in* the Movie. And, sadly, a lot of those are no longer with us. It really was a dream cast of old and new. Quite intimidating for me to come face to face with so many familiar faces that I'd grown up watching on TV.

The first thing I did was approach the Proclaimers to ask if they were up for it and appearing in the video. They didn't mind at all and were lovely. Like an identical Scottish Chas & Dave.

My friend Paul came up with the brilliant idea: why not have '500 Miles' sung by Brian Potter and Andy Pipkin (from *Little Britain*). I rang Matt Lucas to ask him if he fancied it. He definitely did, and not only that (and here's a weird coincidence), he's also an enormous fan of the Proclaimers. So much so that, when we were chatting on the phone, he emailed me a picture of himself with the Proclaimers. He'd even written the sleeve notes for one of their albums.

Just like with 'Amarillo', I wanted to use the original recording. This meant I had to go to Abbey Road Studios in London, where an engineer tracked down the Proclaimers' recordings from the archives. I was more excited about being in Abbey Road, without a doubt the most famous recording studio in the world. I even walked the zebra crossing where the Beatles had. I would have got a picture, but I was on my own. Sadly, I never got to see the main recording studio where the Beatles had recorded so much of their music.

But a couple of years later my mate Paul (the one from two paragraphs back) was working at Radio 2 and wangled some tickets to see Stevie Wonder, who was recording a special live concert at Abbey Road in that very same studio.

We were right at the front of the stage. It was incredible being so close to Stevie Wonder. The chance of a lifetime. He sounded fantastic and performed all of his hits. Then he went into a second hour, and I started thinking, This is great, Stevie, lad, but I've got to drive back to Bolton. Then a third hour, I started getting a bit tetchy. You can have too much of a good thing and this was starting to shape up like Ken Dodd at Stockport Plaza.

On one hand, I'm thinking, This is STEVIE WONDER! He's a legend, Peter, when will this ever happen again? Then on the other hand I'm thinking, I've got work in the morning, for fuck's sake, Stevie, wrap it up. Enough is enough now, son.

You're probably thinking, Surely you could have thrown a sickie? I wouldn't have thought twice about that when I worked in my part-time jobs, but I just couldn't do that anymore. Not even for Stevie Wonder. Besides, I was right at the front of the stage and didn't want to just walk out. Not that he would have seen us. Sorry! I'm sorry. I'm sure there'll be an address at the back of the book if you want to write and complain. I eventually got back home at half five. Shattered.

Filming for '500 Miles' took place at Elstree Studios, where they film *EastEnders*, *Strictly Come Dancing* and *Naked Attraction*. Production had constructed a huge marquee in the middle of a studio, complete with circular tables, a raised area and a stage. Jeremy Hewson returned as lighting cameraman and did a great job of colouring the space with lots of turquoise and magenta (my favourite colours). It looked lush on camera.

I'd enlisted the help of Amanda Neal. Now, I'd worked with Amanda many times, firstly on *Max & Paddy's Road to Nowhere*. She's one of the best first assistant directors in the business (everybody thinks that); also, she's a very good friend.

We always have a good laugh at the situations we continually find ourselves in when filming. The thing I love about her most, though, is her optimism and endless sense of joy. She'd probably disagree with that but it's true. Everybody wants to work with her, but she always puts her family first. That's what I like most about her. It's a demanding job. Not only do first assistant directors schedule the order of all the filming, but they also run the entire shoot. Something I'd never be able to do without Amanda.

The first day, we filmed towards the stage from the audience's perspective. Matt was dressed as Andy, me as Brian. They played the music and we both rolled on stage and sang the first verse straightforward, but we started to giggle and then laugh. The sudden realisation of what we were doing hit us and we just couldn't get through the song for laughing. It took about forty takes.

We'd just managed to contain ourselves when I decided to sing 'Bobby Davro' on the chorus instead of 'Ba-ba-da-da'. This set Matt off laughing. Even more so when I told him that Bobby Davro was coming the next day as part of the celebrity karaoke audience.

On the second chorus, David Walliams came on stage as his character Lou Todd from *Little Britain* and introduced the Proclaimers. Then they took over on lead vocals for the rest of the song. David also re-appeared towards the end of the video to place a blanket around Matt in a spoof of James Brown's stage performances. All in all, it was a great afternoon's filming. Quite easy compared to the showbiz avalanche that would be incoming the next day.

Up bright and early the next day, as we had a lot to get through, we put the celebrities into groups and surrounded them with supporting artists, so they blended into the background. It was a proper surreal mishmash of celebs. There was no real method to it and we literally put together whoever turned up. First up it was Keith Chegwin, the Krankies, Lesley Garrett, June Whitfield and Paul Henry (Benny from *Crossroads* with his green hat). How crazy was that line-up?

The footage that we'd shot the day before was projected onto a giant screen on stage so that the celebrities could see Matt and me singing and react to it. When it was all edited together you could never tell it was filmed separately.

Amanda shouted, 'Action!' and everybody crashed into the party mood.

On the previous day, Matt and I had developed a bit of choreography on the chorus. We acted as if we were riding a horse: arms outstretched, miming holding a jockey's reins. I asked the celebs if they'd like to do the same and they didn't need much encouragement. Before I knew it, wee Jimmy Krankie had gone completely nuts, stood on a chair pretending to ride a horse, while Keith Chegwin had straddled the back of a wooden chair and was literally riding it round in a circle (too much windscreen wash, clearly).

When Bobby Davro arrived he was thrilled when he discovered we'd adapted his name into the chorus. In fact, I think he still plays '500 Miles' at the start of his stage act.

The party atmosphere continued throughout the day. It was contagious as wall-to-wall celebs kept arriving. Too many, in some cases, when five of Bucks Fizz turned up instead of four. Apparently, there had been a miscommunication, and Jay Aston, a Bucks Fizz original, turned up as well as her replacement in the group. There was a lot of tension backstage, so I did what any sane thinking man would do. I said, 'Let's use all of them and stick David Bellamy in the middle of them. Nobody will dare kick off.' And sure enough, nobody did. A truly surreal day.

Terry Nutkins literally drove 500 miles, all the way from the Isle of Skye in Scotland. God love him and God rest him.

David Tennant drove from Cardiff after filming *Doctor Who* all night. He was completely knackered, but he put his kilt on and he gave it his all, alongside Dusty Bin and Rod, Jane and Freddy. Then he drove back to Cardiff for more filming. I'd bet he'd have been glad to have a TARDIS that day (I know that was crap, but I couldn't resist).

It was very kind of everybody to give their time and I was grateful. Cynically, I was also well aware there'd no doubt be a couple of years' panto work off the back of it, but who cared? I certainly didn't.

After a fortnight of meticulously sifting through every bit of footage and driving ourselves completely nuts listening to '500 Miles' about 500 times, we finished editing the video and sent it to Comic Relief. They loved it as much as 'Amarillo'.

The BBC showed it on Comic Relief night with a special intro from Kate Thornton, who was (supposedly) live at a celebrity karaoke just as Brian Potter and Andy Pipkin took to the stage. The song was released as a DVD and single and, just like 'Amarillo', it went straight to number one the following Sunday. '500 Miles' was a joyful achievement for everybody involved and it raised another shedload of money for a very worthy cause. So, where was my knighthood from the Queen? Fuck knows.

Peach and
Lettuce Salad

My 'Mum Wants a Bungalow Tour' ended on 2 July 2003. It was my thirtieth birthday the next day and I was knackered. Proper knackered. I'd played 180 shows in nine months, most of the time six nights a week.

In an effort to try and recharge I went on holiday to France. Lying in the pool on one of those floating chairs, I decided to write a letter to Ronnie Barker. I'd wanted to write to him for a long time. I'd made a few attempts previously, but they'd always ended up in the bin. This time I was going to try not to be as self-conscious and just write it. To my surprise, by the end of the week I got a reply.

Dear Peter,

I was very pleased to get your letter. At first, I thought it was a fan letter but then I thought this man's humorous and interesting, and then when you mentioned being on tour I realised who it was. I loved Phoenix Nights *and find you funny, entertaining and original. I notice too how you like to play more than one character – always my favourite pastime.*

I hope your time in France helped rid you of your tiredness. It will eventually go and now I must immediately go.

Yours, Ronnie
PS Write again!

Wow! I was over the moon and back. Not only to get a response, but how nice he was. I'd mentioned several times how much I'd always admired him, especially his performance as Norman Stanley Fletcher in *Porridge*. His comic timing was perfect, and a testament to how well the series was written is that it's still shown in primetime all these years later and still gets great ratings. Funny is funny.

In fact, just as a side note, I was offered the part of Fletch in a stage version of *Porridge*. I even shared a conference call with *Porridge* writers Dick Clement and Ian La Frenais. That was a bit painful, as Dick was in New York, Ian was in LA and I was in Bolton. We either just kept talking over each other or there were huge gaps. I told them that I was honoured not only to speak to them, but for them to think of me for the part, as it was one of my favourite series. The script they'd written for the stage version was really good too, and took a new storyline that incorporated many of the funniest elements from all of the series. But unfortunately I declined the offer. Nobody could fill Ronnie Barker's shoes, in my opinion.

After receiving my letter from Ronnie Barker I was completely blown away when, the following week, I received another letter, but this one was a bit different. When I opened it I caught a glimpse of headed notepaper inside, 'Home Office HM Prison', and I thought, Who's writing to me from prison? Then, when I looked a little closer, I realised what it was and I burst into tears. The heading at the top of the paper said 'HM

Prison Slade'. It was a letter from Ronnie Barker, but he'd written it in character, as Fletch.

> *Dear Peter,*
>
> *It's always nice to hear from someone on the outside. In that jostling, squashed-up, traffic-burdened claustrophobia they call 'freedom'. Inside here we carry on as normal. I nicked this notepaper from the library while old Barrowclough was daydreaming about his dear wife at home. Wondering how to kill her and get away with it. At least he's got somebody, unlike us lonely mortals.*
>
> *There are three things missing in prison – women. Although three would hardly be enough to go round. Indeed, they would be going around so fast they'd get dizzy and fall flat on their backs, which would save time.*
>
> *Life goes on much the same in here. Old Mackay has always got his eagle eye on me, which only adds to the stress and strain of prison life. Fortunately, I've managed to keep a clean sheet so far. Mainly because I work in the laundry. Not so much as my old job in the kitchen, with its endless opportunities to nick a lot of useful gear. I mean, the laundry! Once you've got a locker full of Lifebuoy soap, that's it, isn't it?*
>
> *Well, I'll have to close up now as I'm running out of paper. As the girl said in the ladies' room, Look after yourself and keep your nose clean (and the rest of you if possible) and see you on the Xmas tree, as they say.*
> *Your old friend*
> *Fletch*

What about that? I was careful not to get my tears on the handwritten letter. Straight away I rang Paddy to tell him. The phone rang and rang and then his gruff voice said, 'Hello.'

'Paddy, you won't believe who I've got a letter off?'

'Who?'

'Ronnie Barker, but he's written to me as Fletch from *Porridge* on prison notepaper!'

'Who gives a fuck?' he said and slammed the phone down. Charming.

I made up some letterheaded paper from the Phoenix Club. It had some clip art at the top, of a keyboard player and some stars. 'The Phoenix Club, Junction 4 off the M61, just past Balti Towers'. I wrote a letter to Fletch as Brian Potter and I even put a Soreen fruity malt loaf in the parcel with a couple of nail files shoved inside it (wink, wink).

Ronnie Barker released an autobiography that Christmas and I was thrilled to find he'd written about our letters. He even mentioned me sending him the fruit loaf with the files inside.

Remarkably, we kept in touch over the next few years, writing letters, sending postcards. It was so lovely. I've got a big pile of them here beside me now and it's very emotional reading through them again.

There's one where Ronnie has cut and pasted a review of the film *The Life and Death of Peter Sellers*. It says, 'What are we going to have next? Peter Kay as Ronnie Barker?' Ronnie has then commented underneath in ink with an arrow pointing to the review: 'If offered this job, do not take it. I'm still doing the Ronnie Barker jokes at the moment.' There's then a PS: 'Have you tried peach and lettuce salad? It's horrible.' Lord knows what that PS meant but its randomness made me laugh.

In 2004 Ronnie Barker was the recipient of a special BAFTA lifetime achievement award. I was invited to speak at the ceremony, which was broadcast on BBC1. What a privilege to be asked.

Normally the recipient of the award would sit in the audience and listen to the various speeches about their career. Ronnie preferred to sit backstage. I was hovering backstage on the night and I asked a member of the crew where Ronnie was; they pointed towards a black curtain in a darkened corner of the studio. Casually, I wandered over and cheekily popped my head around the curtain. There he was. He looked over and gave me a big smile, then waved me over. 'It's so good to finally meet you,' he said. 'You too,' I replied. Then, before we got a chance to say anything else, a producer told me that I was on next.

I was introduced on stage by Ronnie Corbett. I'd written a speech, but Lord knows how it would go down:

It's an honour to stand here tonight as a fan and pay tribute to one of my favourite comedians, Ronnie Barker. Now, I'm not going to be gushing or slushy. I'm not going to be long either, as I'm not getting paid. My earliest memory of Ronnie Barker was when I was a child. On Saturday nights, my mum and dad would be getting ready to go out. My dad would put on his best frock. My mum would have a shave and my grandad would roll up in his wheelchair to babysit. We'd watch *The Two Ronnies* with special musical guest Barbara Dickson – every week.

We'd also watch *The Two Ronnies* on Christmas Day with the whole family. Mr and Mrs Whole, they lived next door. Lovely couple with their son Plug. Sunday night was bath night in our house. Straight after *Songs of Praise* I'd be up the wooden hill and then up the stairs. I remember my mum bringing a black and white portable into the bathroom and plugging it into the extension lead so I could watch *Open All Hours* in the bath. The fact I risked electrocution just so I could watch Ronnie Barker goes to show how much he means to me.

As I got older I started getting into *Porridge*, and that changed my life forever. Not only did I put on four stone, but I also realised what I wanted to do with my life. It was a true revelation, like St Paul on the road to Domestos. It wasn't to be a convict; it was to be a comic actor. I'd like to thank Ronnie (like I know him), but I wouldn't be here tonight if it wasn't for him. He's my inspiration, my hero and my chauffeur.

The biggest influence he's had on me is his ability to say no and put his family first. He did one of the bravest things you can ever do in show business, he retired. Now bankrupt he's back, and if I make half as many people laugh as he has or mean a quarter to as many people as he has then I'll die a confused but happy man.

My speech got a great response. Phew! Ronnie Corbett and David Jason presented Ronnie with his special lifetime achievement BAFTA, and once again I couldn't hold back the tears. It was moving to see the three of them together. After the show, I was asked if I'd like to have my picture taken with Ronnie. So we briefly met again. It's a picture that I'll always treasure, along with all of our letters.

One of my favourite correspondences from Ronnie arrived after he'd watched '(Is This the Way to) Amarillo' on Comic Relief.

Dear Peter,

Your Comic Relief spot was wonderful. We roared with laughter at it.

It was so full of energy, verve and joyfulness that it was irresistible. Please could you send me an autographed copy of the DVD. I would treasure it. Ronnie C falling over was hilarious. I want to watch it again and again.

Well, I must close now as Arkwright used to say about nine o'clock at night.

I'll look forward to the DVD when you get the time.

From your fan

Ronnie

That was a real thrill. Growing up watching *The Two Ronnies* and now I've got Ronnie Barker asking for my autograph on a DVD that's got Ronnie Corbett falling on it. Madness.

We carried on as pen pals for the next few years. Christmas cards, birthday cards. I never lost the absolute bliss I felt when I received some correspondence from Ronnie. One time he wrote to me about *The Two Ronnies Sketchbook*. This was a series the BBC had made celebrating their work across the decades. Both Ronnies reunited and introduced their classic sketches. They were brilliant episodes filled with a lot of laughter and memories. Sadly, it was the last time Ronnie Barker appeared on camera. He did look very frail.

My dear Peter,

How nice to hear from you as usual and the kind words you said about the show.

It got 8 million viewers, which was better than James Bond on the other side. That got 4.7 million – so the Beeb are delighted with us. I'm hoping that a whole new generation will become fans now.

My idea was always to insist on the whole sketch being seen and not, as you put it, 'cut to pieces', interspersed with so-called experts pronouncing the merits of each bit (most of the experts, you've never heard of). Anyway, who cares about the psychology of humour – let's have a laugh, that's what I say.

We did six shows and the audience was the best we've
ever had. Cheering at the end, etc. It did my old heart good
to hear the laughter again.
  All my love
  Ronnie

That was the last letter I received from him. He died a few
months later.

I was heartbroken. Still am. There were plenty of requests
from the media asking for my thoughts on his passing, but I
gave them a swerve. I knew what he meant to me, that's all
that mattered.

The following year I received a request from Ronnie's wife,
Joy, asking if I'd like to speak at a memorial service for Ronnie
at Westminster Abbey. Bloody hellfire! What an absolute
honour. Of course I said yes.

Dear Peter,
  I'm delighted that you've agreed to say something at the
Abbey. Ronnie thought a lot of you and I think it would be
nice if you could perhaps talk about the letters you and
Ronnie wrote to each other. They meant a lot to him.
  Please don't worry about the Abbey – it will just be like
Bolton Albert Hall, only with stained glass windows and
altars and crosses and holy men!
  In case you're into 't'internet' my email address is joy@
dsl.pipex.com (a modern way of getting in touch, which
Ronnie could never get the hang of). The written word was
his thing and it served him well.
  Thank you once again for your kind words. Ronnie was
such a fan of yours and so am I.
  Love
  Joy

The night before the memorial I had a bath in the hotel and lay thinking about what I could say about Ronnie. I wanted it to be from the heart and not necessarily going for laughs.

Susan and I arrived at Westminster Abbey and immediately I was overwhelmed by how many comedy icons were there. Michael Palin, David Frost, June Whitfield, Lenny Henry, Terry Jones, John Cleese, Dawn French, Ben Elton, David Jason. That got my arse twitching straight away. Then I bumped into Ronnie Corbett, thankfully he didn't fall over. We went into the vestry at the Abbey and had a chat. He said he was giving a short eulogy, along with me and Josephine Tewson. Three of us? Is that it?! There's fifty years of British comedy out there. Just as I said that I saw the Goodies walk into the Abbey.

We took our seats next to Michael Grade, across from Terry Wogan. Then the ceremony started. Everybody smiled when we saw the procession led by altar boys carrying four candles. A nod to a classic *Two Ronnies* sketch. The service started, then a mobile phone started to ring, muffled at first. Everybody looking around, disappointed. Talk about inappropriate. It got louder when removed from the person's pocket. It was Terry Wogan's. He was red-faced as he turned off his phone, his wife Helen glaring at him. Then he looked over at me and started to giggle. So did I. Thank the Lord his ring tone wasn't 'The Floral Dance'.

I was told before the service that when it was my turn to speak I would be led to the pulpit by an altar boy. I just didn't expect the altar boy to be an old bloke in his nineties. I expected him to be a boy. The clue was in the title. I stood up, took a deep breath and started to follow him. He was so slow and doddery when he walked. So I decided to copy him. This caused quite a lot of stifled laughter, which I could hear as I walked down the aisle.

243

We reached the pulpit. Christ, that's high, I thought as I looked up. It was about four times as high as the one we used to have at our church. Mind you, we were in Westminster Abbey and not St Ethelbert's. Cautiously I climbed the narrow circular steps as the congregation finished singing the last verse of 'Jerusalem'. I tried not to look at all of the showbiz faces I'd grown up with. I was already nervous enough. I turned my attention to the general public section of the Abbey, who all had normal faces. The entire place was packed. Four thousand people, I was told.

I talked about how I'd written to him as a fan and that we'd become pen pals over the years. Then I took out the letter he'd written to me as Fletch and read it out, slowly and without trying to do a cockney accent (I wasn't brave enough for impressions).

I wanted to speak from the heart. I told them of the previous night, lying in the bath in the hotel trying to think of what to say. How could I celebrate Ronnie? I didn't really know him. I never worked with him, but the one thing that came to mind when I thought about him was always laughter. So I asked all of the congregation to think of one thing that Ronnie had done that made them laugh. Then there was silence and I thought, That's died on its arse, but then slowly I began to hear some titters. Then giggles. Followed by laughter, followed by bigger laughter, and before I knew it the whole Abbey was in an uproar. Then, to top it all, everybody broke into applause. It was very emotional and uplifting, and as I walked down the steps I thought, He'd have loved that.

A week later I got another letter.

Dear Peter,

What a star! If you can get the congregation at Westminster Abbey to give you a round of applause, then there really is no end to your talents. I thought you were magnificent and the funny walk up the aisle was terrific. Ronnie would have enjoyed that.

I'm very grateful for your agreeing to do it. I truly am.

My best love to you, Susan and the family.

Don't be a stranger.

Joy xx

Joy passed a few years later. They'll be together now, both avoiding the peach and lettuce salad.

Hitler Was a Housepainter

Four years had passed since I'd done anything new for TV and I missed it. I appreciated how lucky I was having two careers, being able to do stand-up and create for TV. (I also have a certificate for operating a meat slicer. You always need something to fall back on. Hitler was a housepainter.)

By 2008, TV was obsessed with reality talent shows. They were all the rage, every channel had one. From *Pop Idol* to *The X Factor*, from *Strictly Come Dancing* to *Dancing on Ice*, and from *Fame Academy* to *Soapstar Superstar*. The BBC even had one where you chose the lead in a musical (which was basically just a big advert for Andrew Lloyd Webber). *Britain's Got Talent* was the latest addition. The public lapped these shows up and still do.

For me, it felt like the perfect TV to parody. I'd never been a satirist, but these shows were crying out for a piss-take. We'd all become familiar with the formats. The sad stories, the underdog turned hero. We voted in our millions and made overnight stars of the winners. Some are still around, some have long since faded.

The other element I loved was music. They had lots of it.

After the success of 'Amarillo', '500 Miles' and 'Sleep', I knew how powerful music and comedy could be when they were put together. I'd always wanted to do a musical and this could be the next best thing.

To pull off something like this successfully would mean creating everything in detail, which I knew would be a huge undertaking. I also knew that I'd have to create a new character. But what?

Something that would stretch me as a performer. Something at the opposite end of the spectrum to anything I'd done before. I came up with Geraldine McQueen, a Northern Irish dinner lady who'd had a transgender operation. You couldn't get further away from Max and Brian Potter if you tried. It'd be a stretch, but I relished the challenge. Well, I did before I started filming. Then when I had to get up at four o'clock in the morning to spend four hours in make-up and then cripple myself in high heels, I had a very different opinion of the word 'relish'.

The first thing I did was go to Ireland with a few of my friends and a suitcase full of DVDs of these very shows. We watched them all that weekend and furiously scribbled down ideas. I decided to make the show the series finale of a fictitious talent show. That meant we'd get to see the three finalists' journeys and how they'd evolved over the previous weeks. I wrote down every idea, every cliché recognised. This show would have to be made with total affection. It had to be, in order to make it work as a comedy. By the time we flew home I had the whole thing mapped out and I even knew who was going to win.

Paul Coleman was and is a huge part of my life. A close friend since my first year at school, he was my best man at my wedding and is godfather to my children. Not only all that, but he's a very funny writer who I love dearly. He'd helped me

The camera rig for *Car Share* – a huge technical achievement, which just meant we couldn't see out of the windscreen.

HOME OFFICE
H.M. PRISON SLADE
CUMBERLAND
BADLEY 4444
Governor - Mr. G. Venables

Dear Peter,

It's always nice to hear from the outside, in that jostling

Som...

squ...

He...

Co...

i...

The Phoenix Club

13 Hilda St
Bolton
BL2 5RY

Phone: 01204 6555402 (pay-phone– please wait)

Open: Thurs; Fri; Sat; Coach Party's and Charity's welcome

www.comeondown.com

The Queen's Diamond Jubilee – a happy moment, though it looks like Jimmy Carr wants to kill her.

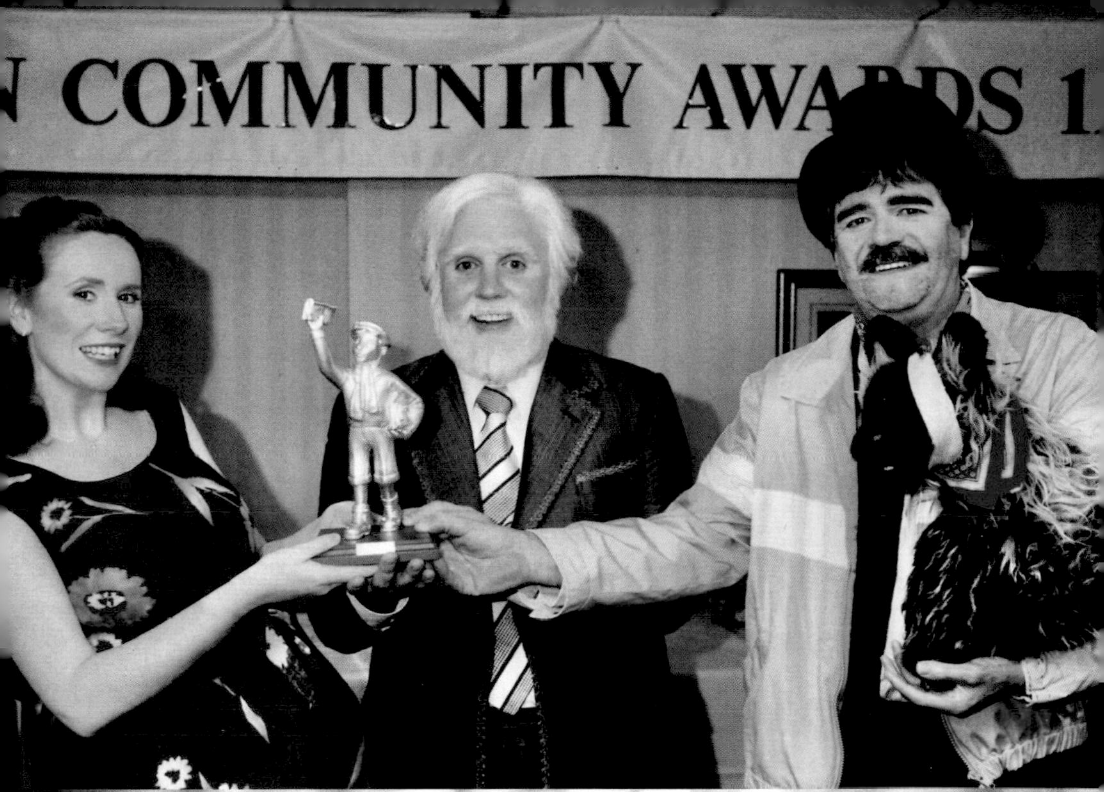
COMMUNITY AWARDS

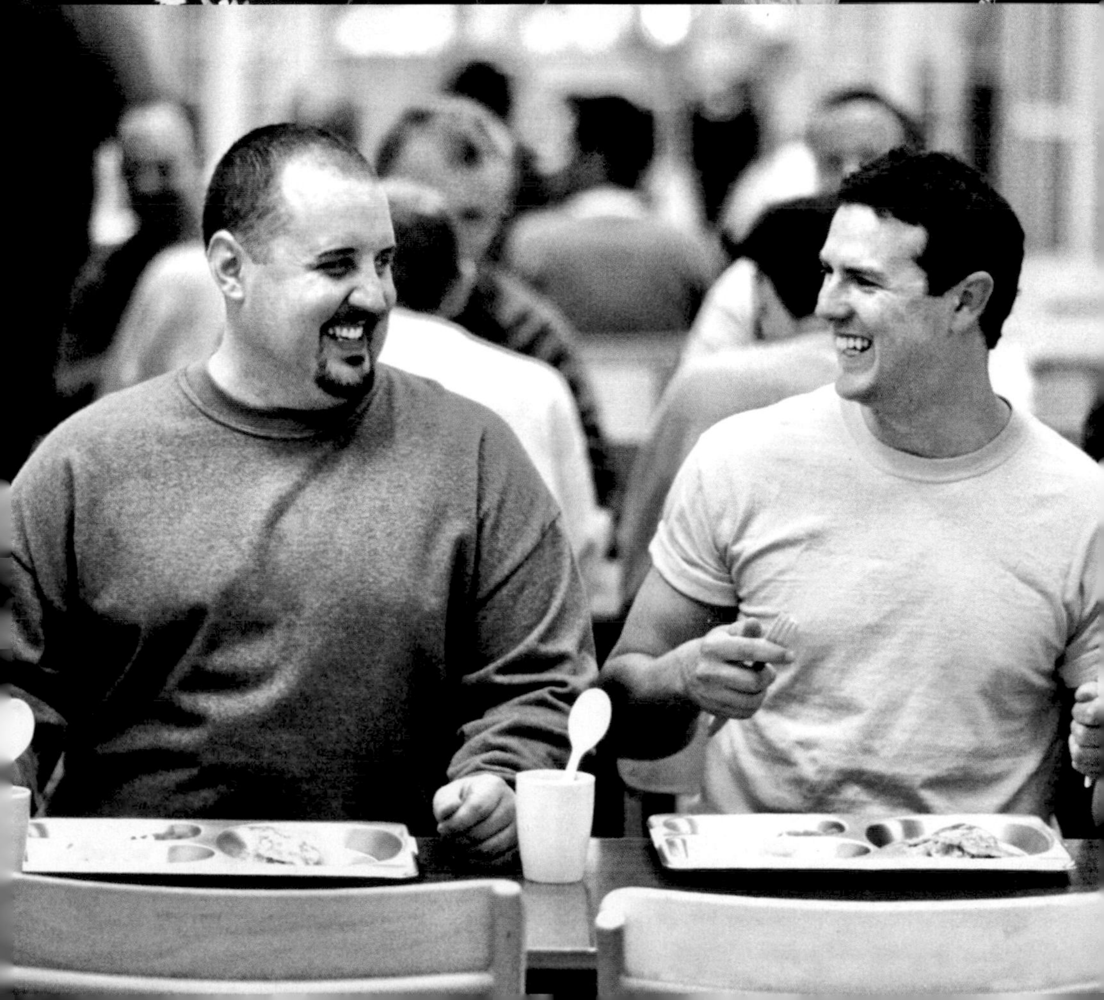

with scripts for everything I'd ever written, coming up with some great material and also suggestions on what to cut or add. After seeing the value he'd added over the years I asked him if he'd officially script edit *Max & Paddy's Road to Nowhere* in 2004. Then, when the idea for a spoof talent show came around, I asked him if he'd like to write it with me. We found an office in Manchester and started writing full-time.

Another good friend, who I'd known since my days at Salford University, was Karl Lucas. He also accompanied me to Ireland and contributed some fantastic ideas to the script. He'd occasionally join Paul and me, developing the series over the next few months.

Britain's Got the Pop Factor and Possibly a New Celebrity Jesus Christ Soapstar Superstar Strictly on Ice was written in the spring of 2008. During the writing I approached Channel 4. Kevin Lygo, who'd commissioned *That Peter Kay Thing*, was back in charge. Which was quite handy, as he seemed to enjoy me playing women. He came up to Manchester and I gave him the big sell. Still never keen on that bit. Luckily, he liked the idea, thank God.

It was to be a single two-hour special, completely replicating a finale filmed at Granada TV, who now rented out their studios for filming. I booked their biggest studio for June that year.

I still can't believe I just typed that. Just thinking I'd gone from standing outside Granada TV when my dad took a photo (which is on the back of this book) to now filming my own show there. Sadly, *Britain's Got the Pop Factor* (I've shortened the title) was to be one of Granada's last ever big productions.

I'd never worked on something so enormous. Such a big, bright, colourful extravaganza. I even hired set designers to, guess what? Design the set. They built a model of the studio but forgot to add stairs off the stage. But I used it and it actually turned out to be one of my favourite jokes in the show. As the finalists literally had nowhere to go and repeatedly ended up standing awkwardly with their heads bowed in the corner of the stage. Very silly.

For maximum authenticity, I invited the three original judges from *Pop Idol*, Pete Waterman, Nicki Chapman and Neil 'Doctor' Fox to recreate those roles once again. Fortunately, they all said yes, which was a huge advantage. I didn't ask Simon Cowell, as he was making *The X Factor* at the time. I also didn't think he'd be too keen. I was correct in my assumption, but more of that later.

Each of the fictitious finalists had a video shown of their journey in the competition before they performed a final medley of their favourite songs. This gave viewers an opportunity to understand their back story. It was also exactly what they did in every final show we watched.

The first contestant in *Britain's Got the Pop Factor* was R Wayne. A Geordie jack the lad who worked in a local care home helping his mum. He impressed the judges in his first audition but was booted out of boot camp because he simply didn't have a sad enough story. 'Back to bingo and wiping arses,' R Wayne says tearfully as he travels back home to tell his family. The bad news causes his 'R Gran' to have a massive heart attack and die. Then her funeral is interrupted by Pete Waterman, who's travelled up from London to tell R Wayne that he now has a sad enough story to get back into the competition.

Two Up, Two Down are the second finalists, a husband-and-wife quartet. Neil Fox comments that the ladies are in wheelchairs. They tell the tragic story of their joint honeymoon and a water-skiing accident at Niagara Falls that sadly left the ladies without the use of their legs. They then sing 'Tragedy'.

The third and final finalist is Geraldine McQueen, introduced by Nicki Chapman as 'the part-time dinner lady, full-time diva'. We see Geraldine's first audition, where she performs 'Man in the Mirror', as well as the press uncovering the story of her transgender operation and the fact that she used to be a man, Gerry King, a popular pianist on the Irish ferry circuit. We see newspaper headlines, 'Britain's Got the Cock Factor', and Geraldine is forced to appear on ITV's *Tonight*, in a tell-all episode entitled 'Snip Tackle and Pop'.

Voiceover

With a four-year waiting list on the NHS, Geraldine's quest for surgery led her to a Bangkok hospital

Geraldine

One night in Bangkok? Try three months. I've never known pain like it

I owe everything to Dr Fung-Me-Wow. He certainly knew his onions … and now he's got mine

But the truth only makes the British public love Geraldine even more.

I think a long enough time has passed now for me to confess that I hired an editor who actually worked on *The X Factor* and put all of these video packages together for the show. He knew the rhythms and style of the edits so well that he was perfect for our spoof. He'd travel up to Manchester and work with me for a few days before heading back to work on *The X Factor* at the weekend. He also refused to take a credit on *Britain's Got the Pop Factor*, fearful in case Simon Cowell's team found out and he'd get sacked.

As you know, music was important, so I hired a musical director called Mike Stevens. He worked with Take That and now tours with Jeff Lynne's ELO. He instantly understood it, and with his brother he created some of the brilliant medleys for the show. I'd spent hours with Karl working on deliberately bad transitions for the medleys, segueing songs together that had no business being together, like 'Born Free' into 'Free Nelson Mandela' and then taking the 'ela' off Mandela and taking it into 'Umbrella' by Rhianna. I'll never forget seeing a full sixty-piece string orchestra bursting out laughing when they heard the transitions they had to play in the medley.

For authenticity, I approached Kate Thornton to host *Britain's Got the Pop Factor*, as she'd hosted *The X Factor*, but she was pregnant at the time and had to decline. She kindly suggested Cat Deeley. I'd met Cat briefly a few years earlier and she was lovely. I spoke to her agent and called her in LA, where she lived. Cat was very successful in America, presenting a series called *So You Think You Can Dance*. We chatted on the phone and she completely got the idea. The only problem was that she was incredibly busy, but after jigging her schedule around she was able to fly to Manchester for two days of filming. Jesus, that was tight.

When Cat arrived, she was out of her mind with jetlag. I went round to her hotel to go through the script with her and she was off her face, hyper and laughing hysterically. I'd spent weeks watching episodes of *So You Think You Can Dance* on YouTube and writing links completely in her style. Cat had two full-on days at Granada. It was lovely because she also knew a lot of the crew from when she'd presented *Stars in Their Eyes*.

We got on great and I encouraged Cat to improvise too. Like in the sequence when she's about to announce the winner and decides to tell the audience absolutely everything that she's doing: 'I'm holding a golden envelope and I'm making my way to the centre of the stage, I'm going down the steps, I'm walking towards the finalists. I'm here.' Then when she opens the envelope she pulls out an oddly shaped scrap of paper. I'd put that in just to make her laugh. If you ever see it, you'll see it's just a random ripped piece of paper with the results on.

My favourite moment of Cat's was when she swore at the audience. I'd noticed how loud the audiences get at times on these shows, especially when the winner is about to be announced, jeering and cheering for who they wanted to win. So when that moment arrived, Cat said, 'Could we have quiet, please, in the studio? Please could you be quiet? FUCKING SHUT UP!' You couldn't hear a cockroach fart. Lord, that was funny. It even made it on to YouTube as 'TV Presenter Loses It with Studio Audience'. People thought it was real. I still can't thank her enough for doing that. I was nervous about asking her, but she was well up for it. Mind you, it was probably more the jetlag that I had to thank.

The show was all-consuming. Every aspect needed attention, like all of the costumes. Even though a clip might only last a few seconds, all of the dancers had to have a bespoke costume made. I massively underestimated how much work that would be. Fiona Dealey, who I'd first worked with on *That Peter Kay Thing*, was the costume designer, and she certainly had her work cut out, as the final was filled with excerpts from fictional weekly shows in the contest. Some of the excerpts only lasted a few seconds, but still all of the dancers and finalists had to look exactly right, or the parody would never have worked. Fiona and her team grafted around the clock to get things ready in time. There ended up being over two hundred costumes in the show. From fifties-style dancers to superheroes, from a pastiche of the Village People to six dancers dressed as chimney pots.

The make-up department also had a very heavy schedule, as we had a huge cast, each needing to be made-up before appearing on camera. They completely took over the whole make-up department in Granada. I'd started a few make-up tests months before so I could decide how Geraldine should look. I wanted her to be as believable as possible and not a caricature, especially as she was transgender.

Make-up designer Jill Sweeney and I tried lots of ideas but settled on a very natural-looking ginger wig in a bobbed style. It's hard to explain, but you instantly know when you've found the right look for a character. I knew that I wanted Geraldine to be Northern Irish, an accent I'd done before. It came naturally to me because of my mum.

The first thing I had to do was get waxed. Mother of God, that's an experience I'll never forget. Two Russian girls in a hotel in Manchester. It sounds dodgy but it was all above board. Jill was with me. The two girls were quite shocked when Jill told them how much was coming off. Back, chest, legs, arms. When they ripped the first strip off, I thought, Fuck me, what have I done? Agony. It might have been a hot summer's night, but I was shivering like a shitting dog when I drove home, with the heating on full-blast. I even had to call in at the all-night chemist and buy two tubs of aloe vera just to ease the pain.

My eyebrows were also waxed for the duration of filming. I remember catching a glimpse of my reflection when filling up with diesel. I just looked constantly surprised that summer.

Pop Factor (I've shortened it again) was a mammoth production with a mammoth cast, featuring familiar faces from all my previous series. My friend Sian, who had completely given up on acting at this point, played Wendy in Two Up, Two Down. It took a lot of persuading to convince her she'd be great for the part, and she was. Working with her again was joyful. Jo Enright played her sister-in-law. Alex Lowe turned in a cameo as psychic Clinton Baptiste. He consoles R Wayne on R Gran's progress in the spirit world: 'She says she's very proud of you, but she's got to go, as she's just off to a pub quiz with Thora Hird and Heath Ledger.' Pearce Quigley appeared briefly too, auditioning a magic dog act. Even my father-in-law turned up playing the accordion with his brothers.

Marc Pickering was a wonderful discovery as R Wayne. He had a brilliant singing voice and great comic timing. Karl Lucas and David Hulston were fantastic as the husband half of Two Up, Two Down. Karl had also gone to Salford Uni with Sian and me. I felt lucky being surrounded by so many close friends in the cast and the crew, and it made the job a lot of fun. Hard work, but fun.

Amanda Neal returned as my irreplaceable first assistant director. Jeremy Hewson was on camera again. Pete Hallworth was back in the edit. It was also on this project that I was introduced to a new editor, Matt Brown, who's become an important part of my life in the years that've followed.

As well as the judges we also had a few celebrities in the cast. Lionel Blair as a very demanding choreographer: 'They say you can't polish a turd, well, I've polished hundreds, thousands.' Rustie Lee turned up as a parody of Sinitta (who was always with Simon Cowell). Musical guests included Ricky Wilson from the Kaiser Chiefs singing the Muppets classic 'Mahna Mahna' with Geraldine; Rick Astley duetted with Two Up, Two Down; and the Cheeky Girls appeared as singing mentors for R Wayne. The irony, as their only big chart success had been 'Cheeky Song (Touch My Bum)'.

But I wanted a big fish. An A-list celebrity cameo would give the show credibility. Months before, I wrote to a few big names to ask them to appear, but I'd had no response. I'd almost given up when, one Saturday afternoon, I was sat typing at the kitchen table and I heard the ping of an email. It was Paul McCartney. Well, that's what it said in the email, but obviously I thought it was a wind-up. When I read the email, though, it really was him. He said he appreciated my request and would love a part in my new musical show. I couldn't believe it.

Paul McCartney had never even appeared on *The X Factor* or any of those types of shows, so to have him appear on a spoof would be an extraordinary coup. I was bursting to tell people but didn't. I wanted to keep it a surprise.

I spoke with his office in London and they said that filming could take place there. We set a date and took a limited crew to London; just Amanda, Jeremy and Jill, who'd been doing my make-up. I got ready into Geraldine at a hotel around the corner and then casually walked to his office in Soho Square. Just like when I met the cast of *Corrie* it was like meeting a real-life waxwork. He took us up to a flat on the top floor of the building. It had a lounge, but most importantly a piano.

He was exactly as you'd expect him to be. Funny, laid-back and very self-effacing.

The idea for the sequence was that Paul McCartney is mentoring Geraldine during her TV themes week (each week *The X Factor* had a theme). The camera started recording and we improvised around his piano. I got him to play the theme to *Blankety Blank* and we sang along, and then he said, 'I think you'd be better doing more of a ballad.' Geraldine said, 'Like *Home and Away*.' So I sang the theme from *Home and Away* as he played the piano and joined in.

The whole scene took about half an hour to film and then we were off, with solid gold in the can. I guarded that tape with my life. It was so lovely meeting Paul McCartney and we've kept in touch ever since. In fact, a few years later he asked me if I'd like to introduce him at the Queen's Diamond Jubilee outside Buckingham Palace for a big live TV celebration. That was another huge honour. I know I say that a lot in this book, but honestly it's the truth, every time.

I'd learnt over the years that being last on a bill can be tough, as practically every gag will have been done by the time it's your turn. I knew I needed a gimmick.

As this was a royal celebration I decided to dress up as a Beefeater. You know, those royal yeoman guards in red that protect the Queen's jewels. Paul McCartney didn't get in touch until a few days before the concert, so I had very little time to get a costume. I did try hiring one, but as it was Jubilee weekend they were already on hire. So I got in touch with my secret weapon, a seamstress in Rawtenstall called Cath. She measured me up in her back bedroom and knocked up an astonishing Beefeater costume in forty-eight hours (just like the film). Fair play to her, it was perfect. She even sewed a big gold letter 'Q' on the front, for 'Queen', but on stage I said it was for 'Quorn', as Paul is a vegetarian. She only charged a hundred quid, so I gave her a hundred and twenty and a Dairy Box from the Co-op. I met Her Majesty after the show and told her how much the costume cost. It's on YouTube, apparently.

Don't ask me why, but I thought it'd be funny to pretend to play 'Let It Be' on the panpipes before introducing Paul McCartney. I'd found a piss poor version of it. I even got a set of panpipes Velcroed to the top of my big Beefeater mitre, so I could just yank them off and mime playing.

Before the concert, I was sat backstage in a Portakabin shitting myself when I got the message that Paul McCartney would like to see me and have a chat. So I went round to his 'much larger' Portakabin. It was good to see him and we ran through what the plans were for me introducing him. I was to go on stage after Madness, who were singing 'Our House' on the roof of Buckingham Palace (that truly was madness). I'd introduce Paul. Then he went through the list of songs he was planning on performing and one of them was 'Let It Be'.

'But I'm doing that,' I said in a mild panic.

'What do you mean?'

'I'm miming to that on the panpipes before you come on. We can't both do it. Do you have to do it?'

'Well, I'd like to,' he said.

'But you've hundreds of songs!'

Then I took a step back. I thought, This, right now, this is probably the most mental thing that has ever happened to me. I'm backstage at Buckingham Palace in a Portakabin, telling Paul McCartney not to sing 'Let It Be' (by the Beatles, mind), because I wanted to mime playing a piss-poor version of it on the panpipes. Guess who backed down first? Well, he did write it, after all.

Every year the *X Factor* winner would release a song. We've had such classics as Joe McElderry's 'The Climb', Leona Lewis's 'A Moment Like This' and Shayne Ward's 'That's My Goal'. I knew I needed my own winner's song in the same style, so I got in touch with Gary Barlow (as you do).

We'd become good friends since I bumped into him at an Elton John concert in Bolton. We hit it off, with both of us having a big affection for working men's clubs. Gary later reformed Take That and we'd kept in touch. When I spoke to him about *Pop Factor* he was well up for it and even invited me down to his home studio. Very decent of him. He had his synthesiser, I had my rhyming dictionary. We both put on our tracksuit bottoms and started to make magic.

Gary had already come up with a demo for what was to be called 'The Winner's Song'. It was a beautiful regal tune. I suggested having a double key change. They always had an obligatory key change, so I thought it'd be funny to have two.

I started on the words and, to be honest, we had most of it sorted by the end of the day.

I loved the process. It was going so well I thought it'd be a good idea to write a Christmas song for Geraldine too. So we set about writing what would become 'Once Upon a Christmas Song', which was incredibly catchy. And would no doubt have people singing it 'over and over and over again'.

Channel 4 and Kevin Lygo loved the finished version of *Pop Factor* and were equally surprised by Paul McCartney's appearance. Someone at Channel 4 thought he hadn't actually been there and it had been done with a green screen. Fools.

That reminds me of the time I sent a rough edit of an episode of *Phoenix Nights* to the head of comedy and one of his notes was, 'What's with the big black gap in the middle?' That's where the adverts will go. Dickhead.

Pop Factor was broadcast on Sunday, 12 October 2008 at 9 p.m. It was broadcast in two sections on the night an hour apart, as I insisted on having a gap before the fictitious results show an hour later.

The overall viewing figures were staggering. It got over eight million, so Channel 4 were over the moon. These were the highest viewing figures I'd ever got for anything, and it wasn't even Christmas.

I was very happy with the final show. It had been a slog, the hardest production I'd ever worked on, and even when I see it now my chest automatically tightens at how much time, effort and stress went into it all. My only criticism of *Pop Factor* is that I think I went a bit nuts on the attention to detail. It was so real that it left many viewers confused. Even to the point that some were trying to vote for their favourite finalist by pushing the purple button on their remote controls. Mind you, you'd have to be fucking stupid if you tried to vote via the purple button. What purple button?

True to the form, Geraldine's 'The Winner's Song' was released the next day. Astonishingly, it went to number two in the charts. Higher than Leon Jackson, the previous year's *X Factor* winner, who had released his new single. If you're reading this, Leon, I'm sorry. I had no intention of damaging you in any way. I didn't even know you had a single out.

Simon Cowell wasn't too pleased. He popped up in the press, venting his anger at both *Pop Factor* and 'The Winner's Song' damaging Leon Jackson's chances. I just found it fascinating, art imitating life to such a degree of absurdity.

The day after the show was broadcast, I was back in Geraldine's bra again (with false breasts, I hasten to add), this time to film the video for 'Once Upon a Christmas Song' in October. For eight hours we drove an open-backed truck around the streets of Greater Manchester. Myself, the girls from Two Up, Two Down, two elves and a snowman, all miming to the song. The crew would run ahead up the road, handing out tinsel and Christmas decorations for the public as we drove past, singing along with the cameras rolling. Then the tinsel would quickly be collected and dished out again further up the road (hey, tinsel's a lot dearer than you think). People got into a merry mood despite the autumnal weather and we got some very festive footage.

The next night we set up in a cul-de-sac in Bolton that was legendary for its Christmas decorations. The neighbours all pulled together each year to raise funds for charity and, to be fair, they really did a fantastic job of decorating their houses. We hired a company called Snow Business to whiten things up with their fake snow, and the whole place looked like a Hallmark Christmas card for the video. I even managed to get Father Christmas and his reindeer in at the end when they flew past a full moon in the sky.

With the success of *Pop Factor* in the ratings, Channel 4 enquired about the possibility of a Christmas special.

Fortunately, we'd filmed so much footage when we were making the show, including full versions of songs we'd only used excerpts from. I said yes to the special. It would also give Geraldine a chance to tell the viewers what she'd been up to since winning the show.

Bizarrely, I got a request from Stella McCartney asking if Geraldine (not me) might like to turn on the Christmas lights at her shop in London. Of course I said yes, not only because it was Stella McCartney, who's a really lovely person, but also because I thought it'd make great footage for the *Pop Factor* Christmas special. It was a cold, dark December night when I turned up in full Geraldine regalia. There was a bit of a soiree in Stella's shop before the big switch-on. Lulu was there (without her dog) and Kate Moss. Quite a surreal mix.

Then we all piled outside in front of tons of paparazzi and counted down from ten, I flicked the switch, the lights went on and, as I was singing a quick rendition of 'Jingle Bells', a black cab pulled up. There followed a flurry of flashbulbs and Paul McCartney emerged through the crowd. He came up on stage with me and we hugged like long-lost friends before diving into an impromptu version of 'Wonderful Christmastime'. Magical. It could only have been more perfect if it snowed, and then it did.

Top of the Pops was a huge deal, particularly to people of my generation. We watched it every week growing up. Every Thursday night without fail. So imagine my reaction when I was asked to appear on it as Geraldine. Unbelievable!

And it was to be the Christmas special, which features the biggest songs of the year and always goes out on Christmas Day.

Michele Thorne, a brilliant choreographer, had done an amazing job with the cast of *Pop Factor*, so I invited her to work up a routine for our appearance. I say 'our', as I wasn't going to go on *Top of the Pops* without Sian. If I was living the dream, then she was coming with me. So I had the girls from Two Up, Two Down and six dancing snowmen.

Sian travelled down with me, and we finally made use of my portable DVD player by watching *Mamma Mia!*, this time without any interruptions from the driver. We arrived at BBC Television Centre. I showed Sian the big fountain in the middle of the circle where Roy Castle tap-danced on *Record Breakers*. We were both very giddy as we walked around the corridors, reading signs for what was filming in the studios. *Strictly Come Dancing, Tomorrow's World*, and then we arrived, *Top of the Pops*.

Geraldine was on in between Adele and Girls Aloud – hilarious. We did the routine twice and I even got the studio audience to do a bit of choreography along with us the second time. We couldn't believe it then and we still can't now.

Then, if it's possible to top *TOTPs*, I was asked (well, Geraldine was) to top the bill on that year's Royal Variety Performance. Double woo-hoo! (Geraldine was starting to get more work than me.)

As the recording of both shows fell close together it seemed logical to have the same routine for both. I'd been on the Royal Variety before, in 1999 performing stand-up, but to be asked to top the bill was a huge honour. Plus, it was to be at the London Palladium, one of the most famous theatres in the world.

Geraldine

Well, I've not stopped since I won the competition. I've been whisked here, there and everywhere. I've hardly had time to catch my breath, which is a worry, as I'm asthmatic. But the highlight of everything I've done so far has got to be appearing on the Royal Variety Performance in front of Prince Charles. I

still get emotional just thinking about it. To think I used to sit
at home when I was a little boy and dream about being
on that show one day

*We see Geraldine on stage at the London Palladium, sat at a
grand piano, playing the opening chords of 'The Winner's Song'.*

Geraldine
Hello, well, who'd have thought it. Little old me on the Royal
Variety Performance

How lovely to perform in front of His Royal Highness. You'll get
your crown eventually. I got mine

Cuts to close-up of Prince Charles laughing.

I met Prince Charles and Camilla later in the line-up, still
dressed as Geraldine, and I honestly don't think they knew
what to make of me. All I remember is Charles was wearing
slippers. I'll never forget it. I suppose he must have thought,
I'm only nipping down the road to the Palladium. I'll keep
these on.

I understood. I used to do the same when I'd nip to the back
shop for a bottle of semi-skimmed milk. Comfort is king and
now Charles is.

I wanted to make the routine for 'Once Upon a Christmas
Song' special, so I asked production if they could please make
three massive parcels to go on stage. Then, when a point
arrived in the song, Pete Waterman, Nicki Chapman and Neil
Fox all popped out like jack-in-the-boxes. It got a huge cheer
and gave the musical number a lovely finish.

All of the proceeds from 'Once Upon a Christmas Song'
went to the NSPCC, and the song made it to number two in

the charts on Christmas Eve. Ironically, it was held off the top spot by that year's *X Factor* winner, Alexandra Burke with 'Hallelujah'. But I didn't care. I'd been on *Top of the Pops* with my best friend Sian. Now that's a memory to treasure.

My new year's resolution: wave goodbye to Geraldine and finally grow my eyebrows back.

15

She Rode Elvis

So, I was talking about being on the Royal Variety in the previous chapter. I've been involved with it a few times over the years. What I love about it is the eclectic mix of people you get. In 2008, the year I performed as Geraldine, I shared a dressing room with Jimmy Tarbuck and the cast of *The Lion King*. As I was wandering around backstage dressed as Geraldine, I decided to knock on Cliff Richard's dressing room door. Like you do.

I had met Cliff before, so I wasn't a complete nutter. My mother-in-law is a big fan, and for her birthday I got her tickets to see him in Manchester and we got to go backstage to meet him. Cliff was lovely to her, very gracious and modest.

Meanwhile, back at the Royal Variety, Cliff looked puzzled when he opened his dressing room and saw me dressed as Geraldine. He didn't recognise me for a few seconds then invited me in. He was sharing a dressing room with the Shadows. The next thing I knew I was wedged in between Hank Marvin and Bruce Welch, posing for a selfie on Cliff's iPhone. What a memory. That was the last time Cliff and the Shadows ever performed together.

In 2009, I was asked to host the Royal Variety Performance in Blackpool. I know I say this a lot, but it was a huge honour (that's almost becoming a catchphrase). Hang on, I'm going to look up another word for 'honour'. Just let me click on Thesaurus. There's only one more option, 'privilege'. Right, so it was a real privilege, and to be hosting in Blackpool too, a big part of my life and a lot closer to home than London.

I was to appear at the start of the show rising up through the floor, playing the theatre's enormous Wurlitzer organ. I was pretty terrified, sitting under the stage in complete darkness as I waited for the Queen and Prince Philip to take their seats, and then I slowly started to rise up playing 'Amarillo'. What an opening.

I got to bring my family to the show, including my nan, and they all sat in front of the Royal Box.

Peter

(that's me, in case you didn't know)

We have got a very, very special lady in the audience. I'm sure you all know who I'm talking about, and I'm sure she won't mind me saying that she looks absolutely stunning tonight. She's spent her winter fuel allowance on a shampoo and set. She's up there in the circle … I'm talking about my nana, ladies and gentlemen

I never thought I'd see my nan and Her Majesty side by side … well, as close as MI5 will allow. Thick as thieves, the pair of them. They'll be swapping Revels by the interval. Hey, she might be in her eighties, but she still pulls her wheelie bin out once a week. I just wish my nan would do the same

It was also the first time I ever met the Queen. Though I'm sad to say I can't remember a thing she said, as I was completely overwhelmed. But I do remember Prince Philip asking Diversity if they were all related. WTF?!

In 2011, I was invited to host the Royal Variety again. This time from Salford's Lowry Theatre. I said, 'If this show gets any closer to Bolton I'll be on the roof of my mum's bungalow.' That was a great show to host and I was much more at ease the second time. There were a few cock-ups, though. Like when Barry Manilow was supposed to be singing with some old footage of himself on a big screen, but he couldn't get his timing right or sing in the right key. He tried six times before he got it right. I think Princess Anne was nodding off.

Then Nicole Scherzinger was singing 'The Phantom of the Opera', but something technical went wrong with the revolving stage and she just kept going round. They closed the curtains and I was asked to fill in for a few minutes. A few minutes became ten minutes and then, out of sheer frustration, I walked off stage into the wings, saw the show's producer Andrew Lloyd Webber and literally dragged him out on stage with me. I said, 'It's your show, you fill in for it.' He wasn't so chuffed, especially as he was on crutches at the time with a broken leg.

The sad thing about that year was that Tony Bennett was supposed to be performing a duet with George Michael for the finale. But George threw a sickie and pulled out. What a shame. That could have been magic. Unlike Barry Manilow.

The only other show I presented around this time was the BRITs. A huge deal, not only within the music industry but also on TV. Sadly, that turned out to be something I didn't really enjoy, as there was a lot of politics and hierarchy backstage during the rehearsals that afternoon. I remember an American record company executive moaning about my introduction to Lady Gaga. I said, 'She is America's answer to Su Pollard,' and they were whinging, 'Who's this Su Pollard? Somebody google her … what the hell's *Hi-de-Hi!*?' (Imagine all that in an American accent.) I reassured them that I'd drop the introduction for the broadcast that night. Did I balls. The show was live, sod them.

Liam Gallagher won an award. He swaggered on stage to collect it, then threw it into the audience and walked off. He could have hit somebody in the face with it. What a nobhead, I thought. So I said just that when I walked back to the mic: 'What a nobhead.' I wasn't trying to be controversial or stir trouble, I just said what was on my mind. That might be the reason why I've never been invited back to present the BRITs again.

After I finished *Pop Factor*, I decided to take a break from making any TV for a while. I was also back on tour. *Pop Factor* did receive some fantastic prestige, remarkably in America, where the show was nominated for an LA BAFTA. That was a bit of a whirlwind trip. Suffering from jetlag, I have vague recollections of sitting at a swanky table at the Hilton Hotel in Beverly Hills between Cat Deeley and 'nasty' Nigel Lythgoe (the producer and judge from the original *Pop Idol* on ITV). He was with his then girlfriend, Priscilla Presley, and all I kept thinking was, She rode Elvis.

Pop Factor won the award. Woo-hoo! I thanked Cat Deeley in my speech and then, still off my head with jetlag, I thanked my pilot for the choice of films on the flight over. Also, I shared what I hoped they might be showing on the flight home.

While I was there Nigel Lythgoe (who wasn't really nasty at all) arranged a meeting with a big producer from NBC to discuss the possibility of bringing Geraldine to American TV. Nigel loved *Pop Factor* and was quite keen to get it going in the States. *Little Britain* had recently done the same with a US version of their series. There was talk about a big development deal but all I was interested in was getting back home. Don't get me wrong, I was flattered, but the thought of working in America wasn't for me. I'm a homebird. Family first. Plus, you can't beat living in the real world. Like today, my auntie Kath was coming out of the Market Hall in Bolton when a woman collapsed in front of her. A few people gathered, one of them giving CPR. My auntie bent over and said, 'Can I help at all?' and the woman on the floor said, 'No thanks, love, we're filming,' and nodded to a camera crew across the street. They were filming a drama for ITV.

I'd been offered a few films (I know the book is called *T.V.*, but the films always end up on TV so get out of that). Usually they've been comedic bit parts in Disney films, the *Paddington* movies, once a big-budget American comedy, but I've never fancied being away from home for weeks on end. The first one I ever did was *24 Hour Party People*, with Steve Coogan playing the *Granada Reports* presenter and music svengali Tony Wilson. Tony founded Factory Records as well as the Manchester nightclub the Haçienda. He also aided and abetted quite a lot of indie bands, including Joy Division, New Order and Happy Mondays.

The biopic was directed by Michael Winterbottom and his style was very improvisational, which suited me, as I could make it up. I played Don Tonay, a Manchester gangster who let Tony Wilson use one of his clubs for his music acts. In one scene Tony brings Joy Division down to the club, and I remember improvising a line telling Ian Curtis to 'cheer up, for fuck's sake – you look like you're gonna kill yourself'. Funnily enough, they didn't keep it in the film.

In another scene I was in the back of a van with Tony Wilson, having sex with a couple of prostitutes. Like you do. Now, the problem was, I never read the script and didn't know anything about that scene until a girl from make-up handed me some flesh-coloured underpants for the sex scene. 'What sex scene?' I said, throwing them back at her. She showed me the script and I thought, Bugger that. I was on the phone to my mum and mentioned the sex scene. She immediately asked to speak to the director. So I handed the phone to Michael Winterbottom.

I'll never forget how sheepish he was speaking to my mum: 'Well … yes, I understand, Mrs Kay … sorry, I mean Deirdre, but it has always been in the script … well, I'm sure he can keep his clothes on if that'll help.' Hilarious.

If you ever see the film, I'm in the back of this van with Steve Coogan. He's getting undressed with these two half-naked girls and I'm fully clothed, sat well away from them. Then I had to open a big bottle of champagne. Which I'd never done before. So I'm playing this hard-as-nails gangster who's trying to open a bottle of champagne with one eye shut in case it explodes. If there's one thing I learnt that day, it's always read the script, every bit of it.

The next film I was offered sounded like a belter. It was for Miramax and it had an incredible cast, Alan Rickman, Bill Nighy, Rachel Griffiths, Natasha Richardson, Warren Clarke, Hugh Bonneville and a Hollywood heartthrob at the time, Josh Hartnett. It was called *Blow Dry*. Never heard of it? Neither has anybody else, as it turned out to be a right load of old shit. Which just shows you that having a stellar cast means nothing.

It was written by Simon Beaufoy, who wrote *The Full Monty*, which was a huge success, so I think somebody must have been thinking everything he wrote must be gold dust. I did have my suspicions. An international hairdressing competition set in Keighley in Yorkshire wouldn't have had me running to the cinema.

But I thought, Keighley's quite local to me on a map of Europe so I'll take a little trip over the Pennines, but sadly no. The exterior shots were done in Keighley, while the interior shots were to be filmed in Shoreditch in London, in some shithole of a building doubling as Keighley Town Hall. I was sat in a tiny little Portakabin for days on end just waiting. Waiting and more waiting. Plus, it always seemed to be raining. Nobody spoke to me, and by the fourth day I wanted to go home. Why was it taking so long?

When I finally got on to the location to film it was on the same day the executive producer, Harvey Weinstein, was coming on set. Probably *literally*, knowing what he's like. It was my job to shift all the potted plants. I was in a big final scene where they were announcing the winner of the hairdressing competition. I was stood right next to Josh Hartnett in the crowd. The director said, 'Action!' and Josh Hartnett turned to me and said, 'Ow did wi do?' in the shittest Yorkshire accent I'd ever heard. I just burst out laughing and said, 'Are you having a laugh? Go on, say it proper.' Josh stared at me. Ironically, I don't think he understood *my* accent. Somebody shouted, 'Cut!' and I was ushered to one side. The director said, 'Look, please don't draw attention, but we've had a lot of trouble with Josh's accent over the past few months. He's on his third voice coach.'

I said, 'Well, you wanna get your money back, he sounds shocking.'

We did another take and I literally had to bite my lip to stop myself laughing.

That's where they went wrong. Casting an American actor as a Yorkshire lad just because he was a bit of a pin-up. They should have checked to see if he could do the accent first.

I got offered a few more films after *Blow Dry*. I was offered the part of a butcher in *102 Dalmatians*, a removal man in

Garfield: The Movie, a pirate in the Caribbean, but I turned them all down. The thought of sitting around a film set doing nothing for days on end wasn't for me.

Saying that, I did say yes to one more film, which went on to win an Oscar. *Wallace & Gromit: The Curse of the Were-Rabbit*. Now that was an honour (I know, but there's only privilege and I used that last). Everybody loves Wallace & Gromit. How could you not? Nick Park created the most glorious, meticulous characters that will stand the test of time forever. The BBC knows, that's why they show them every bank holiday. They're right up there with the best. Disney, Pixar and DreamWorks (who, incidentally, made this film). I did the voice for PC Mackintosh, the local village bobby who sounded remarkably like Brian Potter. I didn't mind, I was just chuffed it was set in Lancashire, which meant a lot.

Especially to Nick Park, as he's from Preston.

It was an easy job. I said my lines in a studio in Manchester while they were recorded in London. When the film was finished, I had to re-record some more noises, such as screams, yelps, woos, wees, gasps, sneezes … a few hours down in London. It was great to finally meet Nick Park.

Working on *Wallace & Gromit* gave me a desire to try and do more children's projects. Then fortunately I was approached to do the voice of Big Chris, a mechanic in a new pre-school show called *Roary the Racing Car*. It was a lovely, bright, colourful show with lots of humour and songs. It was set at Silver Hatch racetrack by the sea. Big Chris looked after all the different racing cars, including Roary, Maxi, Cici and Tin Top. Other characters included a very naughty rabbit called Flash, who was always causing trouble; Marsha, who organised everything; Farmer Green; and the owner of Silver Hatch, Mr Carburettor, who always arrived in a helicopter called Hellie the Helicopter (I bet they were up all night thinking of that).

Over the next four years, 108 episodes were made. The thing I loved the most about working on *Roary* was the people I worked with. The voice actors. I'll never forget that first day we met, we all sat around tables and rehearsed the script. There were a lot of characters on the page and yet only four other voice actors. I couldn't fathom it. But what I didn't realise was that they'd all be doing multiple voices. I remember being blown away by how skilfully they leapt from voice to voice across the pages of the script. I felt like a right lazy sod, just doing my own voice.

We were recorded reading the scripts and then the animation was done later. That process took about a year. The series was shown on Nick Jr as part of *Milkshake!* on Channel 5. If I'm honest, I really did it for my own children. In fact, for a while they thought working at Silver Hatch racetrack was my real job.

What *Roary* allowed me was a unique insight into how stop animation was created. It also gave me an idea for a new charity single. Well, actually, my children did. One of them asked me if Fireman Sam actually knew Bob the Builder. That was all it took. I thought, What if they did? What if all the children's TV characters knew each other? What if Postman Pat was friends with Fireman Sam? I thought it would be fantastic if you could show that. Get them all together.

I remembered that excitement people had when the Band Aid single was released and we saw all the different pop stars come together, George Michael, Bono, Paul Young, Duran Duran and Spandau Ballet, etc. I thought, What if I made a video that did the same but with all different children's animation characters? Children would love that. My children would love that. So I pitched my idea to Keith Chapman on our lunch break during *Roary* (he was the head of the production company). He loved the idea. I said they could all meet at Silver Hatch racetrack.

Originally, I considered the idea for Comic Relief but then thought it'd be much better for Children in Need. In fact, it'd be perfect for children to see at the start of the programme. So I gave Sir Terry Wogan a ring (like you do). It was quite funny because I rang him at home and his wife, Helen, answered and said he wasn't in, but he'd call me back. Later on, I got a message from him on our answer machine, but I couldn't tell if he was saying 'sir' or 'er'. 'Hello, it's Sir/er Terry Wogan here.'

Eventually, we spoke. He loved the idea, which was a relief, and said he would tell the heads of Children in Need. The project was official and would be released as a DVD and audio single. The first thing we had to do was come up with a song. But what song? Maybe a medley would be better. I listened to a lot of upbeat, happy songs. In particular, I listened to the lyrics. I had to be careful that the characters wouldn't be singing anything dodgy like 'Bump n' Grind' or 'Gang Bang'. The songs that were eventually chosen were 'Can You Feel It', 'Don't Stop', 'Jai Ho!' (popular that year), 'Tubthumping', 'Never Forget', 'One Day Like This' and 'Hey Jude'. I got in touch with a fantastic musical director called Nigel Wright, who arranged all of the backing tracks for *The X Factor*. We worked on a medley and then we got all of the cast to record their vocals over several months.

We got some great names: Bernard Cribbins, he'd voiced *The Wombles*; Neil Morrissey – Bob the Builder; Casey Kasem as Shaggy from *Scooby-Doo*. We even got Ringo Starr as Thomas the Tank Engine. Plus all of the cast from *Roary*.

Can you believe it took two years to complete the project? With so much meticulous attention to detail, the filming process of working with stop animation requires hours upon hours to co-ordinate and film. Each frame is individually taken, then each character is repositioned. This can be painstaking for everybody involved, especially if there are multiple characters in a scene. But it also took a while just to get all the permissions from the owners of the characters. It was an eye-opener to discover that a lot of them were rivals. They were a bit picky about *their* characters mixing with other rival characters. Who'd have thought it with pre-school children's shows? A few times I had to get in touch and say, 'Can we just all calm down, please? This is for Children in Need, for fuck's sake.' Or words similar.

We also had a task finding some of the original puppets. We found Bagpuss in an attic stuffed behind a water tank. He was so tatty we couldn't use him, so he had to be remade. As did some of the original Thunderbirds. The puppets arrived in boxes, some from all over the world in all kinds of conditions. Some had to be repainted. It was like that old man off *Toy Story 2* who restores Woody. The costume department at the studios had to make them tiny new clothes. Such a lovely department. They even had teeny-tiny ironing boards to press the puppet's clothes. I used to love going over to see how the animation was coming along. It was all produced in Altrincham in Cheshire, which isn't far from home.

I'd watch what they'd filmed and suggest things. Like the bit when Paddington arrives like a rock star flashed by paparazzi and later gets a cloak placed around him like James Brown.

Some characters weren't puppets, like Peppa Pig and Scooby-Doo, so I came up with the idea of having them appear via a mobile phone or on TV. That meant we could really mix the styles and we managed to get over a hundred characters in the final video.

The video was finished in time for Children in Need. I watched it with Tim Harper, the director, and the rest of the team who'd worked so incredibly hard on it for so long. Although I knew it would be special, I never realised how much joy it would bring to children, not only my own but so many others, and adults too. It was truly joyous and remains the best thing I've ever made in my career in TV.

The single, which still didn't have a title, was eventually called 'The Official Children in Need Medley' by Peter Kay's Animated All Star Band.

Gary Barlow had organised a big gala at the Royal Albert Hall called Children in Need Rocks. This was going out live on BBC1. It had a great line-up, including my old pal Paul McCartney, Take That, Shirley Bassey and Cheryl Cole (no, I'm not kidding). I was invited to introduce Paul McCartney, but before the show I had a wander backstage. I'd brought my laptop and DVD of the animated single and I knocked on Paul McCartney's dressing room door. I showed him the new video, which he loved, especially the end bit when all of the characters sing 'Hey Jude'. That was a precious moment, sharing that with him.

A couple of hours later I was stood by the side of Paul McCartney's piano singing 'Hey Jude' with the rest of the cast. Sir/er Terry Wogan and I sharing a microphone. Funny old world.

The video received its official premiere the following night on *Children in Need*. I asked them if they'd please try and put it on early in the evening, as I wanted children to see it before they went to bed. Sir/er Terry introduced me and we introduced the video. Twenty minutes later I was on the M40 home. Job done.

The video was extremely well received and reached number one the following Sunday. I was in New York when I found out. Reggie Yates phoned me live on Radio 1's Top 40 Chart Show. I was there because, incredibly, *Pop Factor* had been nominated for an Emmy for best comedy, but sadly it didn't win. So finding out the Animated All Star Band had gone to number one was a wonderful consolation.

The song remained at the top of the charts for a further three weeks and apparently earned a gold disc (well, that's what I've just read on Wikipedia). That's news to me. I never got a gold disc?

Doggin'

February 2011, I was in the middle of a stand-up tour, travelling back from Birmingham and chuckling to myself as I read a script called *Car Share*. My friend Paul Coleman had sent it to me. He'd written it with a fella called Tim Reid. They'd written six episodes. Paul has always been a bit of a dark horse. I didn't even know he was writing, so I was really surprised when he sent me a full series. He wanted my opinion and to see if I knew any way he could possibly get it made for TV.

I fell in love with the premise immediately. It was so simple, two people travelling to work and back each day, car sharing. That was it! I was drawn in by its simplicity, the confined space of the car. The spiralling conversations.

It also reminded me a lot of 'A Night In', the episode of *Porridge* where Fletch and Godber spend the entire episode talking in their cell. That had a huge influence on me and I'd been searching for something similar ever since. I'd kind of got there already with *Max & Paddy*, but this was much more restrained.

A few months later I met up with Sian for one of our regular catch-ups. They usually consisted of lunch followed by a drive, where we'd put the world to rights to a playlist of classic hits that we'd both sing along to. That's when it suddenly dawned on me. This was, in essence, *Car Share*. We could do this series. The both of us. Paul knew Sian. In fact, he'd already lifted a few of her comments and put them in the script. I knew Sian would be perfect. All I had to do now was try and convince Sian herself. She'd completely given up acting. The last thing she'd worked on was *Pop Factor* and she was now working full time in a call centre.

At first, Sian was unsure. This would be a huge starring role with a ton of lines. Just the two of us, on screen almost all of the time. That's a lot of pressure for anyone, let alone someone who's not done any TV work for a long time. But I knew we could make it work. We'd have each other to lean on and I truly believed that she could do it. I've always believed in Sian (even if she sometimes doesn't believe in herself). I know how talented she is. Finally, other people would be able to see that. After a lot of conversations and reassurance, Sian finally said yes and agreed to come out of 'early' retirement.

I thought *Car Share* would be perfect for the BBC. Its pace was quite gentle and its characters endearing. I didn't relish the idea of a noisy commercial break tearing through the middle of it. I also thought the series could go out on their 'then new' iPlayer platform and forgo the pressures of being 'Peter Kay's new series'.

Shane Allen had become a good friend during my time at Channel 4, and we'd kept in touch when he moved to the BBC and got the prestigious job of head of comedy. I phoned to congratulate him while doing the school run and casually pitched him the idea of *Car Share*. Immediately he said yes.

Now, don't get me wrong, I do recognise how lucky I was to get a yes as quickly as that, especially over just a short call on the school run, but I had racked up some credentials over the years. Still, I was very grateful.

Now the only issue I did have was convincing people that Sian was right for the other role. Suspicions were aroused, such as 'Who?', 'Never heard of her' and 'Shouldn't you go for somebody who's well known?' I'd had it all those years before with Paddy. But I knew Sian was right and if we could capture just a bit of our real-life chemistry then that could be the secret ingredient to the show's success.

Car Share had been conceived with a much younger couple in mind, so Sian and I slowly started to rewrite the script, delving into our own lives for stories and conversations. The scripts would be completely bespoke to us. We would write a scene and then read it out, hearing exactly how everything would sound so we could tailor it for ourselves. We even recorded the new scripts (to check for length), sending each of them to Paul and Tim for approval. Even though we ended up losing a lot of their original material they were fine with our changes. Then we spent time with Paul rewriting the scripts.

On the production side, I planned to film early summer, as we'd need plenty of light for filming inside a car. I began to rally all of my favourite crew to see if they'd be available to work on the new series. Most of them were back on board. I even got a new producer, Gill Isles. She has a big passion for TV too and turned out to be as detailed as me. We worked well together, slowly getting everything into shape.

I toyed with the idea of using a green screen for all of the interior car scenes. They had some really sophisticated set-ups on TV shows and I'd seen how they could cleverly superimpose the moving footage behind actors. They're very believable.

Filming it this way meant we could spend a lot of time in the controlled environment of a studio and not fall foul to the weather. I spoke to a lot of companies in America about the techniques available. It would be costly. I was also concerned about scenes when the characters exited the car and entered a real-life location. Would we be able to see the join?

One day I bumped into an editor friend and was telling him about my dilemma, and he said, 'Why don't you just put some cameras on the dashboard? You'll be surprised what you can get.' He was right. I was thinking about it too much.

We needed to crack on and find a car that could fit all the cameras inside. At first I thought of an SUV, as I imagined there'd be plenty of room, but deceptively they have widely sloped windscreens so there isn't much room. (Now how could you not be enthralled by that last sentence?) In the end, we discovered the only car with enough space to suitably fit our cameras inside was a Fiat 500. So that's why John ended up with that car he has in the series. I thought it only added to the comedy.

One problem we did have to solve was how we could film while on the move with the crew. So I bought a minibus and removed all of the seats inside. We then redesigned the interior so we could accommodate the crew and their kit. We had three focus pullers (working the cameras inside the Fiat), a sound man, a lighting cameraman and a script supervisor (so they could check whether we were saying the right lines, as there was a lot of script). This minibus would be connected to the Fiat via cables that ran through the car's headlights, and then the minibus would tow the Fiat around via an A-frame. It took a lot of figuring out and tests in advance, but somehow we cracked it.

We also had a silver people carrier following the Fiat with costume, make-up and other crew inside. If you watch the series you'll almost always see the silver people carrier following the Fiat through the back window. That's why John's back window is always dirty, to try and disguise the fact.

The whole crew was in convoy, but it was the only way we could figure out how to make it look real. We also had a second Fiat, so we could film scenes with the camera in the back over our shoulders. You'd see Kayleigh, me driving, and you'd get a 360-degree sense of the whole car when it was edited together.

One thing we never counted on was the shocking condition of the roads. So many potholes everywhere. We'd be juddering and banging over them constantly. All of the cameras would shake themselves loose. So we'd all have to pull over and re-tighten all of the equipment before it fell off.

The majority of the filming took place on the A6 from Salford to Bolton. It was important for me to stay in and around Bolton after all these years. There's even a scene where the Fiat drives up the same hill Brian Potter went up in his motorised wheelchair in the opening shot of the very first episode of *Phoenix Nights*. Mercia Street. I've actually been thinking of doing tours around the locations where I've filmed, in an old milk float at the weekends. Fancy it?

In *Car Share* John and Kayleigh both work in a supermarket, though it never states which one and we never see inside. I loved that idea. Now we just needed to find a location that looked like a supermarket with a decent car park. We found an empty unit in a small retail park in Altrincham. We covered the windows with huge images of carrots, apples and tomatoes (I copied the idea from the side of a Tesco near me). I also wanted the uniforms to be ambiguous and only suggest a national supermarket chain. We must have created a believable location because we'd often get the public parking up, taking one of our prop trolleys and trying to head inside our fictitious supermarket. Only to find it was completely empty inside. How they never noticed a full camera crew in the car park I'll never know.

We filmed long days and would often stay out until the last of the daylight fell and the cameraman would call time. Fortunately, the weather was great for most of the filming and we didn't get much rain at all. So a lot of the series looks really lush, which I think adds to the enjoyment. Sunshine makes everything look good.

Car Share was two people in a car, but I always think there was a third character, the radio, in our case Forever FM, which played constantly throughout every episode. That was a crucial element, as radio is so much a part of people's daily commute. People spend their lives driving and listening to the radio every day. Even when it's something they don't particularly like, they rarely change stations. There's an abiding loyalty. Originally, I wanted to bring back Chorley FM but was told I couldn't, as Chorley FM had become an official radio station and BBC legislation meant I couldn't cross-promote it. How mad is that? I'd created it! Fortunately, the real Chorley FM never used the line 'Coming in Your Ears'. Mind you, who would?

So, as an alternative, I came up with Forever FM. It was crucial that it sounded completely credible as an FM station. Paul suggested a radio producer called Gavin Matthews. He knew exactly what we were after. The station had to be 100 per cent believable, right down to the jingles; the news, weather, traffic and travel; the quizzes, competitions and especially the adverts. Everything had to be written and cast. It was a mammoth undertaking but completely worth it, as I knew this element would drive *Car Share* (if you'll forgive the pun). He captured it perfectly, making it just that little bit naff without being overly comical. We handpicked the songs – Forever FM played 'timeless hits now and forever' – so Sian, Paul and I were able to feature all of the songs we loved.

Forever FM had to be audible wallpaper that would gel the whole thing together. Did we get it right? Well, I used to play the recordings of Forever FM occasionally and people listening would ask, 'What radio station is this? They play some good songs.' So I knew we'd nailed it.

Sian and I would listen to the radio when we were filming and quite often we'd improvise, reacting to an item on the news or a song. These were always my favourite moments filming *Car Share*. The following extract never made it into the final series, as we were sadly short on time.

News presenter
Police discovered a homegrown cannabis farm in the mum-of-five's attic. Said to be in the value of twenty-six thousand pounds

Kayleigh
In her attic?

John
They're all at it. There was one down the road from me. The house burnt down when they were on holiday and everyone within a two-mile radius was stoned. I went out to walk the dog and came home off my tits

Have you ever dabbled in drugs?

Kayleigh
What? Me? Never

Pause.

Well, just the once. I got stoned by accident. I had a massive chocolate hash cake when I was on a hen do in Amsterdam. I had no idea what it was. Well, I did really, but it just looked so nice. We all went out dressed as Charlie's Angels and ended up in this bar chatting to these French Asian lads. I remember one chatting to me, he had the most beautiful blue eyes, he looked just like George Michael in a turban, and all I kept thinking was that I couldn't feel my teeth. The next thing I knew I was at the top of a human pyramid in the middle of the red-light district. Have you ever dabbled, John?

John
I've had the odd puff

Kayleigh
Anyone I know?

John
Funny. No, I've smoked the odd joint, yeah … well, I'm in a band, aren't I? Rules of the road

Kayleigh
Ganja?

John
If you like

Kayleigh
When?

John
Once, when I got dumped …

Kayleigh

By who?

John

Nicola Farrell, a girl I'd been going out with. Then she came
back six months later, said she'd changed her mind

Kayleigh

Bitch. I hope you told her where to go?

John

No, I met up with her

Kayleigh

Why?!

John

Because I'm an idiot, that's why. I suppose I wanted to try and
show her I'd changed, show her what she was missing, so I
borrowed some of my mate's clothes …

Kayleigh

What for?

John

He was a skater, wore trendy clothes, long baggy shorts,
hooded tops, baseball cap … and all that gear

Kayleigh

OMG

John
(embarrassed)
I looked like one of Mc bloody Busted …

Kayleigh
That's hysterical

John
I bought a joint off him. I thought if she saw me with it she'd
think I was cool … what a dick

Kayleigh laughs.

Kayleigh
How old were you?

John
Thirty-two

Kayleigh laughs again.

John
I'm kidding, I was … twenty-one, twenty-two … when was the
Freddie Mercury tribute –? Anyway, whatever, it was that year.
We drove up onto the hills in her dad's Sierra, she took two
drags and then coughed her guts up. What a waste. Three quid
that joint cost me. Twenty minutes later we were back at her
mam and dad's watching *Heartbeat*

Kayleigh
Sunday night

John

Correct. I made my excuses, she offered me a lift home.
Worst bit was when I got halfway down the path and her dad
came tearing after us, waving the joint over his head: 'Whose is
this?' It had only bloody fallen out of my friggin' skater shorts
and onto the front room carpet. They were that low down,
you see …

Kayleigh

You are joking me!

John

She said, 'Isn't it one of Nana's?' He said, 'No, Grandma
smokes menthol'

Kayleigh

What did you do?

John

I just skated home quick as I could

Kayleigh

That's hilarious

John

Not seen her since … or been near a skateboard

Kayleigh

Oh, I went out with a skater once …

John

Did you?

Kayleigh

Yeah, he was a right perv. He took me to the pictures on a first date and was all over me, wandering hands

John

German lad, was he?

Kayleigh

No, he was from the Wirral

John

I meant hands as in ... never mind. And why did you stay with him?

Kayleigh

Dunno.

John

Did he do the old yawn?

Kayleigh

The what?

John

The old yawn trick

John demonstrates.

Kayleigh

Oh, yes. He did keep yawning, I thought he was just bored with the film

John

No, that's page one, that, textbook. I've used that one on many
a first date. I remember trying to feel one girl up in the middle
of *The Goonies*

Kayleigh

That's not very romantic

John

Romantic? I was in third year, I used to get a hard-on just
unzipping a pencil case

Kayleigh

(covers her ears)
I'm not listening to this

John

I had my hand on her breast for twenty minutes, then it turned
out to be her bag

Kayleigh

Could you not tell?

John

Only when I realised her nipple was a press stud. I flicked it
open and all her Revels fell out …

Another section I enjoyed filming was the music video
sequences. This was just pure indulgence on the part of Sian
and me. As you know, I've always loved filming music videos.
They were born from daydreaming during the journey.
Everybody drifts off in traffic.

They weren't easy to film but they were a lot of fun. We had dancers and fancy locations, like Gorton Monastery, which looked incredible when it was lit up on camera, Sian pretending to be Anastacia, all for the half-minute it ended up on the screen. I went all out on 'MMMBop' by Hanson. Kayleigh has a panic attack in a car wash and tries to overcome it by thinking calm thoughts. She imagines herself swimming underwater in a fully animated world. This effect took months to develop, working with an animation company who created all of the different types of sea creatures. It looked so colourful and vibrant when it was finished, and if you ever want to see the full versions of the video sequences they're on the complete series DVD, or YouTube, no doubt.

We also had a lot of outtakes, especially when my old pal Reece Shearsmith made an appearance as 'Stink' Ray, the supermarket's fishmonger. He's waiting for a bus when he catches a glimpse of John and Kayleigh in traffic. Reluctantly, they give him a lift to work, but he stinks the car out. Immediately, they open all the windows. Kayleigh even takes John's Magic Tree air freshener and hangs it around her neck. We couldn't film that scene for laughing. Especially when Ray turns the radio up and sings along to 'Here Comes the Hot Stepper' by Ini Kamoze. 'I was a very naughty boy to this song many moons ago in Okinawa.' He then sang what he thought were the lyrics, and that's when Sian and I really lost it. Uncontrollable laughter. I even heard that song earlier today and laughed out loud. 'Lyrical danceflap'.

The scene when Kayleigh insists that doggin' and dog walking are both the same was also difficult to film for laughing.

John

How was your make-up party last night?

Kayleigh

It's next Monday. I got my weeks mixed up, so I just went doggin' instead

John

Come again?

Kayleigh

What?

John

You went doggin'?

Kayleigh

Yeah, I went with Ken, my neighbour. There was nothing on telly so we just went up the back field

John

Doggin'?

Kayleigh

Yeah

John

As in dogg-in'?

Kayleigh

Yeah, doggin'

John

Well, you've opened my eyes

Kayleigh

What do you mean?

John

You went doggin'?

Kayleigh

Yes!

John

… and who's this Ken fella?

Kayleigh

Ken, my next-door neighbour. Aw, he's in his eighties now but
he's very active

John

Sounds like it

Kayleigh

I have to link him through the woods

John

I bet you do, the dirty old bastard

Kayleigh

What? What's your problem?

John

Nothing

Kayleigh

It is a shame for him, he usually takes Maggie doggin',
but she's on her last legs

John

Who's Maggie?

Kayleigh

His Cocker Spaniel

John

(realisation)

So doggin's with a dog?

Kayleigh

Yeah? Are you slow? Of course doggin's with a dog,
what else would doggin' be?

John

So you don't have sex outdoors with people watching?

Kayleigh

(incredulous)

WHAT?! Are you out of your mind? What, why are you asking
me that? Sex? Outside? With Ken?

(makes a retching noise)

Are you sick, John?

John

You said you went doggin' with Ken, what am
I supposed to think?

Kayleigh

Doggin' with my dog, with Misty

John

So you go dog walking, you don't go doggin'?

Kayleigh

They're the same thing

John

They're not the same thing, they're a million miles apart.
Where have you been living, on the moon?

Kayleigh

Dog walkers are doggers. I've even got a car sticker that
says 'Doggin's for Life, Not Just for Christmas'. People
are always beeping

John

(laughing)

I bloody bet they are

Unlike any other series I'd previously made, *Car Share* was edited at home. My home, that is, not just some random house. Up in the spare bedroom, in fact. Technology had moved on so much since *Phoenix Nights* that it was possible to work from home. Matt Brown would arrive every morning and we'd work till about seven in the evening, meticulously sifting through all of the footage. Making sure we got the absolute best. As usual, I had my notebooks and would be jotting everything down. Matt brought so much to *Car Share*. He's incredibly talented and would put so much time and effort into crafting a scene. The sad thing is you don't really notice when you watch the series, when they've finished and everything looks perfect. That's the skill of a good editor. *Car Share* might look simple – two people in the car – but trust me, it isn't, and Matt made it all look so easy.

As much as I tried to get the BBC to premiere *Car Share* on iPlayer, they wanted it on BBC1. I was nervous. Would people take to two people talking in a car? We compromised. *Car Share* went out on BBC1 on Monday nights and all of the first series went on iPlayer at the same time. That was actually the first time that had ever happened, and I think it really helped the series. Viewers love to binge-watch everything at once. That happens all of the time now, but it was a huge novelty then. In fact, I think *Car Share* was the most downloaded series for a while on the iPlayer.

Remarkably, *Car Share* went on to win a ton of awards, including three National Television Awards for Best Comedy. I was truly delighted, especially after working in TV for almost twenty years and to have one of the greatest successes now. Though nothing could have thrilled me more than when Sian won a Royal Television Society Award for her performance as Kayleigh. What an incredible achievement. I was so proud of her and loved that viewers enjoyed her as Kayleigh.

Something also happened that I'd never experienced before. I started to get people telling me how much the series meant to them. How much they cared for John and Kayleigh and how much they wanted them to fall in love. The series seemed to transcend comedy. Wow! All I'd ever wanted *Car Share* to be was joyful, but now it was becoming something more. People cared about John and Kayleigh and seemed to love being in their company. They too wanted to car share.

The BBC was very keen for series two of *Car Share*, but unfortunately they'd have to wait, as I had some other work in the pipeline.

Danny Baker and I had become good friends since we'd first met filming the John Smith's advert. We had a similar sense of humour and we both had an encyclopaedic knowledge of film, music and, in particular, comedy. We'd spend hours on the phone telling stories and laughing a lot.

Danny had written his autobiography, and he'd just finished writing a TV adaptation with Jeff Pope, called *Cradle to Grave*. Jeff had become quite a successful producer and writer, with series and films such as *Philomena*, *Appropriate Adult* and *Cilla* to his ever-growing list of credits. I'd read Danny's book and it was really funny, rich with great stories and characters born out of real-life experiences growing up with his family in Bermondsey, London, in the early seventies.

Danny and Jeff asked me to play Danny's dad, Spud Baker. I was flattered, to say the least. Apart from a few projects I'd never taken any acting roles outside of my own work, let alone a big starring role. I was nervous initially but also intrigued by the offer, plus the scripts they'd written were top class. In fact, they reminded me a lot of Dick Clement and Ian La Frenais's writing.

I agreed to play the part and then the roof caved in. On the first day of filming the reality of what I'd undertaken hit me. I was never completely confident about my accent and had been given a voice coach. He was great at what he did, and we worked very hard on every line, trying to perfect the East London accent. As soon as my first take was over, he took me to one side and gave me a few notes on my vowels and how to deliver certain words in a certain way. I took note.

Then the script supervisor quietly reminded me of the correct lines when I said anything wrong. I took note. Then

Danny came over and gently told me how his dad would gesture and what he wouldn't do. I took another note. Then the director, Sandy Johnson, would ask me if I could watch where I moved so I could stay in a well-lit area. By now I was dumbfounded. They were all really lovely and considerate, but the realisation hit me: Oh, my God, what have I done? There's so much pressure. I'd never experienced anything like it before. I really didn't want to let Jeff and Danny down. Particularly Danny, as I was playing his dad. But we did another take and the notes continued and they continued. Immediately, I regretted my decision but told nobody. I just stayed professional, dealt with everything that was thrown at me over the next few months and got a shitload of cold sores.

I tried my best and ultimately I'm proud of my achievements (even though I think I sound like Dick Van Dyke in *Mary Poppins*), but the experience just wasn't very enjoyable. The only time I had any fun was in between takes, having a laugh with Danny and Jeff, but as soon as we had to go for a take my heart would sink a little.

During the filming I wrote down a few reasons why I didn't want to work on a second series. Reminders of the stress, which I knew I'd forget. Sure enough, Jeff and Danny had approached me to do another series, so before the first series was broadcast I rang them both and told them how I felt: 'No matter how successful the series might be I just don't fancy doing it again.' They weren't so chuffed, but I thought it better to be completely honest with them.

The series turned out to be a belter. Lucy Speed, who played my wife, did an incredible job. The production values looked great and nobody would ever have guessed that 1970s Bermondsey was actually 2015's Ashton-under-Lyne (well, not unless you lived in Ashton-under-Lyne). Mysteriously, the series was buried in the schedules, Thursday nights at nine on

BBC2. Even at ten it would have stood a better chance, but it just seemed to disappear. I'm confident that if it had been screened in a better slot it would have been a huge success.

Ah, well. I didn't have much time to ponder, as I was straight back to *Car Share* to write a second series. This time Sian, Paul and I wrote it together. We already had quite a lot of ideas, and one thing we did want was the second series to be more heartfelt.

I also wanted to ring the changes visually and film at night. We came up with the idea of John and Kayleigh going on a works do, in fancy dress (Harry Potter and Hagrid). Kayleigh gets drunk and talks John into giving Elsie (a drunken female Smurf) a lift home. Conleth Hill played Elsie and he was hilarious. I'd worked with him briefly on *Pop Factor*, when he played Geraldine's mum, and I really wanted to work with him again. He was perfect with his strong Northern Irish accent and his ability to improvise.

Kayleigh
Any man would be lucky to have you, Elsie

Elsie
I wouldn't have one. I just want a wee dog at my age.
Something that'll lick me and doesn't want anything back.
John, could you turn that heating down, I'm sweating like a
blind lesbian in a fish shop

Lines like that only lead to giddiness and a ton of outtakes from the three of us.

In another episode, Kayleigh talks John into bunking off work and going to the seaside. Reluctantly, John agrees and eventually they end up at a safari park. We filmed the safari park scenes at Blair Drummond in Scotland, as they were the only one who'd let us film. They couldn't have been more helpful over our two-day visit. They let us film with all of the animals, including the lions (we were carefully escorted) and the monkeys. They had a great time climbing all over the Fiat. Later in the episode, John and Kayleigh are shocked to discover a monkey on the roof of the car. The scenes that followed ended up being some of the funniest in both series.

John and Kayleigh look dishevelled. The monkey is now in the back, wearing a seatbelt.

John
Christ, that was a struggle. Little swine

Kayleigh
Are you alright?

John
Do I look alright? I'm cut to bloody ribbons. Look at my clothes. We're gonna get screwed for this. Kidnapping a monkey is a serious crime

Kayleigh
It wasn't our fault

John
I can't believe we drove all that way with him on the roof and nobody stopped us

Kayleigh
I wondered why all those cars were flashing us. How are we gonna get him back?

John

You'd think they'd notice a missing monkey. Do they not do a headcount?

Kayleigh

Maybe he's not from there

John gives Kayleigh a dumbfounded look.

Then the monkey urinates on them both from the back seat.

John

Oh, my God! The dirty little bastard

Kayleigh

What just happened?

John

It's leaving its scent. That is potent. That is strong piss

Kayleigh

John, is this dangerous? Will we have a monkey virus?

The second series of *Car Share* went from strength to strength and proved to be even more successful than the first. But just like *Phoenix Nights*, I knew that two series were enough. For now, anyway (wink, wink).

The series ended on a bit of a sad note, much to the viewers' dismay. John frustratingly ignores all of Kayleigh's amorous intentions, so finally she gives up on him and gets out of the car. John does feel the same way but finds it hard showing it. That was very emotional, filming that scene, but for me that ending was real life. There was an outcry from fans. They even started a petition for another episode to be made. How flattering that people cared enough about the characters.

Little did they know, we'd already filmed another secret episode. In fact, the BBC didn't even know. We kept it secret until they showed a repeat of the series and then we revealed the extra episode. They flipped. Now we could hopefully have the resolution that people wanted. The series also featured one of the most memorable scenes ever. When Kayleigh gets out of John's car at the traffic lights to save a hedgehog in the road, a car swerves to avoid her and hits a second car. Then when John gets out of his car, his door is struck by a passing van and is completely ripped off, sending it hurtling down the road. The scene was chosen by BAFTA as one of the TV Memorable Moments of the year. How incredible was that?

When I write this and recall my memories of *Car Share*, I can't help but think how much it meant to me. Being with my closest friends. Working with a fantastic crew in and around my home town. Work can't get much better than that.

Epilogue

After *Car Share*, I was invited to work on a short project close to my heart, *Goodbye Granadaland*. Sadly, Granada TV was about to close and move to a new home at Media City in Salford. ITV wanted to make a one-off programme saying a final goodbye to the iconic studios. They invited me to host it. Having been a huge fan all of my life, I was honoured, as it truly was the end of an era.

The programme celebrated all that Granada had created over the years – *Brideshead Revisited*, *Cracker*, *Stars in Their Eyes*, *Prime Suspect*, *7 Up*, *World in Action*, *Band of Gold* – and toasted some of the legendary artists who'd appeared there over the years. The Beatles, Woody Allen, Joy Division and Jeremy Kyle.

It was slightly melancholy to film. Walking around the empty studios, tinged with so many happy memories, just for myself. I went to the rehearsal space for my first job at Granada as a getaway driver in 'Two Minutes', where I met Paul Shane and Alexei Sayle. Studio 12, where we'd filmed *Britain's Got the Pop Factor*, one of Granada's last big productions. Up to the editing department, where I'd worked on *Phoenix Nights* and *Max & Paddy*. Then over to *Coronation Street*, where I once dropped a piece of fish behind the counter in the corner shop. So much emotion walking the corridors where we'd filmed '(Is This the Way to) Amarillo'. I was truly thrilled to just be a tiny part of Granada's history in some way. From an ecstatic little boy posing for a photograph outside the front entrance, to eventually working at the Hollywood of the North. And now it's all gone, forever. Last time I heard, it was a *Crystal Maze* experience.

A few weeks later I found myself sitting in the audience at the BAFTA ceremony in London. *Car Share* had been nominated, twice, and astonishingly it won twice. Once for Best Scripted Comedy, and then, just as I sat back down, I heard, 'And the winner of Best Comedy Performance is ... Peter Kay.'

Best Comedy Performance. The very same award I'd watched Ronnie Barker win all those years before. Now it was my turn. I looked out at a packed auditorium, and for a few seconds I was genuinely speechless. How had it come to this?

It seemed as if everything in my life had come full circle and I felt a completeness I'd never felt before. All those years I'd spent watching, recording and studying TV had paid off (square eyes, my arse). A childhood spent idolising TV had inspired a life of working in TV. That wooden box in the corner of the front room had been my real education. It literally changed my life forever, but now I was ready for a rest. There was only one thing left to do, sit down and watch some TV.

Script and Picture Credits

While every effort has been made to trace the owners of copyright material reproduced herein and secure permissions, the publishers would like to apologise for any omissions and will be pleased to incorporate missing acknowledgements in any future edition of this book.

Scripts

Barking (Ep 5), written by Peter Kay, © Channel X/ Screenocean/Channel 4, 1998

Peter Kay The Early Years, written by Peter Kay and Iain Coyle, © Channel X/Screenocean/Channel 4, 1997

The Sunday Show (*Junior MasterChef* clip), written by Peter Kay, © BBC Motion Gallery/Getty Images, 1997

The Services (Pilot for *That Peter Kay Thing*), written by Peter Kay, © Open Mike Productions/Screenocean/ Channel 4, 1998

That Peter Kay Thing (Ep 2, Ep 3, Ep 6), written by Peter Kay, Dave Spikey, Neil Anthony (Fitzmaurice) and Gareth Hughes, © Open Mike Productions/Screenocean/ Channel 4, 2000

That Peter Kay Thing (Ep 1, Ep 5, Ep 4), written by Peter
  Kay, Dave Spikey and Neil Anthony (Fitzmaurice), © Open
  Mike Productions/Screenocean/Channel 4, 2000
Phoenix Nights (Series 1 Ep 1, Ep 2, Ep 3, Ep 4, Ep 6),
  written by Peter Kay, Dave Spikey and Neil Fitzmaurice,
  © Goodnight Vienna Productions, 2001
Phoenix Nights (S 2 Ep 2), written by Peter Kay, Dave Spikey
  and Neil Fitzmaurice, © Goodnight Vienna Productions,
  2002
Max & Paddy's Road to Nowhere (Ep 3, Ep 4, Ep 5, Ep 6),
  written by Peter Kay and Paddy McGuinness,
  © Goodnight Vienna Productions, 2004
The Catherine Tate Show (S 2 Ep 6), written by Catherine
  Tate, Derren Litten and Peter Kay, © BBC Motion Gallery/
  Getty Images/© Tiger Aspect Productions Ltd, 2005
Coronation Street, written by Daran Little, © ITV Archive,
  2004
Parkinson: The Final Conversation, written by Peter Kay and
  Michael Parkinson, © Parkinson Productions, 2007
*Britain's Got the Pop Factor and Possibly a New Celebrity
  Jesus Christ Soapstar Superstar Strictly on Ice* (Pt 1 and
  Pt 2), written by Peter Kay and Paul Coleman,
  © Goodnight Vienna Productions, 2008
The Royal Variety Show (Blackpool 2009), written by Peter
  Kay, © ITV Archive/Royal Variety Charity, 2009
Peter Kay's Car Share (S 1 Ep 2, S 2 Ep 3, Audio Special),
  written by Peter Kay, Sian Gibson, Paul Coleman and Tim
  Reid, © Goodnight Vienna Productions, 2015
John Smith's Adverts, © John Smith's/TBWA/
  Adam&EveDDB, 2002